Perspectives on the Entangled History of Communism and Nazism

Perspectives on the Entangled History of Communism and Nazism

A Comnaz Analysis

Edited by Klas-Göran Karlsson, Johan Stenfeldt, and Ulf Zander

LEXINGTON BOOKS
Lanham • Boulder • New York • London

Published by Lexington Books
An imprint of The Rowman & Littlefield Publishing Group, Inc.
4501 Forbes Boulevard, Suite 200, Lanham, Maryland 20706
www.rowman.com

Unit A, Whitacre Mews, 26-34 Stannary Street, London SE11 4AB

British Library Cataloguing in Publication Information Available

Library of Congress Cataloging-in-Publication Data

Perspectives on the entangled history of communism and Nazism : a comnaz analysis / edited by
Klas-G?ran Karlsson, Johan Stenfeldt, and Ulf Zander.
pages cm.
Includes bibliographical references and index.
1. Totalitarianism. 2. Communism. 3. National socialism. 4. Soviet Union--Politics and government--
1936-1953. 5. Germany--Politics and government--1933-1945. I. Karlsson, Klas-G?ran, author editor
of compilation. II. Stenfeldt, Johan, 1978- author editor of compilation. III. Zander, Ulf, author editor
of compilation.
JC480.P475 2015
335.4309--dc23

2015015517

∞ ™ The paper used in this publication meets the minimum requirements of American
National Standard for Information Sciences Permanence of Paper for Printed Library
Materials, ANSI/NISO Z39.48-1992.

Printed in the United States of America

Contents

Introduction

Klas-Göran Karlsson, Johan Stenfeldt, and Ulf Zander

This book is the result of a scholarly project on the entangled history of Communism and National Socialism. At the center of attraction is the problem if, why, and how the history of German National Socialism and Soviet Communism should, and could, be situated within one coherent historical narrative. Most of the contributions to the volume were presented at an international conference at Lund University in Sweden in late 2011. The title of the book, *Comnaz*, is a portmanteau word of the kind that we often associate with Soviet Communist prose. However, to our knowledge, it has never been used outside of this endeavor.

Several works on the Communism-National Socialism nexus have been published; held together by an ambition to link Communist and Nazi history. In recent years, quite a few volumes on the theme have been written, which indicates that the topic has a certain relevance in the twenty-first century. It goes without saying that the opening of former Soviet archives has provided scholars with new opportunities to level out the quantitative and qualitative differences between studies of Nazi and of Communist history, and to lay the basis of more balanced comparisons. Furthermore, internal changes in the scholarly world, such as an increased interest in historical comparisons, in transnational interconnections, and in aspects of civilization, may have added to the orientation toward intertwined historical trajectories.

Some of the earlier works belong to the tradition of totalitarianism, with its ambition to lay bare the patterns of totalitarian rule by chiseling out and classifying its crucial components and factors, such as ideology, bureaucracy, and coercion, and combining them in a systemic way. Structural similarities or even identities between the Communist and Nazi regimes often—but certainly not always—stood out as the most scholarly—and politically—relevant, while diversities and unique traits were considered less rewarding.[1]

Another kind of book on the comnaz theme has been biographical, which means that Hitler and Stalin have been portrayed and their origins, lives, and deeds compared or in other ways related to each other. While ascertaining that the leaders played an extremely important role in totalitarian rule, politically as well as symbolically, the best scholars of this approach also use the biographies of the *Führer* and the *Vozhd'* to dive deeper into the power mechanisms of Nazi and Communist societies. Another consideration, mentioned by Richard Overy, is that the character of the modern world's tragedy of fate emerges most clearly from an individual perspective: "To set Stalin and Hitler side by side is to join company with two of the historical giants of the modern age, whose dictatorships met head-to-head in the greatest and costliest of all armed conflicts."[2] A special kind of biographical, or rather autobiographical work seems to have started from personal experiences of life in totalitarian, normally a Communist society. These are passionate studies, based on the conviction that the histories of Communism and National Socialism can teach us useful lessons on how to withstand evil and retain our humanity even in the most diabolic circumstances of totalitarian violence, humiliation, and destruction.[3]

A third, more recent and scholarly distanced type of often joint works on the same topic combines the structural and historical approaches by analyzing the Communist and Nazi movements in complex, thematic settings. Some superficial similarities or commonalities are recorded, but it is normally maintained that historically based differences and distinctions are of decisive scholarly importance. In general, the *Sonderweg* thesis of special paths and asymmetric developments is salient, although there is no Russian-Soviet equivalent to the extremely influential interpretation that Hitler owed his political success to Germany's uniquely unbalanced modernization. In relation to totalitarianism studies, these analyses have a clear revisionist character. In their co-authored work on the Communist and Nazi dictatorships in comparison, Ian Kershaw and Moshe Lewin already by way of introduction ask the crucial question: "Why compare countries with such different history, geography, social structures, and levels of development as Germany and Russia (subsequently the Soviet Union)?"[4] The answer they provide us with is that Nazi Germany and Stalinist Soviet Union have already been compared, which seems like an extremely defensive answer. Some of these studies, however penetrating they may be, are based on parallel histories and leave much of the work to interconnect the two phenomena to the reader, while others have an overtly eclectic character.[5]

To these explicitly comparative or entangled works should be added a few scholarly analyses which have mainly been oriented towards Soviet Communist history, but where the implicit, preconceived notion of a "twin evil" obviously has called forth the company of a German Nazi history. For some, these books serve as a confirmation of an existing historical affinity between Communism and National Socialism, while for others, the same works rather arouse an interest to refute any accusations of kinship.[6] In this context, concepts such as the "red" Holocaust tend to awaken excitement.[7]

The latter observation is connected to the most recent scholarly approach, in which Communism and Nazism are interrelated in terms of their representations and interpretations in and by posterity.[8] Experiences, memories, and other cultural expressions of Communism and Nazism, not least of their most abominable and repressive manifestations, symbolically often denoted as "Gulag" and "Auschwitz," have recently attracted a widespread interest which certainly is not limited to the academic community. An important framework for this kind of interpretation is European; while Hitler, Nazism, and the Holocaust seem to have gained a position of prominence in the historical consciousness of Western Europe, as a kind of moral or political basis for a more sincere European integration, Stalin and his satellite equivalents, Communism, and Communist terror have a stronger hold on the minds of those living in the eastern parts of Europe. The same conflict can as adequately be expressed in an adverse way: while many leftist intellectuals, politicians, and others in the West often fall silent or even choose to actively rearrange or deny history when the misdeeds carried out in the name of Communism are addressed, many east Europeans find it painful to discuss the Holocaust, being aware that the genocide of the European Jews was not only the work of SS and Gestapo executioners, but also of various nationalist and anti-Semitic collaborators in their countries. In that respect, comnaz is certainly not only a scholarly but also a political entanglement of our time.

Few or none of the mentioned works have the ambition of this book, namely to integrate the two histories into a theoretically and analytically coherent study of different kinds of historical interconnections and entanglements. The book is certainly a collection of different essays, but it is held together by a common idea and an overarching problem and perspective. In the first chapter, this overall approach will be further elaborated, but a few general hints will be given here. The idea is twofold: on one hand to demonstrate how Communism and National Socialism have interconnected in modern European history, mutually influencing each other as historical and structural phenomena, on the other hand to analyze how they have *come to be* entangled in terms of historical narratives and other constructs. In the book, Communism and National Socialism will thus be analyzed in terms of "real" historical phenomena such as ideologies, movements, and regimes of their time, but also as conceptual, cultural, and ideological symbols and other constructs interpreted, represented, and used by both contemporaries and posterity.

The Communist and National Socialist histories will be handled as entangled phenomena. In this ambition, we are guided by three basic perspectives: a genetic, a structural, and a genealogical one. Each of them can separately be derived from the analyses just presented. Focusing on roots and historical developments, the genetic perspective highlights traditional scholarly values, such as the need for historical understanding from a contemporaneous, prospective standpoint, and a diachronic historical thinking in general. When two historical developments such as the German National Socialist and the Soviet Communist ones are located side by side, when and why do they merge and when and why do they repel from one another? Do they influence, react on, or learn from each other? The second structural perspective implies a change of focus from a process-oriented to a synchronic perspective of totalitarianism. This change of perspective indicates an attempt to narrow down "operational" parallels of the two political systems and rules in the way they handled ideology to construct social utopia, used propaganda, and techniques of terror. The third perspective is genealogical, emphasizing the retrospective processing of history in terms of meaning and memory. When we address the past genealogically, we do not do so in an unprejudiced way, but consciously start from *our* predicament. We do not always search where professional historians have identified the scholarly important history, and not where history textbooks have taught us to. Our search for relevance in history has other qualities. Rather, we make use of history within a history culture, a communicative arena in which the past is ascribed meaning and significance. In history culture, individuals, and collectives make sense of history or evaluate what past is worth remembering, teaching and learning, celebrating, exhibiting, and debating.

An entanglement indicates that these three analytically perspectives are applied together, strengthening and clarifying each other. Genealogical perspectives are useful, or rather necessary, in order to highlight questions of relevance and meaning, to demonstrate how a dead past can change into a living history. On the reverse, a genealogical study needs a genetic perspective, because otherwise urgent questions of why history is interpreted, represented, or used in a particular time and place cannot be analytically dealt with in an adequate manner. Besides, the choice of what history is made use of is not made arbitrarily, but from the genetic and structural perspectives of what we collectively and culturally perceive as our important and necessary history. In the following chapters, the entangled character is made empirically and analytically operable in different ways, but the common denominator is the challenge to deal with Communist and National Socialist history as interdependent entities.

THE CONTENTS

In the first long chapter, *Klas-Göran Karlsson* provides an overview of the comnaz scholarly field, evaluating international research on the theme and introducing the main theoretical and analytical instruments used in the book. He also scrutinizes the French and German comnaz debates of the 1970s and 1980s. Karlsson begins with the presupposition that our understanding of National Socialism and of Communism differs fundamentally. There is a distinction between on one hand an evil and malevolent Nazi intention, and on the other, a good and benevolent Communist one. While communists sought to build a new, improved humanity, progressive utopian thinking turned into retrogressive dystopia only as a result of deviations from Communist ideology or of external aggression from the ideological opponents. On the contrary, the Nazis' dreamland was originally only meant for the Aryan race and primarily built on violence and war in order to reach utopia. The distinction between Nazi intentionalism and Communist functionalism is discussed in the chapter. Certainly, it helps to explain why Communism and Nazism are treated differently in history culture.

Jörn Rüsen departs from some of Karlsson's interpretations when he addresses the comnaz historical complex from a theoretical and metahistorical perspective. In particular, he takes issue with the threefold genetic-structural-genealogical perspective, and with its interconnections. The main questions how to compare and evaluate Nazism and Communism are, in Rüsen's analysis, synthesized in the genealogical perspective, in which the two historical phenomena have been made sense of and kept alive in history culture. Cultural processes such as concealment, moralization, and historization are mentioned and made operable as scholarly instruments to bridge temporal distances and grasp the meaning of Nazi and Communist inhumanity in and for our time.

Johan Stenfeldt's chapter focuses on the concept of the "dystopian trilemma," an analytic framework developed in his recent thesis as a mode of interpreting the relation between the totalitarian, Nazi-communist comparison and other ways of understanding the ideological twentieth century. The underlying idea is that experiences from Nazi and Communist societies may, on a general level, be regarded as dystopian experiences that in turn have lead up to the dystopian ideologies anti-Nazism and anti-Communism. Experiences, a concept used in the tradition of German hermeneutics, are, however, never unquestionable. The intentionalist explanation that lies inherent in the dystopian ideologies may be questioned, or at least put in a wider context, by focusing on functionalist modes of explaining by questioning death tolls, by emphasizing emancipatory consequences of repressive actions, or by focusing on crimes against humanity committed by someone else, most likely Western colonialists. In sum, the chapter will try to identify a number of patterns or rhetorical strategies that are used when Communism and Nazism are discussed.

Anton Weiss-Wendt approaches the comnaz complex not only from a scholarly, but also from an existential perspective. He tells the moving story of his grandfather Helmut Weiss and of his double victimization by the Nazi and Communist regimes. The process started when Weiss as a young man with communist sympathies moved from Germany to the

Soviet Union in the 1930s to escape Nazi persecution and instead found himself victim of the Stalinist terror. The chapter is certainly a biographical case study, but it also provides the reader with general comparative knowledge, in particular of what Weiss-Wendt calls "the perverted logic of political mass violence."

Johan Dietsch's structural point of departure is that the two propaganda figures of the model Soviet youth Pavel Morozov and the Nazi-German Herbert Norkus (Hitlerjunge Quex) seem strikingly similar. The respective epic sagas of the boys celebrated the exploits of a model youth and came to inspire millions of young activists in both countries. What set them apart from other types of child heroes was their blind faith in their political systems, which consequently led them to denounce their family members. The chapter explores the similarities and differences between the two propaganda figures who appeared almost simultaneously in the early 1930s in the Soviet Union and Nazi Germany. Comparing the National Socialist Norkus with his Soviet communist counterpart Pavlik from the horizon of political religion makes it possible to explain their elevation to and function as martyrs.

In her contribution, *Nanci Adler* also reflects on the ideological passions and religion-like convictions of Communism and National Socialism, but seen through the prism of the Gulag prisoners and returnees whose stories she has gathered and analyzed. The ideologies are both secular religions, belief systems with the power and function to legitimate authoritarian rule, mass violence, and extreme hardships that strike both enemies and followers. Another key word in Adler's interpretation of the worldviews of individual victims of the terror is meaning; what Gulag internees described as a Bolshevik soul, a total belief in Communism and loyal faith in the Communist Party of the Soviet Union, made their unselfish hard labor make sense. Individual projects have to be sacrificed, for the common Soviet project was the officially promoted gospel of Soviet Communist political religion.

John-Paul Himka's empirical object of study, The Lontsky Street prison museum in Lviv, was opened to the public in 2009 and is one of the fruits of the nationalist history politics of the presidency of Viktor Iushchenko. It is devoted to the history of the repressions conducted here by the Soviet authorities (1939–1941, 1944–1991) and by the German authorities (1941–1944). The museum presentation is extremely one-sided. Its chief focus is on the bloody events of June 1941, when the NKVD massacred thousands of political prisoners in Lviv's three main prisons. It passes over in silence the bloody pogrom that transpired at these same three sites on July 1, 1941, in which the chief *perpetrators* were militiamen of the Organization of Ukrainian Nationalists (OUN). Members of OUN do figure prominently in the exhibition halls, but only as *victims* of both regimes. In order to contextualize the exhibits, not only Ukrainian history culture but also the interests and activities of the Ukrainian diaspora in North America are addressed.

Maria Karlsson's final chapter focuses on ways in which Soviet terror and Nazi genocide have been written, debated, denied, or silenced by, mainly, Western academics during the latter half of the twentieth century. In this case, issues of denialism, trivialization, and ideologically motivated silence are of particular importance as is the relationship between history and its pseudo counterpart. It is discussed how, and why, posterity has viewed and valued the two cases of totalitarian terror and mass violence differently. Why is it, for example, comparatively commonplace to question Stalin's intent to mass murder, while it is viewed as a matter of spiteful obfuscation and denial to question the extermination intention of Hitler? In light of this, the fate of the concept of "revisionism"—rightfully a word of scorn within the study of the Holocaust, but a legitimate and successful school of study within the historiography of the Soviet Union—is presented and discussed.

NOTES

1. The classical works of totalitarianism include Hannah Arendt, *The Origins of Totalitarinism* (New York: Harvest, 1979), and Carl Friedrich and Zbigniew Brzezinski, *Totalitarian Dictatorship and Autocracy* (Cambridge, MA: Harvard University Press, 1965).

2. Richard Overy, *The Dictators: Hitler's Germany and Stalin's Russia* (London: Penguin, 2005), xxxi. For other biographical examples, see Alan Bullock, *Hitler and Stalin: Parallel Lives* (London: Fontana, 1993), and Robert Gellately, *Lenin, Stalin, and Hitler: The Age of Social Catastrophe* (New York: Alfred A. Knopf, 2007).

3. Tzvetan Todorov, *Mémoire du mal, tentation du bien. Enquête sur le siècle* (Paris: Editions Robert Laffont, 2012), and Vladimir Tismaneanu, *The Devil in History: Communism, Fascism, and Some Lessons of the Twentieth Century* (Berkeley, Los Angeles and London: University of California Press, 2012).

4. Ian Kershaw and Moshe Lewin, "Introduction: The Regimes and Their Dictators: Perspectives of Comparison," in *Stalinism and Nazism: Dictatorships in Comparison*, edited by Ian Kershaw and Moshe Lewin (Cambridge: Cambridge University Press, 1997), 3.

5. Except the book mentioned in note 4, the following volumes can be mentioned: Dittmar Dahlmann and Gerhard Hirschfeld, eds., *Lager, Zwangsarbeit, Deportation und Verfolgung: Dimensionen der Massenverbrechen in der Sowjetunion und in Deutschland 1933 bis 1945* (Essen: Klartext, 1999), David D. Roberts, *The Totalitarian Experiment in Twentieth-Century Europe: Understanding the Poverty of Great Politics* (New York and London: Routledge, 2006), Michael Geyer and Sheila Fitzpatrick, eds., *Beyond Totalitarianism: Stalinism and Nazism Compared* (Cambridge: Cambridge University Press, 2009), and Michael David-Fox, Peter Holquist, and Alexander Martin, eds., *Fascination and Enmity: Russia and Germany as Entangled Histories, 1914–1945* (Pittsburgh: University of Pittsburgh Press, 2012).

6. In particular, two French books with worldwide reputation should be mentioned: François Furet, *Le passé d'une illusion. Essai sur l'idée communiste au XXe siècle* (Paris: Robert Laffont/Calmann-Lévy, 1995), and Stéphane Courtois et al., *Le livre noir du communism: crmies, terreur, répression* (Paris: Robert Laffont, 1997). In the German Historikerstreit, Ernst Nolte also provocatively addressed the interconnections of German Nazism and Soviet Communism. Cf. Rudolf Augstein, ed., *"Historikerstreit": Die*

Dokumentation der Kontroverse um die Einzigartigkeit der nationalsozialistischen Judenver-nichtung (Munich: Piper, 1987). The debate continued in François Furet and Ernst Nolte, *Feindliche Nähe. Kommunismus und Faschismus im 20. Jahrhundert* (Munich: F.A. Herbig, 1998).

   7. Horst Möller, ed., *Der rote Holocaust und die Deutschen. Die Debatte um das "Schwarzbuch des Kommunismus"* (Munich and Zürich: Piper, 1999), and Steven Rose-fielde, *Red Holocaust* (London and New York: Routledge, 2010).

   8. Henry Rousso ed., *Stalinism and Nazism: History and Memory Compared* (Lincoln: University of Nebraska Press, 2004), and Muriel Blaive, Christian Gerbel, and Thomas Lindenberger, eds., *Clashes in European Memory: The Case of Communist Repression and the Holocaust* (Innsbruck: Studien Verlag, 2011).

ONE

The Evil Twins of Modern History?

Reflections on the Entangled History of Communism and National Socialism

Klas-Göran Karlsson

ENCYCLOPEDIC DIFFERENCE

In the Swedish National Encyclopedia, *Nationalencyklopedin*, produced in the first part of the 1990s, the two entries "Communism" and "Nazism" face diverse fortunes. The first one, Communism, initially allows generous space for what is described as basic ideas of a society kept together by community, equality, and justice. It takes more than half of the allotted space until the author, Sven Eric Liedman, retired professor of history of ideas at Gothenburg University, abandons a strictly factual historical narrative. In the Stalinist 1930s, he admits, "the struggle against any deviating factions [had] paranoid traits and motivated terrible cleansings." The information springs out of nothing. As an aberration or historical parenthesis, the bloody Communist history of Stalin's era is neither connected to the earlier history nor to what will come. The cleansings were caused by "power concentration," while the role of ideology is repressed. Lenin generally fares well, and Communist regimes other than the Soviet Union such as China and Cuba are merely invoked as new Communist role models after 1968, not as countries in which large-scale crimes against humanity were perpetrated under Communist regimes and millions of innocent people were killed. In the final analysis, the author demonstrates an obvious confusion when he mingles his role as an objective encyclopedist with another role as an ideological partisan of Communism. The basic meaning is hard to extricate when he lets his hope of a resurrected Communism coexist with the existing state of Communist decomposition:

> It is improbable that Communism, and certainly in its Leninist version, has the future at its feet. However, the dream of a world without repression and capitalist exploitation will not come to an end but will find new forms. In Communist practice, the political means recommended by Lenin gradually transformed liberation to slavery and growing wealth to poverty.[1]

The difference compared to the "Nazism" entry could not be more salient. The latter text is at least twice as long as the "Communism" one. Written by the Danish historian Karl Christian Lammers, one of very few non-Swedish encyclopedists, it does not allow any scope for ideological visions. Instead, it goes immediately to the definition: "political movement and ideology which provided the basis of the German Nazi Party." After just a few lines, the reader is informed that Nazism thrived on its antidemocratic and antiparliamentary traits, on history understood as a struggle between racial categories, and on politics of terror and violence. The tension between nationalist and socialist ideas is touched upon, and it is laid down that "the Nazi state ideal was a strong centralized state, based on the leader." Liedman could have made use of the same features in his article, except for the obvious fact that Communists did not rely on social-Darwinist notions of history as much as on Marxist ideas of history as a struggle between classes. However, in both cases, such ideas were used to legitimize large-scale brutalities against enemies of the state and the party. Liedman chooses not to mention this connection between ideology, power, and violence. In contrast, the history of "Nazism" never loses sight of the fact that Nazi rule was dependent on repression and terror, from the streetwise attacks on ideological and political opponents of the first years to the Nazi total war and the Holocaust.[2]

After this comparison, a few brief reflections immediately present themselves. The first is that visionary ideas such as those presented by Liedman in the beginning of his text may be relevant, at least if the ambition is to help the reader to understand the enticement of Communism for both citizens of communist countries and Western radicals, encyclopedists included. A second reflection relates to different roles of the authors as scholarly interpreters and ideological partisans. Lammers has no problems distancing himself from his topic in a way normally considered worthwhile in a scholarly endeavor. Besides, dealing with Nazism, an alternative encyclopedic approach would hardly be possible. Liedman, on the other hand, has a larger scope of interpretation. He is allowed to express his ideological association with a more unspoiled Communism designed from a Leninist fundament, while simultaneously dissociating himself from the post-Leninist deviation from this Communist line. At the same time, it is obvious that Liedman is wrestling with what to him stands out as a painful history. The third comment refers to the context of violence and terror. While these features are rightfully emphasized as an absolute foundation of Nazi ideology and rule, Communist terror in the Soviet Union is reduced to Stalin's power ambitions and to a parenthetic historical setting. No serious attempt is made to accommodate the ideological visions with the harsh historical reality. In accordance with a simplistic revisionist interpretation, Lenin, called "the founder of modern Communism," whose ideas for long were "a standard for the Communist parties," is left entirely outside the terror context. Besides, mass violence in Communist China and Cambodia is not even mentioned. Taken together, it strongly indicates an intention to sweep away the fundamental question why a communist assumption of power never has been consistent with democracy and human rights, but all too often with crimes against humanity. A fourth reflection, intimately related to the third, is that this text on Communism is not exceptional. Rather, it represents a standard revisionist scholarly interpretation, and furthermore a narrative which is predominant also in non-scholarly historical products. The fifth and final reflection is that it would probably be worthwhile to scrutinize the entries of Communism and Nazism and neighboring entries in national encyclopedias all over the world. Such a comparison will surely demonstrate that history cultures are still nationally marked off, but larger patterns of representations of these painful histories will probably also stand out. Some of these patterns will be highlighted here.

THE ENTANGLED CHARACTER

The purpose of this introductory chapter is to present a theoretical and analytical framework for a scholarly endeavor to analyze Communism and National Socialism as entangled histories, written into one comprehensive narrative. Rather than providing a thorough empirical analysis, the chapter is directed toward pointing out general approaches of an entangled history project. The idea is to delve into the questions how the paths of Communism and National Socialism have crossed, influenced, and reacted to each other in modern European history. As will be clear from the following, Communism and Nazism will be widely understood not only as political ideologies, but also as historical movements and regimes. They will be perceived as factual historical phenomena as well as conceptual and cultural constructs interpreted, represented, negotiated, and used by posterity. The various links between the reconstructed and the constructed aspects of Communist and Nazi history is a particularly interesting problem to elaborate on.

In its accentuation of the complex interconnectedness of historical phenomena, the idea is related to what has been called entangled history, but also to a host of concepts which have a similar meaning and which all are widely propagated in current history scholarship: transnational, transcultural, cross-border, universal, global, transfer, relational, intersected, connected, comparative, and shared history. In scholarly discourse, there is certainly no consensus on how all these kindred concepts should be understood in relation to each other, and it is certainly not within the parameters of this text to semantically and theoretically keep them apart. The somewhat simplistic point of departure will be that several of these concepts start out from an ambition to associate or combine various historical phenomena often marked off from or considered incompatible with each other, by concocting not only factual political, socioeconomic, or cultural exchanges and networks reaching over national or other borders, but also by letting various ideas, concepts, and perspectives go beyond traditional boundaries, for example by being unconventionally written into a joint historical narrative.

It is often argued that an "entangled" approach is useful to counteract the strictly national interpretations of history that are prevalent in history scholarship.[3] Other possible gains can be added. By interrelating historical phenomena in an entangled, non-cumulative way, qualitatively new historical features can hopefully be demonstrated, compared with when each historical phenomenon is analyzed in its traditional context, be it national, scholarly, or any other one. Such an analysis would do justice to the notion of cross-fertilization. Furthermore, an entangled study should have particularly good chances of demonstrating not only historical patterns of similarity and dissimilarity, impulses and influences, actions and reactions, convergences and divergences, but also of making visible various kinds of lack of balance and unevenness between historical phenomena. This is probably the reason why "entangled" analyses have been particularly popular among scholars dealing with colonial and post-colonial studies.[4]

In the cultural vein, much has recently been written under the banner of entangled history or *histoire croisée*, the latter defined as an approach in which "a multiplicity of possible viewpoints and the divergences resulting from languages, terminologies, categorizations and conceptualizations, traditions, and disciplinary usages, adds another dimension to the inquiry," or in which the historicity of the research object meets the historicity of the researcher.[5] It goes without saying that such an interpretation of the entangled character of history is conducive to demonstrating that historical entities are not naturally given but dynamic phenomena subjected to processes of exchange and negotiation. This notion corresponds well with a predominant constructivist interpretation of history. However, much less has been accomplished in terms of how historical entanglements should be scholarly operated and developed. This is the concern of this chapter, and of this book.

THE MOTIVES

Apart from the theoretical and general analytical challenges inherent in a notion of entangled history, there are several reasons for conducting a large-scale investigation on the historical entanglements between Soviet Communism and German National Socialism. The first and most obvious is that they played crucial historical roles in twentieth-century European and world history, both when they crossed each other's paths, displaying similarities or dissimilarities, influencing, and adapting to each other, acting in concordance or conflict with each other, and when they followed their own paths irrespective of the other. These intricate patterns are important topics of historical study for anyone interested in contemporary international history.

Of course, this is not unchartered scholarly territory. Theoretical and analytical instruments have been tested. Some of the interconnections between Communism and National Socialism have been discussed since the early 1950s in terms of totalitarianism, a concept with its roots reaching back to the early interwar period. At that time, totalitarianism mainly referred to Italian fascism. At present, the totalitarianism debate is more vibrant than ever and has entered into a post-totalitarianist stage.[6] The renewal is probably due in part to internal scholarly changes and "turns" from the primacy of political and ideological history to the supremacy of social and cultural history, in part to the collapse of Communism in Eastern Europe, with its general weakening of the Communist ideology, in part to historical debates in France and other countries—which will be referred to later in this chapter—on the nature of Communism and Communist rule. One consequence of the weakening of the Soviet Communist regime and the increased openness was that totalitarianism became a frequently used concept also in Eastern Europe among radical intellectual opponents to the ruling party. According to Abbot Gleason, this situation implied an important change in the general political state of the concept, since it no longer only was "used by the more conservative segments of society, those most comfortable with society as it was."[7] In this way, the concept could get rid of some of the Cold War over-politicization.

In contrast to the old totalitarianism, the new one focuses less on static structures than on dynamic movements. The new totalitarianism often also explicitly includes a third ideological position which the two others together define themselves against, a Western liberal ideology. Instead of presupposing a rectilinear relationship between the totalitarian states' rulers and ruled, post-totalitarianist historical analysis focuses on the changing mental, cultural and ideological bonds that attach large citizen groups to the regime, or, the other way around, give the regime legitimacy among broad layers of a population. To this new theoretical orientation belongs also a debate on the relationship between totalitarian ideologies and what for long has been called "political religions." This theoretical development will be further elaborated later in this text, and elsewhere in the volume.

As mentioned in the introduction, since the 1990s, a host of anthologies have been published, held together by an ambition to link Communist and National Socialist history. While some of these works are better described as based on parallel histories than on systematic interconnections, there are a few recent examples of a more successful project to bring the two histories together in one single interpretive framework.[8] These works have demonstrated that there are some synergies to gain from such an analytic approach.

Obviously, the opportunities for conducting balanced studies of this kind have changed in the last two decades. One aspect is the expanding field of knowledge. New archival documentation has made Communist rule in the Soviet Union and Central Europe more transparent, but the new openness has in fact also offered new insights into Nazi rule in the same territories in the war years, including collaboration with native population groups. Another aspect is that Communism and National Socialism after many years obtained the same status as strictly historical ideologies and regimes. Discussing the "short" twentieth century in his introduction to *The Soviet Tragedy*, Martin Malia argues that "the furies unleashed in 1914 were finally appeased" with the fall of Communism in 1989–1991.[9] His confidence in the *Verfremdungseffekt* of the death of Communism was strong: "Soviet history is now for the first time really history, and this closure permits us to see the pattern of 'logic' of its life course."[10] As other scholars have maintained, Malia's analysis and concomitant demand for historical judgment belongs to "a time of large consensus" and may seem somewhat premature in a longer perspective.[11] It goes without saying that the traditional quantitative and qualitative imbalances between studies of Communist and Nazi history have become less salient, which might favor a synthetic entangled project. However, the idea that the passing of the Soviet Union into history in 1991 should serve to calm down all the "furies" connected to Communism and to provide a foundation of a distanced judgment of its historical course, as a separate phenomenon or in relationship to the course of National Socialist history, will probably not be realized.

This observation links up to the second main motive. There is an ongoing debate all over Europe concerning the interconnections between Communism and National Socialism. To a certain extent, it was conditioned by the collapse of the Soviet Communist system. However, the debate has other attributes as well, such as generational processes, ethno-national conflicts turned into wars and genocide in the Balkans, south Caucasia, and Russia, the creation of multicultural societies all over Europe, and the ongoing European integration process. The starting points were not primarily the Communist and Nazi ideologies and regimes, but rather their most destructive manifestations, the systems of repression and mass violence often subsumed under the symbolic concepts "Gulag" and "Auschwitz," respectively. That large-scale interethnic violence grew out of the crisis of the Communist regimes in the Soviet Union and Yugoslavia has probably added to this interest.

Our present fascination with the "evil" history of state-organized terror and genocide, with making sense of large-scale victimhood and suffering, has situated the Holocaust as what Jörn Rüsen has denoted as a borderline event in modern history.[12] One aspect is surely political, since the genocide of European Jewry has been used since the 1990s to promote a supranational, pan-European history culture. As will be further analyzed below, the Council of Europe, the European Parliament, and other EU institutions have all been anxious to depict the idea of the European Union as a direct response to the Nazi atrocities, and to attempts to trivialize or silence the Holocaust by neo-Nazis and others. In West European history politics, Communism and Gulag play less prominent roles. Radical politicians, intellectuals, and scholars, of whom few today introduce themselves as Communists, tend to avoid the topic, and if they touch upon it, they are often, in Anne Applebaum's words, "tempted to make excuses for Stalin's crimes that they would never have made for Hitler's."[13] Nevertheless, the crimes against humanity perpetrated by the Soviet Communist regime often announce themselves, on or between the lines, as the "other" borderline event in European modern history. This is of course especially true in the case of the East and Central European societies and states that were subdued by both Nazi and Communist regimes in the twentieth century. Since the early 1990s, they display a need to come to terms with both this painful double inheritance, and the relative responsibilities and guilt attached to it, by means of trials, restitutions, lustrations, and history commissions.

Furthermore, questions of the relationship between Communism and National Socialism are closely connected to basic orientations in the lives of millions of people. The nexus is intimately related to memory and oblivion, experience and trauma. In current history discourse, in which moral concepts such as apology, penance, shame, and guilt are frequently highlighted, value judgments are generally considered important. Thus, questions such as the following demand an answer: Is Communism a lesser evil than Nazism? Is it possibly the reverse? Or are they to be regarded as absolutely evil twins? It may seem like an idealistic statement, but for the future of Europe, there is a need for a process in which these questions are discussed, with both 'twins' involved as actors on one historical scene.

THE PROBLEM

It is hard to imagine any historical questions that evoke stronger reactions than those involving Communism and National Socialism and their historical contexts. A comparative perspective often automatically announces itself, since currently Nazi, Hitler, and Holocaust metaphors and symbols are so influential that any writing about Communist terror or any other crimes against humanity or even injustices of a much lower rank seems almost naturally to trigger comparative comments. The questions definitely transcend the boundaries of traditional "academic" ones.

Many scholars and intellectuals programmatically dismiss the legitimacy and value of analytically linking the histories of Communism and National Socialism by arguing that the latter—related to capitalism/imperialism/fascism—and the former—related to socialism/Marxism—represent opposites on the politico-ideological spectrum. They contrast Nazi particularism to Communist universalism, Nazi doctrine of hate to Communist doctrine of liberation. Others maintain that Hitler's and Stalin's states and societies had radically different socioeconomic foundations—Russia's "historical backwardness" is often mentioned in this context.[14] Sometimes, this argumentation is strengthened by the fact that leading representatives of both regimes described the other in terms of absolute opposites.

As for the two regimes' practices of mass violence, differences are strongly emphasized, among both those who insist on the unique or unprecedented character of the Holocaust, and those who stress the more benign and legitimate character of the Soviet regime's violence against its own citizenry, or at least its want of death camps. The moral indignation is often conspicuous. A juxtaposition of the two terror processes and systems is considered to aim at "trivializing" or "normalizing" the Nazi regime and the Holocaust. The opposite argumentation is rare. In a review of Timothy Snyder's book on the mass murders mutually perpetrated by the Stalinist and Nazi regimes in the East European territory that Snyder calls the Bloodlands, Omer Bartov takes up such a position when he criticizes a history in which one is as bad as the other: "Snyder drains the war of much of its moral content and inadvertently adopts the apologist's argument that where everyone is a criminal no one can be blamed."[15] It should be underlined that Snyder himself would certainly not accept Bartov's criticism. It goes without saying that the Soviet Gulag lacked the death camps that rightly are depicted as main symbols of totalitarian evil. However, this does not mean, as wisely asserted by Ian Kershaw and Moshe Lewin, that comparisons of mechanisms and systems of Communist and Nazi repression are illegitimate and that Stalinist terror need to be minimized.[16]

More often than not, this argumentation is accompanied by a distinction between on the one hand an evil and malevolent Nazi intention, and on the other a good and benevolent, or at least a lesser evil Communist one. Once upon a time, "the lesser evil" was a popular Soviet formula of historiography. It was mostly used to soften the critical judgment of a historical phenomenon considered backward and negative from a Marxist point of view, due to the intervention of a compensating positive patriotic value of the same phenomenon. Thus, certain extenuating features could make up for the basically negative character of a historical individual or event. It goes without saying that "liminal" Russian czars such as Ivan the Terrible or Peter the Great were leading proponents of an antagonistic and exploiting, "regressive" socioeconomic system. However, these historical figures simultaneously fulfilled the much more "progressive" task of stabilizing Russian society and expanding the boundaries of the Russian state, at the expense of various internal and external enemies.[17] Consequently, they were considered "lesser evils." In a more general sense, the prerequisite of the "lesser evil" formula is the interconnection and competition of two ideologies. In the Soviet case, the notion made possible the coexistence in the same historical narrative of two systems of ideas that to most of us seem hard to bring together: Marxism and Russian nationalism, the latter in the Communist era called Soviet patriotism.[18]

The basic contention of the distinction between the good/lesser evil Communism and the absolutely evil National Socialism is the following: While communists sought to build a new, improved humanity, and progressive utopian thinking turned into retrogressive dystopia only as a result of deviations from Communist ideology or of external aggression from the ideological opponents, the Nazis' dreamland was originally exclusively meant for the Aryan race, and deliberately built on violence and war in order to reach utopia. Richard Overy gives one version of this dictum: "Soviet communism was intended to be an instrument for human progress, however imperfectly crafted it now appears, whereas National Socialism was from its very nature an instrument for the progress of a particular people."[19] Charles Maier twists the argument in a similar direction when he argues for the need to differentiate between "a [National Socialist] philosophy whose logic is monstrous and one [Communist] which can be given a monstrous interpretation."[20] Certainly, scholars often apply functionalist interpretations of the Holocaust, stressing especially the outbreak of the Second World War as a cumulatively radicalizing event, but it would nevertheless not be entirely wrong to argue, at least in the wider intellectual debate, that the basic interpretation of Nazi mass violence is intentionalist: the hatred of Jews was declared at an early stage, and the need to solve the "Jewish question" imbued Nazi ideology already in *Mein Kampf*. Interpreted intentionally, the main question of "Nazism" is how the early evil intention could be maintained, constitute a basis for evil power politics in Auschwitz more than a decade later, without succumbing to various unintended consequences.

In contrast, the fundamental interpretation of Communism is a functionalist one. Along the historical road, the original utopian ideas of liberating humanity from exploitation and repression more or less gradually passed into its dystopian opposite. The widespread ideas that external and internal enemies of the "good" Communist revolution necessitated a change of ideological and political course, or that Stalin hijacked the Russian revolution from its original Communist course and perverted it into something completely different and worse than it was intended, have no equivalents whatsoever in the Nazi-Hitler history. The frequent exchange of "Communism" to "Stalinism" has no equivalent in an ambition to reduce "Nazism" to "Hitlerism." In the German case, there is no Lenin to exclude from the historical context. Another usable historical "function" is the Soviet victory over Nazi Germany in the Great Patriotic War, indicated for example by Ronald Grigor Suny when he maintains that "[t]he USSR abused its anti-fascist credentials, but ultimately it was the Soviet army and people who stopped the Nazi scourge in the name of a quite different view of the world."[21]

To be sure, there are some leftist hard-liners who stick to the idea that there was a correspondence between Communist intention and reality. To implement the intention to modernize Russia and to resist both external and internal ideological enemies, it is maintained, harsh methods were needed and used, which led to the excessively violent establishment of Communist states such as the Soviet Union. Violence was a necessary and "progressive" part of the Soviet modernization process, and Stalin's policies were fully justified by the historic accomplishments, if nothing else the victory over Hitler. Most interpretations nevertheless stress ideas of "mistakes" or "excesses." It means that Nazi atrocities are often analyzed as rectilinear and intentional, while Communist mass violence rather is understood as a result of twisted roads, accidental mistakes and unintended consequences. Other ways of expressing the same idea is to underline the spite of the Nazis' aims and the Communists' means, or that Nazi crimes against humanity were necessitated by the Nazi doctrine, while Soviet Communist crimes were not.[22] One renowned scholar distinguishes between "purposive killing," clearly dominant in the Nazi case, and "deaths from criminal neglect and irresponsibility," which is considered salient in the Soviet Communist case. The motives are depicted accordingly: while Hitler clearly was anti-Semitic, "Stalin was clearly impatient of groups that got in the way of his idea of what needed to be done."[23]

Objections have sometimes been raised against such clear-cut analytical-cum-ideological distinctions. The functional framework of Communism has been questioned. Whether the Communist crimes against humanity should be labeled "genocide" is a crucial problem, since the concept, at least as defined in the UN convention of genocide from 1948, clearly indicates intentionality as a *sine qua non* for this particular kind of mass atrocities. While the Red Khmers' killings in Cambodia in the late 1970s normally are characterized as a genocide, the concept is less frequent when it comes to the Soviet atrocities. However, Norman Naimark does not hesitate to point out both the Stalinist and the Nazi system as

> genocidal by their very character, meaning that their distinct combination of charismatic leaders, . . . dictatorial powers, ideological motivations, and Promethean transformative aspirations, led them to use the mass killings of groups of their own citizens (and others) as a way to achieve the impossible future that defined their very essence.[24]

There is a lot to be said in favor of this interpretation, at least when it is presented in such a nuanced way as in Naimark's case. For example, it is not easy to analyze Stalin's shootings of more than 700,000 Soviet citizens over seventeen months in the great terror years 1937 and 1938, including large segments of the most competent military establishment, in terms of functionality. The extremely brutal wartime forced deportations of entire ethno-national groups in the Soviet Union before and during the Second World War, many of them of north Caucasian origins, provides another example.

Some argumentations have aimed at criticizing the basic benevolence of the Marxist and Leninist foundations of Communism. Some have even insisted that the Communist ideology was instrumental for regimes that committed serious crimes, due to its criminal nature. Others have asked whether mass murders for "progressive" purposes should be considered less evil than Nazi crimes, in which the perpetrators' intentions were based on hatred from the very beginning.[25] The argument that "[i]t is unclear why it is less important or less condemnable to kill those who have been promised happiness instead of killing those who have been promised nothing" has even been substantiated with Marxist ideas, since Marx is said to have repudiated "the morality of intentions" in favor of the idea that "history comes first of all with *praxis*."[26] As firm and stable interpretive patterns, intentionalism, and functionalism certainly often contribute to rendering nuanced historical comparisons difficult. The approach of entangled history can hopefully offer a more multifaceted analytical approach.

Behind critical notions on comparability and entanglements often rests a delicate counterfactual question: Might a more rational and humane form of Communism have emerged, one that could have avoided dysfunctional elements and survived longer? One answer is certainly that Soviet Communism survived its most destructive, Stalinist phase, which, it can be argued, demonstrated the occurrence of a kind of self-correcting process toward a more rational and less violent Communist system from Nikita Khrushchev's era onward. While Communism could adopt new political guises, National Socialism could not. The argumentation can be strengthened with the point that Stalin's regime achieved tangible "results," of which the most significant doubtlessly was its victory over Nazi Germany. The question of adoption, renewal and "results" has no relevance on Nazism, being in itself for most people the great dysfunction of twentieth-century history, with no potential for self-correction, only for self-destruction and general destruction.

THE CHARACTER OF THE ENTANGLEMENTS

There are at least three ways of writing Communism and Nazism into one and the same historical narrative. The first is the outright comparison, which can be made historically by putting the Communist and National Socialist historical developments side by side, analyzing instances of rapprochements and repudiations, or structurally by comparing factors such as ideology or power politics. A systematic comparison needs to be outspoken about its aims and analytical tools.

To compare is certainly not to equate. A historical comparison does not only demonstrate commonalities and similarities, but also points out differences. Nor is comparison necessarily a static, synchronic intellectual operation, even if commentators, in their ambition to dissociate themselves from traditional totalitarianism theory, tend to emphasize the non-dynamic character of comparative work. The tendency to equate a systematic comparative analysis with a more politicized scholarship is understandable from the way comparison between Communist and National Socialist regimes sometimes has been carried out in the past, but it is indeed questionable whether the entire comparative endeavor should be rejected, and the babies thrown out with the bathwater.[27]

The most obvious general use of a historical comparison is to analyze whether and in what sense two or more historical phenomena belong to a similar process, category, or type. Such a comparison can probably mean that we get a better understanding of each of the compared phenomena, individually and together, as processes or structures, and of our possibilities to include them into larger historical aggregates. Jürgen Kocka also calls attention to a heuristic aim to identify problems missed or neglected that can be seen through the double-sided character of the comparison, and a paradigmatic aim to critically distance oneself from the comparative case that one is most familiar with.[28] This means that even if the basic result of a comparison between Communism and National Socialism is that differences and asymmetries outweigh "sameness" and "likeness," the general analytical point of a comparison does not fail to appear. Behind highly esteemed interpretations in post-war historiography, such as ideas of a German exceptional path to modernity, a *Sonderweg*, or of Germany as *die verspätete Nation*, the belated nation, or the notion of the unprecedented character of the National Socialist crimes, rests a comparative thinking, or at least a comparatively colored idea that a "normal," "modern," or "Western" condition can be identified.[29] Similar evaluations of a special Russian-Soviet modernization process are innumerable.

Thus, a historical comparison must be multi-dimensional, comprising the historical roots, processes, and structures of Communism and Nazism, aspects of power politics based on the ideologies, including their predilection for mass violence, and their long-term effects and cultural representations. Among the latter, however, we often find simplistic, politically motivated analogies by relating what is considered an urgent problem of our days not to the lesser evil but to the absolute evil in history. Such a political use of history often draws heavily on Hitler and Auschwitz, more seldom on Stalin and the Gulag.

Particularly controversial are comparisons that aim at scrutinizing the elements of terror and destruction that are often symbolically represented as Auschwitz and Gulag, and sometimes, much more controversially, as the Holocaust and the "Red Holocaust."[30] Another conflict-loaded comparison deals with the two ideologies as such. The basic prerequisite of these controversies is, as pointed out by historian Stéphane Courtois in his introduction to the controversial *Black Book of Communism* from 1997, a call for

> assessing the similarity between the Nazi regime, which since 1945 has been considered the most vicious criminal regime of the century, and the Communist system, which as late as 1991 had preserved its international legitimacy unimpaired and which, even today, is still in power in certain countries and continues to protect its supporters the world over.[31]

A second understanding of how Communism and Nazism are linked to one single narrative is expressed in terms of interactions, which means that actions in one camp trigger reactions in the other. Several historians have given evidence of a dynamic economic and cultural exchange between Russia and Germany up to the clash of the Second World War, including interwar military cooperation and various human transfers between the countries related to war and exile.[32] In this context, Michael Geyer makes a distinction between two kinds of analyses, one focused on the dynamic interaction between the Soviet Communist and National Socialist regimes, the other on the two regimes' static images of each other, but surely studies of imagery and stereotypes can also demonstrate a dynamic entanglement.[33] To be fruitful, such an approach should preferably have a deep historical perspective. In his classical study of patterns of interrelation between Russians and Germans, Walter Laqueur starts by attributing the Russian anarchist Mikhail Bakunin, who was not particularly fond of Germans, the following argument: "I say, as Voltaire said to God, that if there were no Germans we should have to invent them, since nothing so successfully unites the Slavs as the rooted hatred of Germans."[34] However, Laqueur adds that there was a great deal of ambivalence involved, since Russians also admired the Germans, just as the Germans both hated and feared the Russians. The transformation of czarist Russia to Communist Soviet Union added new dimensions to this duality but did not change the mobilizing power of these images of the "Other." Attitudes of superiority coexisted with feelings of vulnerability. While Karl Schlögel tries to do justice to German-Soviet interwar connections in terms of precarious "special relations," Laqueur calls the Nazi-Communist history from the late 1920s "a study in misunderstanding," with culturally—or, in his words, ideologically—based conceptions and images that lived their own lives, independently of changeable interwar realities.[35] While Soviet society was mobilized under the banner of anti-fascism, connecting fascism to monopoly capitalism, German Nazi society was mobilized under the banner of anti-Communism and anti-Semitism. Many people in interwar Europe became Nazis through a fear of Communism, and Communists through a fear of Nazism. The interwar political rivalry between the Soviet Union and Germany leading up to the Molotov-Ribbentrop pact, well described by Robert Gellately in terms of answers and responses, indicates the relevance of this approach.[36]

A third way of linking Communism and Nazism is by relating to ideas of imitation or learning processes, meaning that one camp borrows from the ideas and practices of the other. This is still an underdeveloped field of research. So far, more has been written about how various Communist regimes learned from each other, or about how the Nazi genocide perpetrators learned from German practice in colonial African Germany (the Herero) or in late Ottoman Empire (the Armenians).[37]

THE DEBATES

In the intellectual and scholarly discussion of entanglements between Communism and National Socialism, the years around 1990 certainly did not constitute an absolute turning point. The topic was touched upon already after the war by eye-witnesses of the two terror systems such as the German Communist Margarete Buber-Neumann and the Russian Jew Vasily Grossman. In the decades leading up to the demise of Communist Eastern Europe, the Communism-Nazism nexus was articulated in a broad public debate. One instance was connected to the publishing of Aleksandr Solzhenitsyn's *The Gulag Archipelago*, written between 1958 and 1968 but not published until 1973 in Paris. In a contemporaneous review, Stephen Cohen described the three-volume work as

> a non-fictional account from and about the other great holocaust of our century—the imprisonment, brutalization and very often murder of tens of millions of innocent Soviet citizens by their own Government, mostly during Stalin's rule from 1929 to 1953.[38]

Cohen was not the only one to draw parallels between the Gulag that Solzhenitsyn had written about from his own experiences, and the Nazi concentration camps. Robert Conquest compared the Ukraine of the years of the terror-famine 1932–1933 to "one vast Belsen."[39] Especially in France, in the backwash of Solzhenitsyn's work, the so-called new philosophers held reckoning of the Soviet-style Communist ideology that had had a strong position in French intellectual life and that they once had rallied around themselves. Their main criticism concerned partly the Soviet Communist ideology as such, with its deterministic leanings, partly its absolute trust in repressive means. To intellectuals such as Bernard-Henri Lévy and André Glucksmann, the parallels between Communist and National Socialist ideology and rule were conspicuous, and Communism was certainly not excused as a lesser evil.[40]

The second large debate to address the same nexus was the German *Historikerstreit*. One of its main contestants was Ernst Nolte, who has gained a certain distinction by analyzing the years 1917–1945 as a period of a European civil war, in which Germany interacted with both the West and the East but Soviet Communists and German Nazis were the main belligerents.[41] In order to understand the distinctive path of German history that concluded in the Nazi era, Nolte maintained, the relevant point of reference is neither Western countries such as France or Great Britain, nor earlier German history, but the contemporary Soviet Union. To him, Nazi politics stood out as a "defensive" or "secondary" reaction to Soviet Communist politics. The idea that the Soviet Union posed a deadly threat to Germany, or to the bourgeoisie as a class, pushed many Germans to side with the Nazis, Nolte argued. He also integrated the Holocaust into this causal explanation; there was a strong German conviction that Soviet Communism had many Jewish admirers, which meant that Jews would support the Soviet Union in a coming war. Only Hitler could defeat "Judaeo-Bolshevism," was a widespread conclusion. Thus, Nolte did not hesitate to point out the Nazi destruction of European Jewry as a rational "punishing and preventive measure," given the contemporary German worldview and the social panic created by the perceived Communist threat.[42] Later, he took one step further by stressing that the "rationality" of the Holocaust can be deduced not only from collective notions of fear but also from "the factual reality of the large role played by a certain number of personalities of Jewish origin at the center of the communist and socialist movement."[43]

The hard criticism against Nolte probably has combined to discourage others from discussing relations between Communism and Nazism in terms of reactions and influences. Even closely related questions of borrowing and imitation have probably been considered too sensitive. The German scholar's provocative interpretation of Auschwitz as "the fear-borne reaction to the acts of annihilation that took place during the Russian revolution" did not attract much support outside conservative and nationalist circles, although he admitted that Soviet terror *de facto* was a lesser evil than the German "copy."[44] His more radical opponents' idea that Nolte and his colleagues represented an apologetic tendency in German history writing, and that Hitler was best explained by a long-term German *Sonderweg* of unbalanced modernization, has proved to be much more successful. However, Timothy Snyder's recent reappraisal of a Nazi-Communist pattern of actions and reactions when he concludes that "[a]s so often, Stalin's crimes were enabled by Hitler's policies,"[45] will probably provide these perspectives with a new urgency.

One scholar who after 1990 bridged the "French" and the "German" lines of debate was the French historian François Furet. In 1995, he published *Le passé d'une illusion*, The Passing of an Illusion, in which he historically rooted the "totalitarian twins" communism and fascism in the trenches of the First World War. The main task was to analyze the irresistibility of the Communist idea, not primarily in East Europe, but among intellectuals in the Western world. One important explanation comes close to Nolte's perspective, although Furet turned it upside down, when he argued that "the movement to stop Hitler gave Communism its most glorious moment and its militants whatever nobility illusions could endow."[46] However, in a much more modest booklet which contained a correspondence between Furet and Nolte, the French historian is anxious to draw an analytical dividing line between on the one hand interconnections based on patterns of reaction, which he often finds fruitful, on the other a linear causality: Nazism had not been Nazism if there had been no Soviet Communism. Or, in a more incisive version: if not Soviet Communism, then no Nazi killings of Jews. Thus, Communism may serve to exonerate Nazism and the evil deeds of Hitler, Furet maintains.[47]

Up to now, the "French" line has had its most clear-cut expression in the collective work called *Le livre noir du communisme*, The Black Book of Communism, published in 1997. For the editor Stéphane Courtois, comparability is no problem, which leads him to the notorious conclusion that

> the genocide of a "class" may well be tantamount to the genocide of a "race"—the deliberate starvation of a child of a Ukrainian kulak as a result of the famine caused by Stalin's regime "is equal to" the starvation of a Jewish child in the Warsaw ghetto as a result of the famine caused by the Nazi regime.[48]

What he wants to question with his provocative comparison is the idea that it is a lesser evil to commit evil in the name of good, as for deeds often attributed to Communist regimes, than to commit deeds in the name of evil, as for deeds attributed to the Nazi regime. The main problem that echoes from what has been dealt with above is again whether evil deeds of political regimes should be judged from their intentions or from their historical practice. As mentioned, this problem of unintended consequences has never been considered acute in the case of the Nazi regime, since the double evilness of intention and action has seldom been questioned.

THE SCOPE

The debates on the links between Communism and National Socialism bring to the fore another general problem: What is the relevant chronological and geographical scope of the entangled endeavor? When in rare circumstances Communism and National Socialism have been written into the same historical narrative, the former object of comparison is more often than not transformed into "Stalinism," to indicate that the interconnection specifically concerns Joseph Stalin's many years of Soviet rule. No doubt, this conceptualization has certain advantages, of which the most important is that Stalin's and Hitler's rules were reasonably contemporaneous. This contiguity in time is probably beneficial for the genetic and structural comparison, including the question whether and how the two regimes immediately affected each other.

Whether National Socialism should be analyzed in terms of a delimited and parenthetic period of Nazi rule 1933–1945, or if it had its important roots in the larger German history of the *Kaiserreich* and the Weimar Republic, was the fundamental bone of contention of the *Historikerstreit*. The successful radical position has been the latter, that Hitler and Nazism in all essentials should be understood in a diachronic perspective. In this perspective, not Nazism but the entire German modern history stands out as a deviation.

There is an interesting difference in perspective when the same problem is applied on Stalin and Stalinism. In this context, the successful radical, revisionist interpretation has rather been synchronic in its endeavor to relate the Stalinist "deviation" to contemporary factors in general, and to the hostility from the surrounding world in particular. Stalinism should be interpreted as a civilization of its own. Often, behind such an interpretation has rested an ambition to avoid to involve Lenin and Leninism, especially from the violent, state-terrorist history of the successor.

In an entangled narrative, however, the analytical disadvantages of reducing Soviet Communism to Stalinism are considerable. The Stalinist regime defined itself as Communist, legitimated itself by relating to a larger Communist history, and was defined by the surrounding world, not least by Nazi Germany, as Communist. Henry Rousso has drawn a similar conclusion that while Hitler founded a Nazi system that came to power with him in 1933 and disappeared with him in 1945, Stalin inherited a Communist system that furthermore survived him with almost forty years.[49] To be sure, Rousso's aim is not to analyze Nazi Germany as a historical parenthesis without connections to the past. Rather, he underlines that Hitler, as Chancellor from January 1933 and as *Führer* after Hindenburg's death in August 1934, and to a certain extent his party and bureaucracy, created the political, organizational, and institutional frames in which the Holocaust was perpetrated. In contrast, in these aspects, the way for Stalin's despotic rule was already prepared when he gradually conquered absolute power during the 1920s. It means that Stalinist Communism must be followed back into its Leninist origins. In the comparative perspective, the Leninist period until 1924 must be analyzed as an integrated, even formative period, since the ideological, institutional, and politico-cultural continuity from Lenin's to Stalin's era is conspicuous. From solid empirical documentation, and with support from several modern studies on the relationship between Lenin and Stalin, Robert Gellately states that "far from perverting or undermining Lenin's legacy, as is sometimes assumed, Stalin was Lenin's logical heir."[50] Consequently, the Soviet Communist regime under Stalin was part and parcel of a historical totality which span the entire period from the Bolsheviks' *coup d'état* in November 1917 to the dissolution of the Soviet Union in late 1991. In this respect, there is reason to agree with Wim Berkelaar when he keeps Stalin apart from Hitler:

> However one analyses Stalin, he was part of a tradition of Marx and Lenin. And however much he perverted Marxism, that tradition set limits to his capriciousness. In contrast, National Socialism had neither tradition nor future. Hitler was the Marx, Lenin and Stalin of National Socialism.[51]

It goes without saying that the entangled history of Communism and National Socialism has an unusually large scope. It extends over important parts of twentieth-century European history and touches upon fundamental, recurrent tensions and conflicts of the century, such as the struggle between democracy and dictatorship, war and peace, socialism/Communism and nationalism, Left and Right, and modernity and tradition. In the center of Europe, the German National Socialism was followed immediately by the East German Communism when the Second World War turned into the Cold War. Also other parts of Central and Eastern Europe underwent the same development of a double political and cultural "stratification." In this sense, Communism and National Socialism are definitely parts of the same entangled history.

The next question is whether other Communisms than the Soviet one should be addressed. In addition to the general risk that the entangled work in that case will exceed all analytical bounds, it can be argued that an introduction of a multitude of new times and places and root systems, related also to Communist regimes in China, Cambodia, North Korea, and Cuba, would water down the approach. Besides, the dimension of influence and transfer in relation to Nazi Germany would be less interesting. This does not mean that the problem of whether there is, with Sté-phane Courtois's words, a "genetic code of Communism," introduced in Russia in the revolutionary year 1917 is without interest.[52] The principally same consideration is behind the decision whether to include Nazism in a larger concept of fascism. Whether Nazism shares what Robert Paxton has called "the anatomy of fascism" is an intricate question with scholarly as well as ideological underpinnings, but another full-fledged entangled study within the realm of the main Communism-National Socialism entanglement is probably difficult to handle.[53]

THE PERSPECTIVES

Writing an entangled history of Communism and National Socialism, there is an obvious risk that the similarities as well as the differences between the two phenomena form an endless, superficial compilation. The other danger is that politico-ideological preferences are at the head of the work. Therefore, theoretical and analytical considerations are necessary. Of basic importance is the distinction between a genetic, a structural, and a genealogical perspective. They can all be applied separately, and have so far normally been used in that way, but the analytical idea behind the complex approach of entangled history is that they reciprocally presuppose and reinforce each other, and therefore should be used or applied together.

A Genetic Approach

The first perspective is genetic, focusing on roots and historical developments. It also involves patterns of contacts and confrontations, interpreted in terms of reciprocal perceptions, imitations, and learning processes. The genetic perspective, which should not be understood in terms of Courtois' biologically oriented thinking, highlights traditional scholarly historical values, such as the need for historical understanding from a contemporaneous standpoint, explanation, and a diachronic, process-oriented thinking in general. The idea is to derive a historical phenomenon from its roots, demonstrating its growth, rise, or development up to a temporary focal point in terms of causes and effects, intentions and real outcomes, continuity and change. Mostly, the genetic perspective has been used to analyze a historical phenomenon in terms of a unique historical development, to demonstrate what could be called "separate grounds." However, genetic perspectives can also be applied to highlight processes and successions that can involve both Communist and Nazi history.

The most striking example of historical entanglement is the Soviet and Nazi regimes' successive brutal occupations of the Baltic and the east

central European borderline areas from Estonia in the north to Moldavia
in the south in the Second World War years: the Soviet occupation from
1939 to 1941, the German occupation between 1941 and 1944, and the
Soviet reoccupation from 1944 onward. After the Red Army came the
Wehrmacht, and then the Red Army returned. Nazi Gestapo and the Soviet secret police NKVD followed in the bloody paths of the armies.
Focusing on this historically precarious geographical location, several
scholars have recently analyzed what one of them, Jan T. Gross, has
denoted as "the tangled web" of Communist-Nazi juxtapositions.[54] By
concentrating on local massacres such as the German slaughter of Jews in
the Babi Yar ravine outside Kiev, the Nazi wartime blockade of Leningrad and the Soviet killings of Poles in the Katyn forests outside Smo-
lensk, or on the larger patterns of systematic, large-scale massacres, all of
them have depicted the area as a zone of recurrent mass violence within
which borders were drawn by force and where the human suffering
reached tremendous proportions when the Soviet and Nazi regimes, successively,

> aimed at the total altering of their respective domains and turned the
> borderlands into the testing grounds for massive relocation of popula-
> tions, state-terror on an unprecedented scale, and ferocious internal
> conflicts.[55]

According to Timothy Snyder, Communist and Nazi mass murder
together accounted for fourteen million civilian deaths—Belarusians, Estonians, Jews, Latvians, Lithuanians, Poles, Russians, Ukrainians; German as well as Soviet prisoners of war—in the "bloodlands" during a
dozen years, from the deadly famine in Ukraine and Hitler's rise to power in 1933 to the end of the Second World War in 1945.[56] It is certainly
Snyder's intention to argue that the Communist-Nazi tandem must be
understood in a genetic and dynamic way. Most important for him is to
demonstrate that the entangled character of the various processes of mass
murder—most obviously when new atrocities were committed against
groups accused of sympathies for or collaboration with the former mass
murderers—caused many more deaths than what the German Nazi or
Soviet Communist regimes could have carried out on their own. Another
thing is that his narrative might invite readers to apply a logic of consequence that reminds of the one applied above by Stéphane Courtois, as
pursued by one of the reviewers of *Bloodlands*:

> For the purpose of ridding the country of all elements potentially inim-
> ical to German and Russian supremacy, it mattered little whether a
> Polish-speaking merchant in Lwów (Lviv) was deported for being a
> bourgeois or for being a Jew, or whether a Polish peasant in the Bialys-
> tok region was shot for being a kulak or for being a subhuman Slav.[57]

Another illustrative genetic example of entanglement is provided by the "special camps" in eastern Germany maintained by the Soviet military administration after the Second World War, and situated on the same locations where the Nazi concentration camps previously had worked. After 1989, this has inevitably led to what has been described as a "complex, uneasy confrontation between eastern Germany's Nazi and Communist pasts."[58] As a matter of fact, the same individuals could find themselves captives of the same camp twice, first as enemies of National Socialism, then as agents of anti-Communist ideas. There are also many examples of the genetic notion that post-war victims of Communism had been wartime collaborators with Nazism.

In genetic historiography, there is a tendency to let the "results" of the historical narrative decide the disposition and degree of entanglement between Soviet Communism and German National Socialism. Scholars focusing on the Molotov-Ribbentrop Pact of August 1939 often regard this event as an expression of the fundamental spirit of community between Communism and Nazism, of their proximity and similarity. This is a common idea in the east European countries which were immediately affected by the implementation of the pact, but also other scholars adhere to this idea. One of them connects Nazi Germany and Communist Russia through Stalin's efforts to uphold the antagonism between the German Communists and Social Democrats, a politics that according to him made it easier for Hitler to seize power. This development, together with a psychological notion that Stalin "may have felt more comfortable working with Hitler, a fellow dictator, than with the Western democracies,"[59] left historical traces such as an interwar military cooperation between the Soviet Union and Germany, and the occupation of the territories between the two countries according to the agreement of the secret protocol of the 1939 pact.

Other scholars rather describe the interwar interrelations between Communist and Nazi politicians in terms of ambivalence or dualism: confrontation and hate went hand-in-hand with fascination and a desire for increased contacts. The dictators had not abandoned their ideological postulates but chose to subordinate them to tactical dispositions: while Hitler realized that he could use a widespread fear of Communism for his political purposes, Stalin preferred to associate himself with Hitler to the Western democracies due to his ambition to keep the Soviet Union out of the coming war and reap the harvest of this outside position after the war.[60]

A third group of scholars depart from another historical "result": the Great Patriotic War that started in June 1941. In that case, the interpretation of the Communist-Nazi interconnection is mostly quite different. The total war is rather seen as a final eruption of the fundamental difference and lack of solidarity between the two states. Such an idea is based on the existence of basic ideological and political patterns of conflict between Soviet Communism and German Nazism, but is obviously consistent with a notion that the Soviet-German pact is best explained as a functional solution in a precarious situation: Hitler did not want his army to fight on two fronts, and Stalin needed time to strengthen the Soviet military capacity before the inevitable final settlement with the Nazi arch enemy.

A Structural Approach

A genuinely entangled study presupposes an increased, indeed programmatic openness toward what has been called "common grounds."[61] This approach brings the concept of totalitarianism to the fore. In historiography, this has often also implied a change of focus from a process-oriented to a structural or functional perspective, when scholars have tried synchronically to narrow down "operational" parallels of the two political systems and rules in the way they handled ideology to construct social utopia, organized party life, used propaganda and techniques of terror and extermination.[62]

However, as mentioned above, the totalitarianism approach is not necessarily synonymous with a synchronic analysis of factors that, taken together, demonstrate parallels between Communist Soviet Union and National Socialist Germany that qualify them as integrated parts of a totalitarian system. A few scholars have successfully applied dynamic, historical perspectives on totalitarian states, without abandoning the "common grounds" perspective. One prominent example is Michael Mann, who has identified what he calls a continuous revolution which in neither the Soviet nor the Nazi instance allows any long-term compromises, and common, basically self-destructive tensions between ideology and bureaucracy, between revolution and institutionalization, and between anarchy and efficiency.[63]

In the point of intersection between genetic and structural perspectives, a focus on the similar historical backgrounds of empire, war, and revolution might be useful to explain the birth of the two popular dictatorial systems in pursuit of "holistic" societies. Closely related to the "common grounds" perspective, François Furet has detected a common "matrix," grown out of the experiences and lessons of the First World War, of "familiarity with violence, the simplicity of extreme passions, the submission of the individual to the collective and, finally, the bitterness of futile or betrayed sacrifices."[64] Consequently, in Furet's analysis, "progress" into the "mass" age of "democracy" did not emerge as a result of education, wealth, and peace, but out of memories of war, revolution, and injury. Other historians reinforce this interpretation by maintaining that if it had not been for the war, both Lenin and Hitler had remained marginal figures without any prospects of entering political life.[65]

It should be stressed that structural perspectives do not only have to relate to political and social dimensions, but also to cultural and linguistic phenomena. The tensions between on the one hand the "permanence" and "unfinishedness" of socio-political revolution, a notion that scholarly has been extended to include ideas of a "cultural revolution" in both the Soviet Communist and the Nazi case, and on the other hand a far-reaching conservatism in cultural life and art, are particularly interesting aspects of totalitarian rule. In recent years, cultural studies of Soviet Communist and German Nazi society, often inspired by historian George Mosse's analyses of the Nazi movement and thinking, have focused on phenomena such as aesthetics, body, consumption, masculinity, rituals, and symbols.[66] The importance of the cultural and linguistic dimensions has been aptly emphasized by Luisa Passerini, echoing Arendt's famous declaration that spontaneity is the main enemy of totalitarian aspirations:

> Totalitarianisms need the comedy of unanimity, and that is why they consider every invention and creativity, including poetry and jokes, as dangerous, while they have to encourage the capacity for copying and repeating.[67]

Behind these observations rest a few basic structural questions: Is it possible to reveal a fundamental linguistic or cultural grammar or mode of representation of the totalitarian regimes investigated in this program? If so, what about the interrelations between future-oriented revolutionary and history-oriented facets of such linguistic and cultural representations and constructs?[68]

The totalitarianism approach still retains some scholarly value, despite the obvious formalistic shortcomings. After more than a half-century, Hannah Arendt's critique of the Communist and Nazi ideologies still stands out as penetrating and well-informed, continuously influencing scholarly thinking. However, as mentioned above, during the last decades totalitarianism has been renewed in a way that makes it more attractive. The new totalitarianism, or post-totalitarianism, focuses less on structures than on movements. Ideology is investigated anew as a dynamic means of destroying an old politico-cultural order and of establishing a totally new one. The totalitarian ideology is constructed on stereotypical, pedagogically convincing images, narratives, and discourses of good and evil, friend and foe, derived from mythical historical origins, promising a utopian future, and mobilizing generations of intellectuals and others who came to pay service to these ideologies in a way suggested by Furet's book on their delusive powers.

To this new methodological orientation belongs also a debate on the relationship between totalitarian ideologies and what has been called political religions. Like totalitarianism, this is certainly not a new concept but goes back to the interwar years.[69] As a matter of fact, one of its earlier spokesmen, Karl Bracher, has described political religions in words that

are close to common definitions of totalitarianism when he argues that
ideologies such as National Socialism and Leninism-Stalinism constitute

> an all-embrasing movement and an all-embrasing faith, while at the
> same time identifying and resolutely confronting the absolute ideologi-
> cal opponent in an ideology of simultaneous integration and confronta-
> tion.[70]

Recently, several scholars focusing on totalitarianism have rediscov-
ered the concept and connected it to comparative analyses of National
Socialist, Communist, and other totalitarian regimes.[71] In this scholarly
analysis, the totalitarian societies, including Communist Soviet Union
with its allegedly atheist and materialist ideology, went a long way of
reinstating religious dogma, thought, and practice in their deification of
nation and state, celebration of the personality cult, mythologization of
"rebirth" and the "new" man, and diabolization of internal and external
enemies.

Another concept that in its connections to totalitarianism can be derived back to at least the ideas of the Frankfurt school is the modern
condition itself. In the German scholarly context, the idea of a particular
German modernization is advocated by the supporters of a *Sonderweg*
thesis. Without a doubt, Nazi Germany was a more modern state and
society than Communist Soviet Union, irrespective of whether political or
economic dimensions are emphasized. Nevertheless, it makes sense to
bring the two histories together from a genetic perspective. A common
historical interpretation is that both Russia/the Soviet Union and Germany passed through unbalanced and uncompleted modernization processes. They were characterized by efforts by what in the German context has
been called an intervention state to force the pace of economic and military developments, at the expense of the political and cultural growth of
a civic society.[72] No liberal, middle-class revolutions from below took
place, and democratization was not allowed to go hand-in-hand with
industrialization. These unbalanced modernization processes do not explain why the Soviet Union followed a Communist line, while Germany
succumbed to National Socialism, but they certainly go some way to
explaining why non-liberal extreme ideologies took hold of the two
states, and why totalitarian structures, hostile to liberal democracy and
civil rights, were forwarded. The demands and needs of the strong state
and party took priority over those of the individual, and both regimes
regarded human beings merely as what Richard Pipes has denoted as
"expendable raw material for the construction of a new social order."[73]

In his influential but controversial work *Modernity and the Holocaust*
from 1989, Zygmunt Bauman suggests that without modernity, with its
main ingredients industrialization, rationalization, and bureaucratiza-
tion, the "final solution" would be unthinkable. Of basic importance in
Bauman's theory is the growth of an impersonal bureaucratic culture

within modern society, indifferent to moral values, but eager to classify and categorize, in order to discern and destroy what is perceived as "unnatural," "unhealthy," or "unclean." While some of Bauman's critics argue that modernity rather should be related to a Western civilization of rights and freedom, leaving National Socialism rather as a revolt against modernity, others dislike his underestimation of agency and ideology.[74] Nevertheless, the state of modernity is currently a frequently companion to totalitarianism in the scholarly debate, depicting both Communist Soviet Union and Nazi Germany as in various ways modern or modernizing states and regimes.

Naturally enough, Bauman's book has also had considerable repercussions on genocide studies. Traditional debates of obvious relevance for the understanding of the entire Soviet Communist and German Nazi experiences must be addressed: Did Soviet Communist terror under Lenin and Stalin have the genocidal character that as regards the Holocaust cannot be questioned? Should the crimes against humanity committed by the Soviet and Nazi regimes be explained by means of an intentionalist or a functionalist model? Does the traditional scholarly distinction between the Nazi regime's ethnically or racially motivated killings and the Soviet Communist regime's killings of class enemies correspond to empirical findings?

Another area of scholarly interest, closely connected to the modernization theme, relates to the point of intersection between on the one hand regimes with violent and destructive political programs and policies, on the other their contemporaneous introduction of embryos to or full-fledged socioeconomic welfare states, which obviously increased their legitimacy and popularity especially among the Soviet and German populations. This perspective makes it possible to analyze the "evil" and the "good" aspects of the Communist and the National Socialist regimes in an entangled way. The logic of total war went hand-in-hand with the logic of economic development. The two developments were surely interrelated, in the sense that those minorities who were hit by terror had to "pay" for the benefits of the majority. In the words of historian Götz Aly, Hitler's rule provided either "profits" for the people or "fruits of evil," paid for by the confiscation of Jewish property in Germany and later the plunder of the conquered countries, in particular their Jewish populations.[75] In Soviet studies, there is nowadays a large literature on the tensions and controversies between the regime's ambitions to construct an economically—and militarily—viable and rational Communist society, and contemporaneous political and social ambitions that expressed themselves in class war and terror against "oppositional" groups.[76] In this respect, gender relations might prove a fruitful area; were women primarily victims of a terrorist state with its repressive politics, or did they on the contrary mainly provide political support to or even active participation in the misdeeds of the Communist and National Socialist regimes?

In historical research on Nazi Germany, a "victim thesis" has been followed by a "perpetrator thesis" in what has been described as a *Historikerinnenstreit*.[77]

Finally, a few other scholarly areas that have been considerably expanded during the last decades could be exploited. One is *Alltagsgeschichte*, or the history of everyday life, a concept that in this context has an interesting double root system. One of them goes back to the early totalitarianism theory with its interest in everyday life in a totalitarian society.[78] The other root system stretches back to the opponents of totalitarianism, to radical social history revisionism. Its ambition has been to avoid a top-down perspective and to insist that ordinary people did not act only in response to larger structures, but rather acted on their own and resisted the regimes.[79] In a post-revisionist perspective, everyday history has to a greater extent been related to cultural and linguistic aspects. One of the absolute benefits of the everyday perspective is again that it has given women and female resistance a new place in historiography.[80] With this perspective, ordinary practices in extraordinary times such as denunciations have proven fruitful to analyze in an entangled way.[81]

A Genealogical Approach

The third perspective is *genealogical*, emphasizing the processing of history addressed by posterity in terms of meaning and memory. The notion of genealogy is here inspired less by the ideas of Friedrich Nietzsche and Michel Foucault than by hermeneutical thinking on *Wirkungsgeschichte*, effective history, with its insistence on understanding as an open-ended dialogue—or a comparison—between on the one hand self-understanding, on the other an understanding of a temporally distant matter at issue. Problems of influences and transfers seem urgent to dwell upon.

When we address the past genealogically, we do not do it in an unprejudiced and arbitrary way. We do not process the entire history. We do not always search where professional historians have identified the scholarly important history, and do seldom use the methodological standards and norms that permeate good scholarly historical work. Our search for proximity to and relevance in history has other qualities. Rather, we make use of history within a history culture, which can be described as a communicative arena in which the past is ascribed meaning and significance. In history culture, individuals and collectives make sense of and evaluate history by explicitly or, more often, implicitly answering questions such as: What past is worth remembering, inquiring into, filing, teaching and learning, celebrating, exhibiting, and debating? And, on the contrary, what past do we *not* find relevant or useful, but rather choose to rationalize, distort, repress, or forget? What I elsewhere have called a non-use of history is a special case of an ideological history use, carried out in order to rationalize or legitimize a position of power.[82]

History culture manifests itself in history products such as encyclopedias, textbooks, commemorations, exhibits, and films—in this case products connected to the intersection of Soviet Communism and German National Socialism—which can be analyzed by genealogically oriented scholars. To this perspective clearly also belong the voices of those who survived the politics of the Communist and Nazi regimes and later have born witness to the suffering both in the era of the atrocities and afterward. It has been argued that we live in the era of the witness, and much research has recently been carried out on the memories and life stories of survivors, and, more or less directly, on the mechanisms of Communist and Nazi terror.[83]

General questions with genealogical outlooks, concerning crucial aspects of European history cultures, include: What are the manifestations of a present-day preoccupation with the Communism-Nazism nexus in political and other discourses in various European societies and states? What controversies are to be found in European countries in which there is an ongoing settlement of historical accounts with both National Socialism and Communism, and where the conflict between a "nationalization" and a "Europeanization" or "globalization" of history is so obvious in our days? For whom and for what purposes is the Communism-Nazism nexus considered a usable past? In the last section of this chapter, these genealogical questions will be empirically addressed.

OPERATIVE ENTANGLEMENT

The two first historical perspectives, taken together, present us with important aspects of what historian Charles Maier has denoted as the structural narrative of twentieth-century history, with focus on large-scale historical trends and transformations, which in this case amounts to the rise and rule of the Soviet Communist and German National Socialist systems. The third perspective corresponds to what Maier calls a moral narrative, "sought less in the practice of professional history than in the orientation that intellectuals and commentators expect from history . . . turning to history as a sort of liberation or exit strategy from the past."[84]

An entangled historical analysis must make use of all the perspectives and dimensions just mentioned. As a matter of fact, they presuppose and analytically strengthen each other. The genetic-structural perspective answers to traditional scholarly questions about roots and developments, helping us to answer questions related to difference and similarity, cause and effect, process and system, intentionality and functionality, and simultaneousness. The strength is that it does justice to history as a phenomenon in its own historical right, from a position of diachronic progression and synchronic structure. In an entangled analysis, the advantage of the genetic-structural perspective is twofold, related to what has been argued above about the non-arbitrary character of genealogical history. In order to reflect upon why individuals, societies, and states turn to a certain history in a certain way and in a certain situation, to answer to certain needs and interests, genetic and structural observations are instrumental. The second value is that it helps to understand not only that history is meaningful, but also what history that is meaningful in history culture. The genealogical eye is not directed toward history in general, but toward certain historical contents and interpretations, which can only be critically analyzed from a genetic perspective.

The corresponding weakness of the genetic perspective is that it lacks a mechanism for discussing history from a position of relevance other than the strictly internal scholarly one. It gives no hints of why a history is considered painful, in terms of experience, meaning and memory, responsibility, guilt and justice, suffering, trauma, and grief. It gives the wrong impression that the historical dimension lives its own life, separate from the culture and society it nurtures and is nurtured by. Only a genealogical perspective can bring a relevance criterion that makes it possible to discuss why the entangled histories of Communism and National Socialism are considered indifferent, interesting, or even painful. Only a genealogical perspective can illustrate how they are represented in history culture and used in society.

THE DIMENSIONS

These basic perspectives, relevant in any scholarly handling of history, need to have an operational elaboration. Four analytically distinct dimensions can be suggested. The first two concern ideology. The first of them takes ideology out of its genetic context in favor of a structural and functional approach. In order to analyze affinities between Soviet Communism and German National Socialism, these must be scrutinized as absolute systems of ideas with certain functions. How are these one-truth systems organized? Karl Popper's well-known criticism from *The Open Society and Its Enemies* (1945) of what he called historicist ideas of iron laws of what the future has in store for us, prophetical ideas intended to bring about heaven on earth but in reality producing hell, is still valid. Both Communism and National Socialism can obviously be described as macro-historical narratives, establishing a pedagogically convincing, simplified web of connections between a dark—or paradisiacal—past, a struggling present, and a bright, utopian future, but how are these historical perspectives more tangibly illustrated? Where can be found the destructive potentials of these ideologies that made them motive forces for large-scale crimes, if not what Popper described as a blind belief that all policies and actions must be adjusted to them?[85] How is the ethos and moral superiority of these ideologies motivated? What is the balance between deterministic and activist notions, between a history of necessity and of possibility, between ideas of a nationalist and a socialist character?[86] What kinds of utopias are depicted: is a traditional distinction between a "sociological" utopia of Communism and a "biological" one of Nazism relevant? What roles do notions of revolution and war play in order to mobilize masses of people and legitimize the regimes? What kind of enemy images and scapegoats are used regarding race, ethnicity, gender, class, and other categorizations, and how are they related to the master narratives of the ideologies? It goes without saying that Jews are depicted as arch-enemies by the Nazi ideologists, and their evilness often reinforced by a "Jewish Bolshevik" connection to the Soviet Union, but what role do anti-Semitic ideas, and, more generally, notions of ethnicity, nationality, and race, play in Soviet Communism?

In a general work on modern genocide, Eric Weitz has maintained that although Soviet terror lacked the total character of the Holocaust, over time it assumed a more "German" character as stigmatization of enemies increasingly was essentialized and racialized when ethnic and national purges directed against "unreliable" categories of Soviet Koreans, Germans, Poles, and Balts escalated in Stalin's Soviet Union from the latter part of the 1930s.[87] Furthermore, by reversing Ernst Nolte's argument from the German *Historikerstreit* that German anti-Semitism was provoked by fear of Communist Soviet Union, he argues that the increase of nationalist and racist enemy images in Stalin's Soviet state was triggered by the Nazi assumption of power in 1933, and the following Nazi exercise of power in Germany. In particular, the German invasion of the Soviet Union in June 1941 and the outbreak of total war started a chain of "national" reactions when various "punished" peoples were forcibly removed, several of them from Soviet regions that they had been allotted as autonomous territories already in the early Soviet era:

> The impact of the Soviet Union was immediate and devastating, and it aroused enormous fears of betrayal from within, especially from members of diaspora nationalities who, in some cases, had cross-border ties to the military enemies of the Soviet Union and had demonstrated particular hostility toward the "socialist offensive" of the 1930s.[88]

For Weitz, the Stalinist politics of not only identifying specific "enemy nations," but also providing them with hereditary characteristics of enmity and treachery to the Soviet project, gives evidence of a Soviet Communist racial or genocidal practice that is not far from the Nazi categorization of the Jewish victims of genocide: "Under Stalin, the Soviet Regime condemned entire generations of particular nationalities, not on the basis of what they actually did . . . but on the basis of who they were."[89] In her analysis of Soviet sources of the encounter of Soviet Communism and German National Socialism in the Ukrainian borderland, Kate Brown similarly identifies "a primordialism (or ethnic profiling) creeping into official documents" when enemies of forced collectivization were singled out by Communist party leader of different levels of authority.[90] Diaspora Poles and Germans belonged to the foremost Soviet "enemy nations." When Brown concludes her study, she finds that the Soviet killings of Poles and Germans are part of a larger historical, politico-ideological pattern, a pattern reaching beyond the ideology and political practice of the totalitarian Communist and Nazi states:

> Had Soviet officials not deported Poles and Germans for fear of cross-border ethnic ties, they might well have come up with other reasons for deportation—just as Polish politicians fashioned justifications to forcibly push out and Polonize Ukrainian populations, as Nazi German leaders found reasons to annihilate non-Germans during the war, and as Ukrainian and Polish nationalist insurgents rationalized their own part in the creation of purified nation-space. The Soviet deportation of nationalities was part of this larger trend—that of creating distilled nation-space for modern governance, a process which occurred both within and beyond the realm of the Soviet state.[91]

Arguments such as those put forward by Weitz have not passed unnoticed. In a debate in *Soviet Studies*, one of his opponents promptly rejected his interpretation by arguing that in Stalin's wartime Soviet Union "most were persecuted based on their alleged *conduct* and not a premeditated racial notion of these collectives."[92] In this interpretation, Soviet wartime terror was the result of timely pragmatic and functional Soviet needs of homogenization, stabilization, and consolidation in a difficult situation, not of categorizations constructed on absolute ethno-national or racial criteria. The problem is certainly not solved once and for all, but as is indicated by the argumentations above, it may be useful to make a distinction between on the one hand declared motives for terror, on the other hand basic ideological convictions behind the state-sponsored violence. Also in the 1930s, wreckage and treachery were often considered evoked by social backgrounds and political attitudes incompatible with the Soviet Communist project, but in the underlying ideological foundations, ethnicity and national affiliation were given a new impetus in the Soviet ideological construction of "we" and "they," "friend" and "foe." All scholars seem to agree on what Terry Martin in his standard work on the Soviet "affirmative action" empire has described as a "revised Soviet nationalities policy," but whether this revision was an immediate response to a perceived or real increased threat from Japan, Poland, and Germany, a more fundamental adjustment to a politico-ideological worldview with larger similarities to the National Socialist ideology, or both, is still an open question.[93]

Behind these questions and debates rests an understanding that the ideologies must not be regarded as contained in themselves but must be analyzed in their historical and geographical settings. As mentioned, we often stick to a simplistic binary notion that Communist mobilization was accomplished along class lines, while Nazism relied on race and ethnic distinctions to identify friends and enemies. The Nazis demonized Jews and Slavs as racial subhumans, and the Bolsheviks stigmatized "former people," traitors and class enemies through their—alleged—relations to the old czarist regime and the capitalist Western world. However, historians have demonstrated that these categorizations are much less clear-cut when applied to the multiethnic east European battle zone between Communist Soviet Union and Nazi Germany, where social and ethnic identities were interconnected and where ethnicity often became the most important category also for the Soviet authorities to evaluate the loyalty of entire communities, to include and to exclude.[94] Furthermore, Communist Soviet Union was from its outset a multiethnic empire, Nazi Germany became an empire by means of military expansion, and both states were occupied with eradicating cultural and ethnic differences, thus aiming at what has been described as "a permanent order of social, national, and racial homogeneity."[95]

To be sure, there is a need for a supplementing genetic perspective and a historical context to answer some of these questions, since they probably change over time, especially regarding a less consistent and more protracted Soviet Communism. No doubt, a general historical framework is needed, starting from the turbulence and shattering disruption of progress caused by the great total wars, which tended to undermine rational ideas and further the rise of dictatorships. For entangled purposes, a genetic perspective can highlight the origins and births of the ideologies in question. Do totalitarian ideologies go back on old layers of monocratic thought, as suggested by Popper, are they derived from the Enlightenment and the radical egalitarianism of the French Revolution, as Theodor Adorno and Max Horkheimer maintain, or are they rather to be regarded as radical left- or right-wing manifestations of nationalist and socialist mass ideologies of the modern era? In a most original study, Roman Szporluk has analyzed the relationship between Communism and nationalism in their nineteenth-century context of origin, but he also takes an interest in their twentieth-century legacy. In an entangled way, Szporluk concludes that both ideologies developed in close relation to each other: twentieth-century nationalism tended to incorporate socialist/communist notions, while Communism tended to adopt nationalist ideas.[96]

This second ideological dimension also highlights the problem what happened to the new systems of ideas when they "married" with basic traits in the German and Russian national cultures. This is a dimension which is rarely explicitly dealt with in scholarly works. In the Russian case, socialism was imported and transformed by the encounter with a Russian culture, highly influenced by orthodox religious thinking, while in the German case National Socialism has a less clearly "imported" root system, and more of *völkish* nationalist, racist, and anti-Semitic ideas of German extraction. One must note that Marxism was a German philosophy, rooted and situated in German history and culture. Thus, the Soviet state was an offspring of a German project. In this genetic respect, this state can be treated as a "sibling" to the Nazi state.

A third basically genetic dimension concerns the Communist and National Socialist ideologies in power, transformed into political parties and state institutions ruling with reference to ideological foundations. Several influential works from the last decades have demonstrated that both the Soviet Communist and the German Nazi regime managed to convince large numbers of ordinary people to enthusiastically take part in extraordinary events.[97] It must, however, be added that it is far from clear that Lenin or Stalin or Hitler were consequently acting politically in accordance with ideological blueprints worked upon long in advance. What is more clear is that they all hated the previous regimes, and acted out of hatred of what they perceived as disastrous predecessors and from a radical rejection of their political practices. To be sure, war and economic collapse are analytical factors to be dealt with as well as ideological fervor.

The fourth and final main dimension is the genealogical one, focusing on the handling of Soviet Communism and German National Socialism in European history culture. It has already been argued that historical phenomena related to sudden change, turning-points, and crises tend to engage posterity to raise questions of a time-transcending character: When did it start? Where did it go astray? How could it go so wrong? Who is responsible? Are *we* among those responsible? Can it happen again? These are questions recurrently raised in this text, which indicates that problems related to for example the origins of Communism and Nazism are not only genetic, but are also relevant in a genealogical perspective. Certainly, Soviet Communism and German National Socialism, and the misdeeds carried out within their power spheres, belong to these basic borderline phenomena of history which we, particularly in our time, seem to have strong existential, ideological, legal, moral, and political needs and interests to remember, narrate, and make sense of, for purposes of the present and the future. With a few reflexions on this theme this chapter will end where it started, in European and Swedish history culture.

EUROPEAN HISTORY CULTURE

The Berlin Wall has been torn down, but in history culture, a borderline dividing Europe into one eastern and one western part can still be found. Touching upon these differences, Tony Judt has differentiated between a Western Europe with too little memory, and an Eastern Europe with too much memory. In his overview, the West is devoted to a series of unhappy memories from the Second World War years, with Nazism, Hitler, and Auschwitz as the mainly external evil phenomena in the absolute foreground. Eastern Europe, on the contrary, has many histories to refer to and many perpetrators and victims to attach oneself to. In the latter part, history is not another country but "a positive archipelago of vulnerable historical territories, to be preserved from attacks and distortions perpetrated by the occupants of a neighbouring island of memory, a dilemma made the more cruel because the enemy is almost always within."[98] However, since 1989, Communism has provided east European history culture with an all-embracing theme.

The new border is certainly not as definitive and non-transparent as the old one, but it approximately follows the old east-west divide. Let us start west of the border, where the Nazis were the enemy of the Second World War, and where the Nazi genocide of European Jewry has been embraced with a strong, exclusive interest during the last two decades. It can be certified from the Stockholm declaration on the Holocaust, established in the first of four consecutive international Holocaust conferences in the Swedish capital in the year 2000:

> The Holocaust (Shoah) fundamentally challenged the foundations of civilization. The unprecedented character of the Holocaust will always hold universal meaning. After half a century, it remains an event close enough in time that survivors can still bear witness to the horrors that engulfed the Jewish people. The terrible suffering of the many millions of other victims of the Nazis left an indelible scar across Europe as well.[99]

Europeanization is a process in which the genocide of European Jewry has been used to create a supranational, pan-European history culture, starting in the West. The Council of Europe, the European Parliament, and other EU institutions have been anxious to depict the idea of the European Union as a direct response to the Nazi atrocities. As stated in 2005 by Beate Winkler, the former director of the EU institution European Monitoring Centre on Racism and Xenophobia:

> The Shoah is the traumatic experience of Europe's recent history. It has driven the EU's founders to build a united and peaceful Europe and thus been at the very root of the European integration project.[100]

Examples of this historical connection may be multiplied. They were particularly frequent in the year 2005, sixty years after the end of the Second World War. Thus, in a time-transcending mental operation, the Holocaust is supposed to serve as a founding history or myth of a new, integrated Europe, which, inversely, is supposed to serve as a guarantee against the kind of intolerance and lack of respect for human rights that can cause future genocides. Consequently, right-wing extremists who deny or trivialize the Holocaust should not bother entering into the European Union. In the name of a cultural integration into Europe, new-coming, mostly East and Central European states have been urged to come to terms with an old history of collaboration with the Nazis and of indifference to the tragic Jewish destiny. Sweden has been the best country in this class so far. Here, a civil authority, Forum for Living History, has been created to strengthen democratic values among its citizenry by means of sound knowledge of Holocaust history.[101]

In the eastern parts of Europe, the support of this political and cultural offensive as regards the Holocaust is less whole-hearted. Here, Communist terror has been approached with a more vivid interest.[102] It cannot be considered a surprising development, given the fact that the countries in Eastern and Central Europe were subjected to a ruthless Communist rule for several decades. Thus, temporal dimensions have helped to emphasize Communist history, the protracted Communist repression has made functionalist explanations of repression less plausible, and the proximity in time of Communist rule has promoted political, cultural, and legal actions to cope with the Communist experience, such as trials, restitutions, lustrations, and history commissions. In contrast, the Holocaust for many people stands out as a distant history which, moreover, did not involve ethnic nationals. However, the strength of history culture is not mechanically related to temporal phenomena. This is indicated especially by the European Holocaust interest, which has drawn attention to the involvement of traditional bystander states such as Sweden, but also to the many exposures of Ukrainian, Latvian, Lithuanian, or Polish complicity in the Nazi killings, symbolized by the infamous Polish slaughters of Jews in Jedwabne.[103] The precariousness of the Holocaust topic in the east must also be seen in the light of these painful histories, and of a certain disinclination to publicly expose them.

To this explanation must, however, be added that history commissions in east European states actually have dealt with both Communist and Nazi crime histories. They have either been kept together in one commission's work, as in Estonia and Latvia, or in two separate commissions, as in Romania. As far as can be seen, there are no evident tendencies of making one terror history less evil than the other in the Baltic commission works. However, the Latvian commission reflects wisely on the difficulties in this kind of dual work, built on "lesser-evil" unbalances between the handling of Communism and Nazism in West and East European history cultures: "These differences in perceptions and awareness sometimes lead to unfortunate downgrading of either the crimes of the Nazis in the East or the crimes of the Soviet regime in the West."[104]

In West European history cultures, Communism obviously plays a less prominent role. Radical politicians, intellectuals, and scholars, of whom few today introduce themselves as Communists, tend to avoid the topic. Among frequently used strategies, silencing and trivialization should be mentioned. In 2006, the above-mentioned Forum for Living History, a government-sponsored campaign created in 1997 and transformed into a Swedish public authority in 2003 to promote knowledge about the Holocaust among the Swedish youth, was given an additional task by a non-socialist government to "inform of Communist crimes against humanity."[105] As a result, a full year later, more than four hundred Swedish historians and social scientists had undersigned a petition against "state campaign history," published in the biggest Swedish daily newspaper *Dagens Nyheter*. It is true that criticism was generally directed against political involvement in what obviously was perceived as a scholarly prerogative of producing and mediating history, but in reality, the indignation was caused by the decision to focus on a certain historical contents that was judged inappropriate, on Communist crimes. When the Holocaust was made the center of the Living History information campaign by a social democratic government a decade earlier, very few critical voices were heard.

Interestingly, the collective protest has not caused any open debate in Sweden on Communist history, or on the interconnection between Communism and Nazism. The "lesser evil" formula is probably still active, even if the new task assigned to Forum for Living History has caused some stir. To indicate the framework of such a discussion, one has to turn to a "Swedish" argumentation in the Council of Europe, triggered by the Parliamentary Assembly's suggestion in January 2006 to issue a resolution on the need for international condemnation of crimes of totalitarian communist regimes. The Council's *rapporteur*, Göran Lindblad, member of the non-socialist Moderate Party in Sweden and of the Group of the European People's Party, urged the European states to "reassess the history of communism and their own past, clearly distance themselves from the crimes committed by totalitarian communist regimes and condemn them without any ambiguity."[106] In response, Mats Einarsson, member of the Swedish Left Party and a representative of the Group of the Unified European Left, strongly objected that the report lacked a clear demarcation line between on the one hand "regimes labelled as communist" and on the other hand "communism as a political movement." He continued:

> The problem with the report, which makes it unacceptable, is that it uses the atrocities of the past as a tool to attack, marginalise and even

pave the way for the criminalisation of an ideology and political current, the ideals of which are the opposite of these crimes. [107]

Einarsson's interpretation is yet another absurd illustration of Arendt's dictum that what possibly can be called a lesser evil often tends to become an absolute good. The method is well-known: to totally separate Communist ideology from the only dimensions with which we individually and collectively can orientate toward the future: history, memory, experience. And, I could add: to totally separate Communism from National Socialism. Also for this reason, it is an urgent task to bring them historically together, in one comprehensive narrative.

NOTES

1. Sven Eric Liedman, "Kommunism," *Nationalencyklopedin*, Vol. 11 (Höganäs: Bra Böcker, 1993), 209–10.

2. Karl Christian Lammers, "Nazism," *Nationalencyklopedin*, Vol. 14 (Höganäs: Bra Böcker, 1994), 77–78.

3. Cf. Jani Marjanen, "Histoire croisée of concepts as transnational history: Undermining methodological nationalism," in *Transnational Political Spaces: Agents—Structures—Encounters*, ed. Mathias Albert et al. (Frankfurt and New York: Campus, 2009), 239–63.

4. For examples of different orientations, see Shalini Randeria, "Entangled histories of uneven modernities: Civil society, caste solidarities and legal pluralism in postcolonial India," in *Unraveling Ties: From Social Cohesion to New Practices of Connectedness*, ed. Yehuda Elkana et al. (Frankfurt and New York: Campus Verlag, 2002), 284–311, and Reinhart Kössler, "Entangled history and politics: Negotiating the past between Namibia and Germany," *Journal of Contemporary African Studies* 26 (2008): 313–39.

5. Quote from Michael Werner and Bénédicte Zimmermann, "Beyond Comparison: *Histoire Croisée* and the Challenge of Reflexivity," *History & Theory* 45 (2006): 32. See also Michael Werner and Bénédicte Zimmermann, "Penser l'histoire croisée: entre empirie et réflexivité," *Annales HSS* 58 (2003): 7–36.

6. The concept is coined by David D. Roberts in his *The Totalitarian Experiment in Twentieth-Century Europe: Understanding the Poverty of Great Politics* (New York and London: Routledge, 2006), 475.

7. Abbot Gleason, *Totalitarianism: The Inner History of the Cold War* (New York and Oxford: Oxford University Press, 1995), 166.

8. For an example of the former, see Ian Kershaw and Moshe Lewin, eds., *Stalinism and Nazism: Dictatorships in Comparison* (Cambridge: Cambridge University Press, 1997). The best example of the latter is probably Michael Geyer and Sheila Fitzpatrick, eds., *Beyond Totalitarianism: Stalinism and Nazism Compared* (Cambridge: Cambridge University Press, 2009).

9. Martin Malia, *The Soviet Tragedy: A History of Socialism in Russia, 1917–1991* (New York: The Free Press, 1994), 3.

10. Malia, *The Soviet Tragedy*, ix.

11. Cf. Claude Lefort, *Complications: Communism and the Dilemmas of Democracy* (New York: Columbia University Press, 2007), 29–31.

12. Jörn Rüsen, "Holocaust Memory and Identity Building: Metahistorical Considerations in the Case of (West) Germany," in *Disturbing Remains: Memory, History, and Crisis in the Twentieth Century*, ed. Michael S. Roth and Charles G. Salas (Los Angeles: The Getty Research institute, 2001), 252–3.

13. Cf. Anne Applebaum, *Gulag: A History* (New York: Anchor Books, 2004), xxi.

14. One of the latest manifestations is Yoram Gorlitzki and Hans Mommsen, "The Political (Dis)Orders of Stalinism and National Socialism," in *Beyond Totalitarianism: Stalinism and Nazism Compared*, ed. Michael Geyer and Sheila Fitzpatrick (Cambridge: Cambridge University Press, 2009), 42–44.

15. Omer Bartov, review of *Europe between Hitler and Stalin*, by Timothy Snyder, *Slavic Review* 70 (2011), 428.

16. Ian Kershaw and Moshe Lewin, "Introduction: The Regimes and Their Dictators: Perspectives of Comparison," in *Stalinism and Nazism: Dictatorships in Comparison*, ed. Ian Kershaw and Moshe Lewin (Cambridge: Cambridge University Press, 1997), 8.

17. On Ivan and Peter as liminal historical figures in Russian and Soviet historiography and culture, see Kevin Platt, *Terror & Greatness: Ivan and Peter as Russian Myths* (Ithaca and London: Cornell University Press, 2011).

18. For an analysis of the Soviet lesser-evil formula, see Lowell Tillett, *The Great Friendship: Soviet Historians on the Non-Russian Nationalities* (Chapel Hill: University of North Carolina Press, 1969). The formula was introduced into the Communism-National Socialism debate by Martin Malia, "The Lesser Evil?," *Times Literary Supplement*, March 27, 1998.

19. Richard Overy, *The Dictators: Hitler's Germany and Stalin's Russia* (London: Penguin, 2005), xl.

20. Charles S. Maier, *The Unmasterable Past: History, Holocaust, and German National Identity* (Cambridge, MA and London: Harvard University Press, 1997), 78.

21. Ronald Grigor Suny, "Russian Terror/ism and Revisionist Historiography," *Australian Journal of Politics and History* 53 (2007): 9.

22. Cf. Alan Bullock, *Hitler and Stalin. Parallel Lives* (New York: Vintage 1993), 446, and John Connelly, review of *The Dictators: Hitler's Germany, Stalin's Russia*, by Richard Overy, *Kritika: Explorations in Russian and Eurasian History* 7 (2006), 925.

23. Stephen Wheatcroft, "The Scale and Nature of German and Soviet Repression and Mass Killings, 1930–1945," *Europe-Asia Studies* 48 (1996): 1319–53. Quotation 1319.

24. Norman Naimark, *Stalin's Genocides* (Princeton and Oxford: Princeton University Press, 2010), 129.

25. For critical analyses of the "positive heritage" of Communism, see Tzvetan Todorov, *Hope and Memory: Reflections on the Twentieth Century* (London: Atlantic, 2005), 35–36, and Richard Pipes, *Communism: A History* (New York: The Modern Library, 2001), chapter 2. For the argument that mass murders perpetrated by a "progressive intention" is not an ameliorating but rather an aggravating circumstance, see Alain Besançon, *A Century of Horrors: Communism, Nazism, and the Uniqueness of the Shoah* (Wilmington: ISI Books, 2007), 26–30.

26. Alain de Benoist, "Nazism and Communism: Evil Twins?" *Telos* 112 (1998): 183.

27. One example is Michael David-Fox, "Introduction: Entangled Histories in the Age of Extremes," in *Fascination and Enmity: Russia and Germany as Entangled Histories, 1914–1945*, ed. Michael David-Fox, Peter Holquist, and Alexander Martin (Pittsburgh: University of Pittsburgh Press, 2012), 2–3.

28. Jürgen Kocka, "Comparison and Beyond," *History & Theory* 42 (2003): 39–41.

29. See, for example, David Blackbourn and Geoff Eley, *The Pecularities of German History: Bourgeois Society and Politics in Nineteenth-Century Germany* (Oxford: Oxford University Press, 1984), and Jürgen Kocka, "Asymmetrical Historical Comparison: The Case of the German *Sonderweg*," *History & Theory* 38 (1999): 40–50.

30. See Stéphane Courtois et al., *Le livre noir du communisme: crimes, terreur, répression* (Paris: Robert Laffont, 1997), and Paul Rotherhäusler and Hans-Ueli Sonderegger, *Erinnerung an den Roten Holocaust* (Roth: Werner, 2000).

31. Courtois, *The Black Book*, 15. Already the title of the Black Book indicated a need for a comparative approach. In 1947, under the auspices of the Soviet Jewish Antifascist Committee, the Soviet-Jewish writers Vasilii Grossman and Ilya Ehrenburg published a report that exposed Nazi crimes against the Jews in the Soviet Union during the war. This book was suppressed by Stalin a year after its publication and not republished until in the 1990s. Cf. Klas-Göran Karlsson, "The Reception of the Holo-

caust in Russia: Silence, Conspiracy, and Glimpses of Light," in *Bringing the Dark Past to Light: The Reception of the Holocaust in Postcommunist Europe*, ed. John-Paul Himka and Joanna Michlic (Lincoln: Nebraska University Press, 2013), 492–93. To all probability, the authors of the French Black Book on the crimes by Communist regimes alluded to the title of Grossman's and Ehrenburg's book to stress the relationship, and the idea that Communist and Nazi crimes were commensurable, and can and should be compared.

32. Cf. several contributions to Karl Schlögel, ed. *Russian-German Special Relations in the Twentieth Century: A Closed Chapter?* (New York and Oxford: Berg, 2006).

33. Michael Geyer and Sheila Fitzpatrick, "Introduction: After Totalitarianism—Stalinism and Nazism Compared," in *Beyond Totalitarianism: Stalinism and Nazism Compared*, ed. Michael Geyer and Sheila Fitzpatrick (Cambridge: Cambridge University Press, 2009), 35. See also Katerina Clark and Karl Schlögel, "Mutual Perceptions and Projections: Stalin's Russia in the Soviet Union—Nazi Germany in the Soviet Union," in *Beyond Totalitarianism: Stalinism and Nazism Compared*, ed. Michael Geyer and Sheila Fitzpatrick (Cambridge: Cambridge University Press, 2009), 396–441.

34. Walter Laqueur, *Russia & Germany: A Century of Conflict* (New Brunswick: Transaction Publishers, 1990), 25.

35. Laqueur, *Russia & Germany*, 35.

36. Robert Gellately, *Lenin, Stalin, and Hitler: The Age of Social Catastrophe* (New York: Alfred A. Knopf, 2007), chapter 22.

37. For interconnections between Communist regimes, see Robert Service, *Comrades! A History of World Communism* (Cambridge, MA: Harvard University Press, 2007), Archie Brown, *The Rise and Fall of Communism* (London: The Bodley Head, 2009) and David Priestland, *The Red Flag: Communism and the Making of the Modern World* (London: Allen Lane, 2009). For accounts of a German genocidal line, see David Olusoga & Casper Erichsen, *The Kaiser's Holocaust: Germany's Forgotten Genocide* (London: Faber & Faber, 2010).

38. Stephen Cohen, "The Gulag Archipelago," *New York Times*, June 16, 1974.

39. Robert Conquest, *The Harvest of Sorrow: Soviet Collectivization and the Terror-Famine* (London: Arrow Books, 1988), 3.

40. Bernard-Henri Lévy, *La barbarie à visage humain* (Paris: Grasset, 1977), and André Glucksmann, *La cuisiniére et le mangeur d'hommes. Essai sur les rapports entre l'État, le marxisme et les camps de concentration* (Paris: Seuil, 1976).

41. Ernst Nolte, *Der europäische Bürgerkrieg 1917–1945: Nationalsozialismus und Bolschewismus* (Berlin: Propyläen Verlag, 1987).

42. Ernst Nolte, "The Past That Will Not Pass: A Speech That Could Be Written but Not Delivered," in *Forever in the Shadow of Hitler?: Original Documents of the Historikerstreit, the Controversy Concerning the Singularity of the Holocaust* (New Jersey: Humanities Press, 1994), 18–23.

43. Ernst Nolte, "From the Gulag to Auschwitz," in *Fascism and Communism*, by François Furet and Ernst Nolte (Lincoln and London: University of Nebraska Press, 2001), 28.

44. Ernst Nolte, "Between Historical Legend and Revisionism? The Third Reich in the Perspective of 1980," in *Forever in the Shadow of Hitler?*, 14.

45. Timothy Snyder, *Bloodlands: Europe between Hitler and Stalin* (London: The Bodley Head, 2010), 318.

46. François Furet, *The Passing of an Illusion: The Idea of Communism in the Twentieth Century* (Chicago and London: The University of Chicago Press, 1999), 223.

47. François Furet, "On Ernst Nolte's Interpretation of Fascism," in, ed. Furet and Nolte, *Fascism & Communism* 2.

48. Courtois, *The Black Book*, 9.

49. Henry Rousso, "Introduction: The Legitimacy of an Empirical Comparison," in Rousso, *Stalinism & Nazism*, 7.

50. Gellately, *Lenin, Stalin, and Hitler*, 10.

51. Wim Berkelaar, review of *Stalinism and Nazism. Dictatorships in Comparison*, by Ian Kershaw and Moshe Lewin, *International Review of Social History* 44 (1999): 312.

52. Courtois, *Le livre noir*, 754.

53. Robert Paxton, *The Anatomy of Fascism* (London: Penguin, 2005).

54. Jan T. Gross, *Revolution from Abroad: The Soviet Conquest of Poland's Western Ukraine and Western Belorussia* (Princeton and Oxford: Princeton University Press, 1988). For the "tangled web" perspective, see 241–44.

55. Monographs that clearly situate the Soviet Communist and the Nazi regimes in the same narrative of war and repression are Kate Brown, *A Biography of No Place: From Ethnic Borderland to Soviet Heartland* (Cambridge, MA and London: Harvard University Press, 2003), Robert Gellately, *Lenin, Stalin, and Hitler*, Anton Weiss-Wendt, *Murder without Hatred: Estonians and the Holocaust* (Syracuse, NY: Syracuse University Press, 2009), Alexander Prusin, *The Lands Between: Conflict in the East European Borderlands, 1870–1992* (Oxford and New York: Oxford University Press, 2010), and Snyder, *Bloodlands*. Quotation from Prusin, *The Lands Between*, 125.

56. Snyder, *Bloodlands*, vii–viii.

57. Istvan Deak, "The Charnel Continent," *The New Republic*, December 2, 2010.

58. Sarah Farmer, "Symbols That Face Two Ways: Commemorating the Victims of Nazism and Stalinism at Buchenwald and Sachsenhausen," *Representations* 49 (1995): 97.

59. Michael Kort, *The Soviet Colossus: History and Aftermath* (Armonk and London: M.E. Sharpe, 1996), 203.

60. John Lukacs, *June 1941: Hitler and Stalin* (New Haven: Yale University Press, 2006), 18–26.

61. For this concept, see Kershaw and Lewin, *Stalinism and Nazism*, 4–5.

62. The classical works of totalitarianism include Hannah Arendt, *The Origins of Totalitarianism* (New York: Harvest, 1979, first ed. 1951), Carl Friedrich, ed., *Totalitarianism* (Cambridge, MA: Harvard University Press, 1954, Zbigniew Brzezinski, *The Permanent Purge: Politics in Soviet Totalitarianism* (Cambridge, MA: Harvard University Press, 1956), and Carl Friedrich and Zbigniew Brzezinski, *Totalitarian Dictatorship and Autocracy* (New York: Praeger, 1965).

63. Michael Mann, "The Contradictions of Continuous Revolution," in *Stalinism and Nazism: Dictatorships in Comparison*, ed. Ian Kershaw and Moshe Lewin, (Cambridge: Cambridge University Press, 1997), 135–57.

64. Furet, *Le passé d'une illusion*, 163.

65. Gellately, *Lenin, Stalin, and Hitler*, 3; Alan Kramer, *Dynamic of Destruction: Culture and Mass Killing in the First World War* (Oxford: Oxford University Press, 2007), chapter 8.

66. Cf. George L. Mosse, *Toward the Final Solution: A History of European Racism* (New York: Howard Fertig, 1978), and George L. Mosse, *The Image of Man: The Creation of Modern Masculinity* (New York and Oxford: Oxford University Press, 1996). For a concrete example, see Barbara Keys, "The Body as a Political Space: Comparing Physical Education under Nazism and Stalinism," *German History* 27 (2009): 395–413.

67. Luisa Passerini, "Introduction," in *Memory and Totalitarianism*, ed. Luisa Passerini (New Brunswick: Transaction Publishers, 2005), 8.

68. Regarding a linguistic comparison, inspiration could with advantage be drawn from Victor Klemperer's epoch-making book on the Nazi language, *Lingua Tertii Imperii*. See his *LTI. Notizbuch eines Philologen* (Leipzig: Reclam Verlag, 1975, first ed. 1947). See also several chapters in Igal Halfin, ed., *Language and Revolution: Making Modern Political Identities* (London and Portland: Frank Cass, 2002).

69. Hans Maier, "Concepts for the Comparison of Dictatorships: 'Totalitarianism' and 'Political Religions,'" in *Totalitarianism and Political Religions: Concepts for the Comparison of Dictatorships*, ed. Hans Maier (London and New York: Routledge, 2004), 199–215, and Emilio Gentile, "Fascism, Totalitarianism, and Political Religion: Definitions and Critical Reflections on Criticism of an Interpretation," in *Fascism, Totalitarian-*

ism and Political Religion, ed. Roger Griffin (London and New York: Routledge, 2005), 32–81.

70. Karl Dietrich Bracher, *The Age of Ideologies: A History of Political Thought in the Twentieth Century* (London: Weidenfeld and Nicolson, 1984), 32.

71. Cf. Michael Burleigh, *Sacred Causes: The Clash of Religion and Politics, from the Great War to the War on Terror* (New York: HarperCollins, 2007).

72. The classical work in which the growth of the German intervention state is analyzed is Hans-Ulrich Wehler, *Das Deutsche Kaiserreich 1871–1918* (Göttingen: Vandenhoeck & Ruprecht, 1973).

73. Pipes, *Communism*, 103–4.

74. See, respectively, Luciani Pellicano, "Modernity and Totalitarianism," *Telos* 112 (1998): 3–21, and Yehuda Bauer, *Rethinking the Holocaust* (New Haven: Yale University Press, 2001), chapter 4.

75. Götz Aly, *Hitler's Beneficiaries: Plunder, Racial War, and the Nazi Welfare State* (New York: Metropolitan Books, 2006).

76. David Shearer, *Industry, State, and Society in Stalin's Russia, 1926–1934* (Ithaca and London: Cornell University Press, 1996), and Paul Gregory and Valery Lazarev, *The Economics of Forced Labor: The Soviet Gulag* (Stanford: Hoover Institution Press, 2003).

77. Gisela Bock, "Ein Historikerinnenstreit," *Geschichte und Gesellschaft* 18 (1992): 400–404. See also Christina Herkommer, "Women under National Socialism: Women's Scope for Action and the Issue of Gender," in *Ordinary People as Mass Murderers: Perpetrators in Comparative Perspective*, ed. Olaf Jensen and Claus-Christian Szejnmann (London: Palgrave Macmillan, 2008), 99–119.

78. See Alex Inkeles and Raymond Bauer, *The Soviet Citizen: Daily Life in a Totalitarian Society* (Cambridge, MA: Harvard University Press, 1959).

79. A good example from Soviet studies is Lynne Viola, *Peasant Rebels under Stalin: Collectivization and the Culture of Peasant Resistance* (New York and Oxford: Oxford University Press, 1996).

80. Cf. Orlando Figes, *The Whisperers: Private Life in Stalin's Russia* (London: Allen Lane, 2007), Sheila Fitzpatrick, *Everyday Stalinism: Ordinary Life in Extraordinary Times: Soviet Russia in the 1930s* (Oxford and New York: Oxford University Press, 1999), Detlev Peukert, *Inside Nazi Germany: Conformity, Opposition, and Racism in Everyday Life* (New Haven and London: Yale University Press, 1987), and Heinz Schreckenberg, *Ideologie und Alltag im Dritten Reich* (Frankfurt am Main: Lang, 2003).

81. Sheila Fitzpatrick and Robert Gellately, eds., *Accusatory Practices: Denunciation in Modern European History, 1789–1989* (Chicago and London: The University of Chicago Press, 1997).

82. See Klas-Göran Karlsson, "Public Uses of History in Contemporary Europe," in *Contemporary History on Trial. Europe since 1989 and the Role of the Expert Historian*, ed. Harriet Jones, Kjell Östberg, and Nico Randeraad (Manchester: Manchester University Press, 2007), 38–40.

83. Annette Wieviorka, *The Era of the Witness* (Ithaca and London: Cornell University Press, 2006), Nanci Adler, *The Gulag Survivor: Beyond the Soviet System* (New Brunswick and London: Transaction Publishers, 2002), and Nanci Adler, Selma Leydesdorff, Mary Chamberlain, and Leyla Neyzi, eds., *Memories of Mass Repression: Narrating Life Stories in the Aftermath of Atrocity* (New Brunswick and London: Transaction Publishers, 2009).

84. Charles S. Maier, "Consigning the Twentieth Century to History: Alternative Narratives for the Modern Era," *The American Historical Review* 105 (2000): 807–31.

85. Popper's idea was certainly not that we shall stop learning from history, but "only up to the present moment." Karl Popper, "Historicism and the Soviet Union (1991)," in *After The Open Society: Selected Social and Political Writings*, by Karl Popper (London and New York: Routledge, 2008), 378.

86. For a multifaceted analysis of the "ideological" character of the great atrocities of twentieth-century Europe, see Norman Naimark, *Fires of Hatred: Ethnic Cleansing in*

Twentieth-Century Europe (Cambridge, MA and London: Harvard University Press, 2001). The Soviet Communism of Lenin and Stalin have often been characterized as a National Bolshevism. See David Brandenberger, *National Bolshevism: Stalinist Mass Culture and the Formation of National Identity, 1931–1956* (Cambridge, MA: Harvard University Press, 2002).

87. Eric Weitz, *A Century of Genocide: Utopias of Race and Nation* (Princeton: Princeton University Press, 2003), 74–84.

88. Weitz, *A Century of Genocide*, 75.

89. Weitz, *A Century of Genocide*, 84.

90. Brown, *A Biography of No Place*, 127.

91. Brown, *A Biography of No Place*, 230.

92. Amir Weiner, "Nothing but Certainty," *Soviet Studies* 61 (2002): 46–48. Quotation on p. 46. See also Christopher Browning and Lewis Siegelbaum, "Frameworks for Social Engineering: Stalinist Schema of Identification and the Nazi *Volksgemeinschaft*", in *Beyond Totalitarianism: Stalinism and Nazism Compared*, ed. Michael Geyer and Sheila Fitzpatrick (Cambridge: Cambridge University Press, 2009), 253.

93. Terry Martin, *The Affirmative Action Empire: Nations and Nationalism in the Soviet Union, 1923–1939* (Ithaca and London: Cornell University Press 2001), 344.

94. Alexander Prusin, *The Lands Between: Conflict in the East European Borderlands, 1870–1992* (Oxford and New York: Oxford University Press, 2010), 127.

95. Jörg Baberowski and Anselm Doering-Manteuffel, "The Quest for Order and the Pursuit of Terror: National Socialist Germany and the Stalinist Soviet Union as Multiethnic Empires," in *Beyond Totalitarianism: Stalinism and Nazism Compared*, ed. Michael Geyer and Sheila Fitzpatrick (Cambridge: Cambridge University Press, 2009), 181.

96. Roman Szporluk, *Communism and Nationalism: Karl Marx versus Friedrich List* (New York: Oxford University Press, 1991).

97. See, for example, Daniel Jonah Goldhagen, *Hitler's Willing Executioners: Ordinary Germans and the Holocaust* (New York: Vintage Books, 1997), and Steven Kotkin, *Magnetic Mountain: Stalinism as a Civilization* (Berkeley, Los Angeles and London: University of California Press, 1995).

98. Tony Judt, "The Past Is Another Country: Myth and Memory in Post-War Europe," in *Memory & Power in Post-War Europe. Studies in the Presence of the Past*, ed. Jan-Werner Müller (Cambridge: Cambridge University Press, 2002), 172.

99. *The Stockholm International Forum on the Holocaust. A Conference on Education, Remembrance and Research, Stockholm, Sweden, 26–28 January 2000. Proceedings* (Stockholm: Regeringskansliet, 2000), 3.

100. For Beate Winkler's address, see http://www.osce.org/documents/cio/2005/06/16402_en.pdf, 99–103 (accessed 26 January 2015).

101. I have written extensively on the position of the Holocaust in late twentieth-century and early twenty-first-century European history culture, most recently in Klas-Göran Karlsson, "The Uses of History and the Third Wave of Europeanisation," in *A European Memory? Contested Histories and Politics of Remembrance*, ed. Malgorzata Pakier and Bo Stråth (New York and Oxford: Berghahn Books, 2010), 38–55, and Klas-Göran Karlsson, "The Holocaust, the Communist Terror and the Activation of Swedish Historical Culture," in *Geschichtspolitik im erweiteren Ostseeraum und ihre aktuellen Symptome—Historical Memory Culture in the Enlarged Baltic Sea Region and its Symptoms Today*, ed. Oliver Rathkolb and Imbi Sooman (Vienna: Vienna University Press, 2011), 195–212.

102. Muriel Blaive, "The Memory of the Holocaust and of Communist Repression in a Comparative Perspective: The Cases of Hungary, Poland and Czechoslovakia/the Czech Republic," in *Clashes in European Memory: The Case of Communist Repression and the Holocaust*, ed. Muriel Blaive, Christian Gerbel and Thomas Lindenberger (Innsbruck, Wien and Bozen: Studien Verlag, 2011), 154–72.

103. Jan T. Gross, *Neighbors: The Destruction of the Jewish Community in Jebwabne, Poland* (Princeton: Princeton University Press, 2001).

104. *The Progress Report of Latvia's History Commission: Crimes against Humanity Committed in the Territory of Latvia from 1940 to 1956 during the Occupations of the Soviet Union and National Socialist Germany*, http://www.mfa.gov.lv/data/file/e/HC-Progress-Report2001.pdf, accessed 26 January 2015.

105. Uppdrag till Forum för levande historia om kommunismens brott mot mänskligheten, Stockholm: Regeringen, Utbildnings- och kulturdepartementet, 12 December 2006.

106. Doc. 10765: Need for international Condemnation of Crimes of Totalitarian Communist Regimes. Council of Europe, Parliamentary Assembly, 16 December 2005. Report, Political Affairs Committee, http://assembly.coe.int/Documents/Working Docs/Doc05/EDOC10765.htm, accessed 26 January 2015.

107. 2006 Ordinary Session (First Part), AS(2006)CR5. Council of Europe, Parliamentary Assembly, 25 January 2006. Report, Fifth Sitting, http://assembly.coe.int/Documents/Records/2006/E/0601251500E.htm, accessed 26 January 2015.

TWO

Making Sense of Inhumanity

On the Treatment of an Open Wound in Our History Culture

Jörn Rüsen

I am not a specialist on contemporary history, not to mention the specific topics of Nazism and Communism. How should I comment on Klas-Göran Karlsson's concept of interpreting these two highly important issues in the history of the twentieth century? Since this concept is based on some general ideas on how to conceptualize historical research, and since it includes theoretical reflection, I see it as an opportunity to delve into the theoretical and meta-historical arguments.

Such arguments are more than marginal since there is an open question which should be raised concerning the essence of Karlsson's argumentation. His idea of an entangled history is a synthesis of three different perspectives or dimensions of historical interpretation: a genetic, a structural, and a genealogical one. The questions I have in mind follows this threefold approach and is both evident and unavoidable: What keeps these three perspectives together? What integrates them into one coherent frame of interpretation, which may serve as a plot for a historical narrative?

Karlsson does not explicitly raise this question, but he hints to various combining factors, the most important ones being the comparative approach and the issue of evaluation. Comparison needs a parameter, and evaluation needs a set of norms. Both can be mediated into an idea of a comprehensive historical development of the twentieth century. Both have relevance for a historical horizon in which the world of today has to be understood.

GENEALOGY AS SYNTHESIS

Karlsson starts and ends his chapter with the observation that Nazism and Communism, although both equally guilty of crimes against humanity, have received a remarkably different evaluation: Whereas Nazism has been stamped as an overwhelming manifestation of evil, never receiving any positive evaluations in serious historical interpretations, Communism has been evaluated in an exceedingly different way. It goes even as far as to judge Communism a still unfulfilled promise of a better future for humankind. This unequal evaluation seems to be one of the main challenges, which Karlsson has transformed into his complex framework of historical interpretation.

If this observation is correct, the interrelationship of the three perspectives in Karlsson's approach will be characterized by a *synthesizing role of genealogy*. It is this perspective which has kept Nazism and Communism alive in the history culture of today. In the two other perspectives, however, both have become more and more "historized" in the sense of a growing gap between their past and our present.

The growing temporal distance into which Nazism and Communism as interesting historical events are moving is unavoidable. The presence of this past in the living memory, and the voices of the survivors are fading away. The growing complexity of historical knowledge prevents the immediacy of moral consternation.

Here I see an important innovation in Karlsson's approach to give Nazism and Communism their place in our understanding of the twentieth century: with his genetic and structural perspective, he pays tribute to the usual historization. But it is only the genealogical perspective which gives them a new meaning. Here historical understanding from a contemporary standpoint has changed into moving into the historical orientation of the present, thus bridging the growing gap between past and present.

It would be a mistake to understand Karlsson's third perspective as a simple addition to the two others. Genetic and structural thinking are well established in historical studies. That is not the case with genealogical thinking. One of its origins is the discourse of memory in the humanities, a discourse developed against the claim for objectivity in the academic form of historical studies.[1] Memory was addressed as a vital power of the past in present-day life, and historical cognition brought about by the methodical procedures of the established discipline of history was seen as fundamentally lacking this vitality. The other origin of genealogical thinking in history is the discourse of historical consciousness, which

emerged as the basic category for understanding and organizing historical learning and teaching.[2]

Karlsson belongs to the rather few historians who have picked up the
latter discourse and integrated it into the methodical strategies of historical interpretation.[3] By doing so he has avoided the gap between memory
and history and has given history back its vitality in culture, which it
shares with memory on the fundamental level of making sense of the
experience of the past. This is evident in his idea of historically treating
Nazism and Communism. The growing gap between their time and our
time of the twenty-first century is awarded a new feature if the intergenerational relations crossing this gap are taken into account. The people of
the twentieth century have already experienced these ideologies and
their political realizations. Their mentality was shaped by this contempo-
raneity. As a result, Nazism and Communism became factors in the intergenerational development up until the present. But what about the people of the twenty-first century?

On a side note, intellectual attitudes should not be overlooked, given
that a continuity from the time of the world wars to the present is in
concern. As for Nazism—and all the more so fascism—one should not
forget its allure for intellectuals prevalent until today. To mention only
two, who still have a great impact on the intellectual life of today: Martin
Heidegger and Carl Schmitt. If one includes important forerunners to
their way of thinking, the name of Friedrich Nietzsche has to be mentioned as well. In the case of Communism, the continuity of its intellectual power after World War II is evident. Karlsson concentrates on the
political movements and their ideological features, but the surrounding
field of intellectuality is broader and still very effective.

GENERATIONAL AND HISTORICAL IDENTITY

The mental level on which this intergenerational development is taking
place is that of forming one's historical identity.[4] Historical identity is the
place people give themselves in the course of history. It combines experiences of the past and expectations for the future and it defines the temporal horizon of one's own personality and its place in society.

Thus, in the intergenerational dimension, Nazism and Communism
become an issue of historical identity formation. In Karlsson's argumentation, this relationship between past and future is realized by his use of
normative judgments. Values and norms are constitutive elements of human subjectivity. But identity is more. Whereas a normative evaluation of
historical events and developments can place them outside the intergenerational temporality of human subjectivity—so to speak as "pure"
facts—in the realm of identity the past gets its place within this "time of

the human self." In this case normative judgments have become an issue of the inwardness of the human self.

This inwardness is brought about by two ways of introjections, of making the past an element of one's own self in the present. The first is "identification." Here we integrate the past into our subjectivity. The second is "intrusion." Here the past has already become a part of present-day subjectivity before the person or group deliberately relate themselves to it.

Karlsson's interpretation tackles both ways. By normative judgment the historians and their audience relate their subjectivity to the past in the form of a moral commitment. Nazism and Communism are a matter of normative negation. By this negation, the evaluating subjectivity contributes to the shaping of its historical profile. The idea of "we" is defined by its commitment for a value system which contradicts that of Nazism and Communism. They play the role of a paradigmatic "other" contrasting one's own self. "Otherness" is necessary for any concept of identity.

In the genealogical approach, the past of Nazism and Communism is effective in present history culture. Here they have already been allocated to a rather well-established place in public commemoration.[5] As such they belong to the constitutive factors of historical thinking itself.

Introjection and intrusion as two forms of identity formation relate past and present to each other, thus constituting historical consciousness. They move alongside each other, but they emphasize this history in a different way. In moral judgment, the past receives its historical feature by the present, whereas in genealogy, it is the other way around: the past pre-forms its historical feature in the present by conditioning historical thinking.[6]

STRATEGIES OF HISTORY CULTURE

It is worthwhile to synthesize both relationships between past and future into one coherent procedure of historical identity formation. In the case of Nazism and Communism, this procedure is a special one: it refers to *negative* historical experience in an intergenerational perspective. The German example may serve to develop a typological sequence of three generations after the end of World War II.[7]

(a) The reaction to Nazism dominated by the generation which ran the Nazi system was shaped by the attitude of *concealment*. The involvement in the system was neither negated nor suppressed, but it did not have an impact on the prevailing forms of making sense of history in post-war Germany. What happened in the recent past was not connected to the present. The burden of its inhumanity was too heavy to be picked up and worked through. It had to be exterritorialized from the realm of ordinary and identity-relevant German history. This exterritorialization is illustrated by a statement of the prominent sociologist Leopold von Wiese in his opening speech of the first post-war meeting of the German Sociological Society: "The plague came upon the unprepared people from the outside. This is a metaphysical mystery, not to be touched by a sociologist."[8] The theory of totalitarianism served as an intellectual means for this exterritorialization. The Nazis were the others, now situated in Moscow and East Berlin but no longer in Germany.

(b) The attitude of the next generation toward the Nazi period is typologically characterized by a fundamental *moralization*. Here the Nazi past came into an effective relationship with the history culture of (West) Germany. This generation felt guilty without being personally responsible. This has to be seen as a psychologically interesting case of a specifically historical responsibility, which needs to be dealt with much more in the theory of history.[9] In an intergenerational perspective, we seem to be responsible for the crimes that our forerunners have committed in the past. This responsibility is not an issue in our regular notion of morality, where responsibility is limited to what a person or a group has actually done. Social behavior, like a feud, strictly contradicts present-day universal morality. It is its universality, its specific modern character, which makes responsibility plausible beyond social boundaries, but in respect to history this universality has to be temporalized. Without an idea of a temporalized humanity, historical responsibility is groundless.

Despite this theoretical insufficiency, the idea of historical responsibility has spread all over the world. It has led to political activities like demanding and granting official apologies, sometimes even compensation, for what has happened in the past. It goes along with a general trend of victimization in history culture. Belonging to the victims make one's own people innocent and therefore contributes to its self-esteem. By moralizing, a burdening past is related to the present. In this relationship, it receives a place in the historical development, which is relevant for one's own identity. At the same time this negative past is kept distant from the image of oneself, whereas the morality effective in the (negative) judgment belongs to this image. In this way, post-war (West) Germany was understood as representing a political system contrary to Nazism and Communism. It placed itself in the tradition of Western political modernization. The idea of a German *Sonderweg* was now pushed aside, thought to be indicating a wrong perspective on the future. German history was therefore shaped by the principles of discontinuity and rupture. "Critique" became a powerful principle of historical sense generation.

(c) The next generation has overcome this one-sidedness of excluding the Nazi period from the historical image of German identity. Moralization has changed into *historization*. Now the intergenerational connection of the German people plays an important role in their historical identity formation. The Nazis were no longer seen as simply being the others ("*they* killed the Jews"), that is, a shadow of the German history thrown onto the outside of their own history, which darkens the world outside the realm of its self-relationship. This darkness now moved into the image of German identity itself (*"we* killed the Jews"); now it has become a shadow darkening the world inside one's identity-bearing history. The clear distinction between good and evil has been replaced by highly complex ambiguity and ambivalence, which fundamentally changes and overcomes the traditional strategy of ethnocentrism in identity formation.

This typology can be generalized. It can even be applied to the history culture of the victims and their offspring. In this case, the structure of thinking remains the same; only the norms change into the opposite. The third generation of perpetrators and victims both has to struggle when introducing ambivalence into their historical image, overcoming the black-and-white simplifications in historical thinking. That does not mean that the moral standards of humanity have to be given up. Instead, they have to be accommodated to the complexity of historical experience. One could speak of historizing morality so that it does not slowly decompose into pluralism and relativism, but enlightens historical thinking by sharpening the contours of values in the past and their relationship to present-day morality. This enlightenment may bring the genealogical dimension of historical thinking into a new and much closer relationship with the genetic and structural ones than we are used to in the daily academic work.

Karlsson's constellation of three historical perspectives can therefore be understood as a proposal to conceptualize history in general in a new way. To foster this understanding would demand further theoretical consideration of the logic of historical sense generation.

FROM INHUMANITY TO HUMANITY

Genealogy, in the way Karlsson argues for, should no longer play the role of an extraordinary way of approaching history. The specific elements and procedures of the historical sense generation can be discovered in hidden presuppositions and implications of "normal" historical thinking. In order to disclose these presuppositions and implications and to give them increased relevance for the work of the historians, we should confront Karlsson's project with the demand of overcoming the Western perspective which dominates it. Its subject matter is mainly Western, but the ideas of Communism and their political realization have spread all over the world. The same holds true—although to a lesser degree—for Nazism.[10] Karlsson's three dimensions and their interrelationship are logically not limited to Western history, but they can be reformulated through a more global perspective.

This may be done by relating Karlsson's three perspectives to anthropological thinking. In the framework of an anthropologically shaped philosophy of history, Communism and Nazism would become visible as special manifestations of inhumanity with universal importance.[11] An idea of history that can integrate different traditions of historical thinking has to refer to basic principles of making sense of the experience of the past. Where can these principles be found? What do all cultures at all times and in all spaces have in common? It is the cultural nature of human life. It is humanity as an idea of historical sense, which transcends all cultural differences. It constitutes these differences and integrates them at the same time. Humankind is not only the widest horizon of historical experience; it is a normative principle of making sense of this experience.

Humankind takes place in genetic developments, it is manifest in the structural conditions of these developments, and it is a point of reference in forming historical identity.[12] Realizing this, Karlsson's idea can be understood not only as a contribution to our knowledge of an important part of modern Western history, but as a step toward a new philosophy of history. This philosophy explicates universalistic elements effective in historical thinking, the most important of which is the issue of humankind as a factor of historical identity. Both Nazism and Communism generate their historical importance beyond the growing gap of temporal distance, as radical challenges of the basic and universal value of being a human being—we call it human dignity. They confront us with the question: "Who are we that this could have happened?"[13] Karlsson's ideas are an important step towards an answer to this question.

Nazism and Communism are historical experiences challenging the idea of humankind as a principle of historical sense generation. Nazism fundamentally negates a common value of every member of the human race. Its ideology implies a radical devaluation of some parts of humankind, most radically the Jewish people. The Jews were stigmatized as the roots of evil in the human world. In order to eradicate these roots and bring back a livable order of human life, they would have to be annihilated. The Holocaust explicates the consequences of such an ideology. In order to realize a human life form according to the order of nature in terms of what we describe as social Darwinism, inhumanity has to become a necessary means of politics.

A similar element of inhumanity is inherent in Communist ideology. Here all history is seen as an unbroken chain of class struggle, of depravation, suppression and exploitation. This has to be finished, a final step has to be taken turning history—in the words of Marx—from the realm of necessity into the realm of liberty. This revolution defines the present as the time in which the logic of history is changing from the inhumane prehistory in the past to the humane history in the future. To bring about this change—the "last battle"—inhumanity is justified.

Karlsson's ideas may lead to a new understanding of why inhumanity was the dominant feature of Communism and Nazism. In this understanding, our cultural nature as humans is at stake. In this respect we, as historians, are entangled in this web of history.

Taking this approach to historical thinking seriously, it may open a new dimension of historical experience which is not explicitly addressed in Karlsson's concept: the dimension of human *suffering*. Normally history deals with human agency. Suffering has very rarely—if at all—received fundamental attention, although it is an elementary part of human life and a permanent challenge for making sense of the human world. Nazism and Communism both claim to offer the solution for overcoming human suffering; both have to be understood as secular religions. Both have addressed humankind as an issue of historical thinking. Both draw from their understanding of the past a future perspective with a redemptive character. Through this ideological framework, their political practice has brought about human suffering to a hitherto unbelievable degree.

The historical thinking of today is confronted with this experience. How can we make sense of it by placing it in a historical frame of significance which includes our present and our future perspective? If we take Karlsson's ideas seriously, they should be continued by an argumentation which tackles not only the subject matter of historical thinking, but also basic principles of this thinking itself.

NOTES

1. Maurice Halbwachs, *The Collective Memory* (New York: Harper & Row Colophon Books, 1980), Pierre Nora, "Between Memory and History: Les Lieux de Mémoire," *Representations* 26 (1989), 7–25, Jan Assmann, *Das kulturelle Gedächtnis. Schrift, Erinnerung und politische Identität in frühen Hochkulturen* (Munich: C. H. Beck, 1992), Jan Assmann, "Collective Memory and Cultural Identity," *New German Critique* 65 (1995): 125–33; Aleida Assmann, *Erinnerungsräume. Formen und Wandlungen des kulturellen Gedächtnisses* (Munich: C. H. Beck, 1999), Aleida Assmann and Ute Frevert, *Geschichtsvergessenheit—Geschichtsversessenheit. Vom Umgang mit deutschen Vergangenheiten nach 1945* (Stuttgart: Deutsche Verlagsanstalt, 1999).

2. Karl-Ernst Jeismann, *Geschichte als Horizont der Gegenwart. Über den Zusammenhang von Vergangenheitsdeutung, Gegenwartsverständnis, und Zukunftsperspektive* (Paderborn: Schöningh, 1985), *Geschichtsbewußtsein empirisch*, edited by Bodo vonBorries et al. (Pfaffenweiler: Centaurus, 1991), Bodo von Borries, *Geschichtsbewußtsein im interkulturellen Vergleich. Zwei empirische Pilotstudien* (Pfaffenweiler: Centaurus, 1994), *Geschichtsbewußtsein. Psychologische Grundlagen, Entwicklungskonzepte, empirische Befunde*, edited by Jörn Rüsen (Köln: Böhlau, 2001), *Theorising Historical Consciousness*, edited by Peter Seixas (Toronto: University of Toronto Press, 2004).

3. Klas-Göran Karlsson, "The Holocaust as a Problem of Historical Culture, Theoretical and Analytical Challenges," in *Echoes of the Holocaust. Historical Cultures in Contemporary Europe*, ed. Klas-Göran Karlsson and Ulf Zander (Lund: Nordic Academic Press, 2003), 9–58; Klas-Göran Karlsson, "Historical Consciousness—The Fundament of Historical Thinking and History Teaching," in *The Process of History Teaching. An International Symposion Held at Malmö University, Sweden, March 5–7 2009*, ed. Per Eliasson et al. (Karlstad: Karlstad University Press 2011), 13–34; Klas-Göran Karlsson,

"Processing Time—On the Manifestation and Activation of Historical Consciousness," in *Historicizing the Uses of the Past. Scandinavian Perspectives on History Culture, Historical Consciousness and Didactics of History Related to World War II*, ed. Helle Bjerg et al (Bielefeld: Transcript Verlag, 2011), 129–44.

4. *Identitäten, Erinnerung, Geschichte*, ed. Aleida Assmann and Friese Heidrun (Frankfurt am Main: Suhrkamp Verlag, 1998), *Narration, Identity, and Historical Consciousness*, ed. Jürgen Straub (New York: Berghahn Books, 2005), Jörn Rüsen, *Historik. Theorie der Geschichtswissenschaft* (Köln: Böhlau 2013), 266 ff.

5. The Holocaust Memorial in Berlin, *Denkmal für die ermordeten Juden Europas*, can be seen as a remarkable example.

6. This pre-conditioning is overlooked in constructivism which dominates the meta-historical discourse of today. See my critique in Rüsen, *Historik*, passim.

7. Jörn Rüsen, "Holocaust-Memory and German Identity," in *History: Narration, Interpretation, Orientation*, ed. Jörn Rüsen (New York: Berghahn Books, 2005), 189–204; Jörn Rüsen, "Verstörungen in der Geschichtskultur. Historikerstreit und Holocaust-Deutung im Wechsel der Generationen," in *Singuläres Auschwitz? Ernst Nolte, Jürgen Habermas und 25 Jahre 'Historikerstreit,'* ed. Mathias Brodkorb (Banzkow: Adebor, 2011), 105–14.

8. "Die Pest kam über die Menschen von außen, unvorbereitet, als ein heimtückischer Überfall. Das ist ein metaphysisches Geheimnis, an das der Soziologe nicht zu rühren vermag"; Leopold von Wiese, "Die gegenwärtige Situation, soziologisch betrachtet," in *Verhandlungen des Achten Deutschen Soziologentages vom 19. bis 21. September 1946 in Frankfurt am Main* (Tübingen: J. C. B. Mohr, 1948), 29.

9. Jenny Tillmanns, *Was heißt historische Verantwortung? Historisches Unrecht und seine Folgen für die Gegenwart* (Bielefeld: Transcript Verlag, 2012).

10. A recent example is given by the deputy prime minister and minister of finances in Japan, Taro Aso. According to the "Tokyo Shimbun" he has said that his government could learn from the Nazis to change the Japanese constitution. See *Frankfurter Allgemeine Zeitung*, August 2, 2013.

11. An outline of such a philosophy is presented in Jörn Rüsen, "Humanism: Anthropology—Axial Ages—Modernities," in *Shaping a Humane World. Civilizations—Axial Times—Modernities—Humanisms*, ed. by Oliver Kozlarek et al. (Bielefeld: Transcript Verlag, 2012), 55–79.

12. Rüsen, "Humanism," 55–79, and *Approaching Humankind. Towards an Intercultural Humanism*, ed. Jörn Rüsen (Göttingen: V & R Unipress, Taipei: National Taiwan University Press, 2013).

13. Eelco Runia, "Burying the Dead, Creating the Past," *History and Theory* 46 (2007): 313–25, quotation 317.

THREE

The Dystopian Trilemma

The Guiding Potential of the Nazi-Communist
Equalization and Strategies Used When Questioning It

Johan Stenfeldt

In the summer of 1989, just a few months before the Berlin Wall was torn down, the American journal *National Interest* published an article titled "The End of History?" This article made the at that time seemingly unknown political philosopher Francis Fukuyama an intellectual fixed star on the ideological firmament of the early nineties, a firmament characterized by pro-liberalism and anti-Communism. With his idea Fukuyama revived an intellectual trend from the late fifties, "the end of ideology," stating that the experiences of Nazism and Communism once and for all had turned these ideologies into impossible alternatives when building a prosperous society. The only rational ideological alternative left was liberalism, since the two opponents of liberalism had proved themselves irrational. The dialectic principle of history, based on tension between ideological poles, was eradicated. In this sense history had come to an end.[1]

Of course, Fukuyama's thesis met a lot of critical responses. This is not the place to dissect the critique at any depth, but a couple of things are worthy of note. Firstly, that Fukuyama was a clear exponent for the totalitarianism idea, stating that Nazism and Communism on a scholarly and moral level may be placed adjacent to each other. Secondly, that his liberal ideological conclusion was based on anti-Nazism and anti-Communism, rejections that in turn were based on historical experiences from Nazi and Communist societies. Thirdly, and most importantly, that he was wrong. History did not end, neither in a factual sense nor in the way Fukuyama stated.

A striking example of how debates on Communism and Nazism could be interpreted in terms emanating from the ideological struggle during the Cold War may be the reception of the French anthology *Le livre noir du communisme*, The Black Book of Communism. In the introductory chapter of this volume, the editor, Stéphane Courtois, compared Nazism and Communism in the following terms:

> [T]he genocide of a "class" may well be tantamount to the genocide of a "race"—the deliberate starvation of a child of a Ukrainian kulak as a result of the famine caused by Stalin's regime "is equal to" the starvation of a Jewish child in the Warsaw ghetto as a result of the famine caused by the Nazi regime." [2]

If Fukuyama's prediction about a declining ideological struggle had been true, this statement would hardly have been controversial. But instead, not even the authors of the different chapters in the book agreed with his totalitarianism approach. The controversies also resulted in a number of similar "black books" focusing on atrocities that, according to the authors, should be associated with Western liberalism: *The Black Book of Capitalism* and *The Black Book of Colonialism*.[3] This reaction, almost comparable to a reflex, is crucial and needs to be highlighted. The response to *The Black Book of Communism* and Courtois's totalitarianism approach was not a "white" book of Communism, but instead an attempt to brand different phenomena that could be associated with liberalism—the same liberalism Fukuyama declared as victorious and the sole ideology left at the end of history. To paraphrase a famous quote by Mao Zedong, according to which it is impossible to make an omelet without cracking any eggs, it may be said that, in the debate, it seemed to be more important to point at the eggs that others had cracked than showing the omelet you've been cooking yourself.

The purpose of this chapter may be regarded as twofold, and is based on different aspects mentioned above. Firstly, it may be noted that the critique against Courtois in the examples mentioned is strictly negative: one cannot talk about communist crimes without mentioning the structural violence of capitalism or the atrocities of Western colonialism. The underlying idea is that Communism, when compared to capitalism and colonialism, may be regarded as a lesser evil. Anti-capitalism and anti-colonialism may have a mobilizing function in advantage of Communism or socialism in the same way as the liberal approach advocated by Fukuyama is negatively defined, based on anti-Communism and anti-Nazism. These negative ideological positions, characterized by their anti-prefixes, form what I will call dystopian ideologies in the following. As already mentioned, these dystopian ideologies have played significant roles in the ideological debate in the twentieth century. The first purpose is to summarize different dystopian ideologies into one comprehensive analytic approach that hopefully can work as a useful tool when studying ideological debates.

Another notion, leading up to the second purpose of this article, is that experiences from totalitarian systems seem to play a crucial role in the Fukuyama case. The histories of Nazi and Communist societies have led up to the ideological conclusions of anti-Nazism and anti-Communism, and consequently liberalism is the only ideological alternative that has not been discredited by history. This may sound fairly reasonable, almost as a platitude. There are, however, underlying assumptions in this that may be further investigated. Firstly, that the repressive acts within these systems may be explained by the ideological intentions behind them, if this is about to make sense. If the purges, the terror, the concentration camps, and so forth, are not explained by ideological intentions, there is no rational core in the dystopian ideologies anti-Nazism and anti-Communism any longer. Consequently, there may be ways of questioning this intentionality, or at least to put it in a wider context. These ways may be used as rhetorical strategies or counter-usages of history when discussing crimes committed by these regimes. The second purpose of this chapter is to extract a number of such rhetorical strategies.

Yet another notion made from the Fukuyama case is that liberalism turns out to be the natural ideological implication of rejecting Nazism and Communism. This may of course be questioned, since it reveals an idea that the ideological debate is a closed system with only three positions possible, where rejection of two will have a mobilizing function in favor of the third. Even though this may not logically be the case, it is a striking idea that the ideological debate may be regarded as a more or less deadlocked interplay between three existing parts. This observation may also serve as a launching pad for the further analysis, and will lead up to what I will call the dystopian trilemma.[4]

THE DYSTOPIAN TRILEMMA

The suggested comprehensive analytical approach that I am going to elaborate on the following pages is built upon two, rather intuitive, postulations. The first relies basically on Fukuyama's idea that world politics during the twentieth century may be regarded as a domestic triangle with Nazism, Communism, and liberalism as the main characters. The second postulation is that an ideological position can be taken in principally two different ways, either focusing on what you want to achieve or on what you want to avoid. Your position can be either positively or negatively defined. As the account of the debate from the late nineties and the different black books suggests, I would like to argue that the advocates of the three predominant ideologies to a great extent have

defined themselves against each other, mutually negatively, by the dystopian ideologies associated with their own ideological position.

On a macrolevel, focusing on an overall structure of arguments presented in debates on the atrocities of the twentieth century, these three
ideological poles can be named and summarized in pairs: fascism/Naz-
ism, socialism/Communism, and liberal democracy/liberal capitalism.
The obvious fact that there are a number of tensions and distinctions
within all of these three poles—as within each one of the six "components"—shall be discussed at some extent in the following, but is of lesser
importance given the all-embracing scope applied here. The fact that
there are three potential positions in this pattern, this trilemma, means (1)
that every ideological position is defined against the remaining two
which in turn are regarded as interconnected in some sense or at least
equivalent as dystopian counterparts, and (2) that such a perceptual pattern is disapproved by the advocates of the two remaining ideologies,
which on the contrary define themselves as ideological counterparts to
each other. This provides the trilemma with three rather distinct positions, or viewpoints, and consequently a rather special dynamic.

The liberal viewpoint, to start with, is based on the same comparison
as totalitarianism theory itself, that is, a comparison between Nazism and
Communism, followed by the rejection of both of them, leading to the
ideological conclusion of adopting the dystopian ideologies of anti-Nazism and anti-Communism. During the heydays of the Cold War this
perspective reached its orientating peak and served as a fundament in
American foreign policy. In the field of Soviet studies, the top-down
perspective of totalitarianism became popular through the works of
Merle Fainsod. Two colleagues of his, Carl J. Friedrich and Zbigniew
Brzezinski, extracted a specific six-point syndrome that, according to
them, characterized the Nazi as well as the Communist power system.
The existence of one single mass party, a strong leader, a chiliastic ideology defined by its goal to build a utopian society, prevalence of terror,
total control of armed forces and mass media, and a controlled and bu-
reaucratized economy are all traits of a totalitarian society according to
Friedrich and Brzezinski.[5] An overall definition of totalitarianism that
may be extracted from this six-point syndrome is that it is characterized
by pronounced collectivism and utopianism. The implicit conclusion may
be regarded as the negation of this: individualism, democratic pluralism,
anti-utopianism, and piecemeal engineering.[6]

From a communist or socialist point of view the idea that Nazism and
Communism may be subsumed under the common heading "totalitarianism," based on shared origins or structural similarities, is absolutely
disapproved. Instead socialist, or communist history itself, provides us
with a rather distinct counter-narrative stating that liberalism and fascism (including Nazism) are interconnected by the bonds of capitalism
and imperialism. In his book about the historiography of totalitarianism

theory, the American historian Abbot Gleason characterizes this idea as the "countermyth" of totalitarianism.[7] The most pronounced version of this countermyth was probably formulated during the seventh congress of Comintern in 1935 where the emerging fascist movement, including German Nazism, was characterized as a far-reaching exponent of the most degenerate, chauvinist, and imperialist parts of the Western capitalist bourgeoisie.[8] This idea is also illustrated by the famous front page of *Arbeieter Illustrierte Zeitung* in 1932 and the montage by John Heartfield, showing Hitler receiving a bunch of German *Reichmark* in his hand, stating that he is backed up by millions. However, the ambition to establish a counter-narrative to totalitarianism, focusing on repression caused by imperialism, has got a root-system that goes farther back, even to the *Communist Manifesto* itself. The idea here exposed by Karl Marx and Friedrich Engels, stating that the inner logic of capitalism—to gain profit—will hunt the big business around the globe, leading up to colonialism as a movement, was perhaps most prominently formulated by Vladimir Lenin in his book *Imperialism, the Highest Stage of Capitalism* from 1916.[9] Lenin's book was also a source of inspiration for the historian Marc Ferro, the editor of the previously mentioned *Black Book of Colonialism*, when he wrote this response to his colleague Courtois. Ferro was also eager to emphasize that excluding the role of Western imperialism when discussing totalitarianism indicates somewhat of a one-eyed reading of Hannah Arendt's famous work on totalitarianism and its origins.[10] In Arendt's view, imperialism and anti-Semitism worked as the two historical and ideological cornerstones when totalitarianism was established in the interwar era.[11] In response to the dystopian ideologies of liberalism, anti-Nazism, and anti-Communism, it may consequently be concluded that advocates of a communist or socialist viewpoint regard anti-capitalism, anti-imperialism, and anti-fascism as dystopian ideologies of greater importance. Rejecting capitalism, imperialism, and fascism, all regarded as different facets of the same phenomenon, may also have a mobilizing function in advantage of this left-wing viewpoint. This negativist dynamic is basically the same as when the dystopian ideologies of liberalism are discussed.

From a fascist or Nazi point of view, finally, there are also dystopias which may be identified, even if advocates of this viewpoint are very hard to find, and after 1945 almost non-existent. After the end of the Second World War, Nazism and fascism may rather be compared to the main figure in an ideological version of the game "the old maid": Nazism is transformed into a card that no one wants to have at hand or have in their proximity, but on the contrary is eager to compare their opponent to. It may be noted that anti-Nazism is a dystopian ideology shared by communists as well as liberals and that the question whether Nazism should be interpreted as a "capitalist" or a "totalitarian" phenomenon runs all through the ideological debates of the post-war era. In spite of this, there are also important dystopian traits to be noted from this fascist point of view, since Nazism tends to define liberalism as well as Communism as rationalist, internationalist, and materialist dystopian political projects. From a Nazi point of view liberalism, as well as Marxist socialism, are also regarded as fundamentally Jewish ideologies. In Hitler's *Mein Kampf*, it is even argued that the function of Marxism is to pave the way for the international capital of finance. The Jew can emerge as Karl Marx as well as a wealthy Jewish banker.[12]

To summarize this negativist scheme of definitions, it may be said that from a liberal point of view Communism as well as Nazism may be regarded as equal dystopias based on utopianism, collectivism, and terror; from a communist or socialist point of view liberal capitalism as well as fascism—including Nazism—are regarded as interconnected phenomena tied together by imperialism; and from a Nazi or fascist point of view liberalism as well as Communism share dystopian characteristics such as internationalism, materialism, rationalism, and—from a Nazi point of view at least—Jewishness. This prominent role of negative definitions has actually been highlighted within a totalitarianism discourse, by Friedrich and Brzezinski. In their work *Totalitarian Dictatorship and Autocracy*, they state:

> An additional important symbol for all the totalitarian regimes is negative: the stereotyped image of the enemy. For the Nazis it was the fat rich Jew or the Jewish Bolshevik; for the Fascists it was at first the radical agitator, later the corrupt and weak, degenerate bourgeois; for the Soviets, it is the war-mongering, atom-bomb-wielding American Wallstreeter; for the Chinese Communists, it is the Yankee imperialist and the Western colonial exploiters. In these negative symbols, the ideological basis of all such symbolism is even more evident. It is also found to some extent in the competitive politics of constitutional regimes.[13]

TENSIONS

There are a number of generalizations in this model that may be regarded as far too sweeping. It goes without saying that all the different viewpoints of the trilemma, to some extent already indicated, contain quite a degree of tension. On a factual and empirical level, comprised with qualified scholarly knowledge about the historical process during which ideological concepts have been transformed and related to each other in multiple ways, there is much to say about these tensions. However, this is not the analytical level in this chapter. The purpose, on the contrary, is to study an overall structure of arguments, and arguments presented in the public debate usually reduce rather than add complexity. When focusing a structure of arguments, the mutual negativism of the three ideological viewpoints may very well work as a useful tool. A few of the most striking tensions within the different viewpoints shall, however, be noted below.

Liberalism, to start with, was said to be characterized by democracy and capitalism. The tension within the liberal viewpoint seems to start right here. How far shall democracy reach? To what extent is democracy just an empty concept, if not the economic sphere as well as the political sphere is democratized? Closely interconnected to this is the distinction between positive and negative liberties as elaborated most famously by Isaiah Berlin: Does every restriction on the individual and his possibilities to act reduce the amount of freedom in a society, or is this restriction a necessity to avoid that the freedom of one man does not revoke the freedom of another man?[14] This tension is obvious when discussing the distinction between the liberal and the socialist or communist viewpoints, but it is also valid when discussing the distinction between the equality of political power in liberal democracy and the inequality of liberal capitalism. Similar to this, a distinction between the reformist socialist tradition of Eduard Bernstein and the revolutionary socialist or communist tradition by Vladimir Lenin needs to be noted, in spite of their shared Marxist origins. The mutual suspicion between social democrats and communists may further be illustrated by the German communist leader Ernst Thälmann, who in the thirties stated that a social democrat was no better than a fascist, leading to the concept of "social fascism," or by the social democratic fear of national communist parties and their bonds to the *Comintern* in Moscow.[15] Finally, there are also distinctions to be made within the fascist viewpoint, especially concerning the role of anti-Semitism. If we return to the concept of totalitarianism, it may also be noted that Hannah Arendt herself, in *The Origins of Totalitarianism*, uses the concept exclusively on Nazism and Stalinism, not Italian fascism, since fascism in her view glorifies the state, which Nazism does not. Instead Nazism wants to abrogate the state and transform it into a great German empire.[16]

Mentioning Hannah Arendt, it is also striking how the different viewpoints in the trilemma are not only characterized by their inner tension — they are not absolutely mutually exclusive. According to Arendt, who may serve as an example of this, the nineteenth century was characterized by decline of national states. Social patterns were dissolved. This development, regarded as a consequence of the dynamic of capitalism, also created an alienated group of people who were willing to adopt racism as a kind of substitute for the social patterns that did not exist any longer. This racism, in its pan-German and pan-Slavic versions, together with the dynamic of capitalism, underpinned the development of imperialism — the same imperialism Arendt regards as the fundament of Nazi and Stalinist totalitarianism. From this brief summary, it becomes clear that Arendt's analysis intersects the liberal and the socialist viewpoint. In fact, parts of her analysis recall the Leninist idea of imperialism as the highest stage of capitalism.

THE IDEOLOGICAL PROCESS: UTOPIAN EXPECTATIONS AND DYSTOPIAN EXPERIENCE

So far I have discussed the trilemma mainly as a structure. However, a few things need to be said about its functions as well as about the historical process during which it has been developed. The function is perhaps quite obvious: rejecting, for instance, Nazism and Communism, and adopting the dystopian ideologies of anti-Nazism and anti-Communism will, in turn, have a mobilizing function in advantage of liberalism—as in the Fukuyama case. The historical process during which the trilemma has been formed is less obvious. However, it is fair to assume that the negative and mutual definitions have not always been as predominant as for instance the debate about *The Black Book of Communism* in the nineties indicates. Once upon a time dreams of utopias had not yet been transformed into dystopian experiences. A good starting point for understanding this transformative process could be the statement of the Czech politician Thomas Masaryk who, just after the end of World War I, compared Europe to "a laboratory atop a vast graveyard."[17] The old regimes of Europe had purposely gone to war with flowers in the barrels of their rifles, but ended up in the muddy trenches with a map of Europe that was fundamentally changed. As argued by many totalitarianism theorists, from Hannah Arendt to Ernst Nolte and François Furet, this is a context of great importance when explaining the emergence of totalitarianism. People were eager to adopt new perspectives and ideas, even utopian ideologies. It is important to emphasize that the millenaristic ambitions of German Nazism as well as the ambition to build a communist utopia in the Soviet Union in the twenties or early thirties could not be judged against the background of the horrifying events of the Holocaust or the Great Terror, simply because they had not yet occurred. Successively this changed. Inspired by thoughts from German hermeneutics, most prominently by the works of Hans-Georg Gadamer and Reinhart Koselleck, this may be described as a process of altering experiences, of trial and error, or to be more precise: a way from utopian expectations to dystopian experiences.[18] As Gadamer writes, our experiences constitute our expectations, but our expectations may also be crushed by newly obtained experiences.[19] Suddenly we think we know better, and need to revise our expectations. Since this means that historical experiences have transformed Nazism into the dystopia *par excéllence*, and socialism is regarded as a legitimate viewpoint only when based on its dystopian ideologies anti-capitalism, anti-imperialism, and anti-fascism—not pro-communist utopianism—and liberalism, finally, regards utopianism as dystopian in itself, this altogether may lead up to the conclusion that the dystopias in a sense have been very successful, since these retrospective "lessons of history" are all we have left when navigating politically. In this sense we could even speak of the dystopias, or dystopian experiences, as victorious—a fact that in turn may be regarded as another facet of what Fukuyama called the end of history.

EXPERIENCES AND WAYS OF QUESTIONING THEM

This brief exposition of ideological development and German *Wirkungs-geschichte*, history of effects, leads up to the second purpose of this chapter: to analyze the role of intentions and ways of questioning and debating historical experiences. As previously argued, the core of the dystopian ideologies is the existence of dystopian experiences, that is, repressive actions during history. Historical events, like the extermination of Jews during the forties or the starvation in Ukraine during the thirties (events symmetrically conceptualized as *Holocaust* and *Holodomor* within a totalitarianism discourse), are subject to moral evaluation. Based on the outcome of this evaluation, history will provide us with orientation for the future. Retrospective moralization will lead up to ideological conclusions for the future. In this sense history is really the teacher of our lives.

Historical experiences are not, however, definite in the sense that they are made once and for all or shared by everyone. They are negotiated in debates between people with different positions of power and different views of what history that has the best guiding potential for us as individuals. This means that the underlying assumption behind the dystopian ideologies, that the historical events/historical crimes that are condemned may be explained by the ideological intentions behind them, can be questioned. If we, for instance, would regard the Nazi extermination of the Jews not as a consequence of anti-Semitism or overall racist ideas as declared by Adolf Hitler in *Mein Kampf*, but merely as a response to different structural, cultural, or contextual traits in German society at that time, there would be no rational core in anti-Nazism any longer. To make sure that there is such a core, history needs to be interpreted intentionally, stating that there is a straight line between on one hand the ideological intention and on the other hand repression or genocide. Altogether, this indicates that there may be different ways of questioning intentionality or at least to put it in a wider context, and that these ways may be used as rhetorical or moral counter-strategies when historical events are subject to moral evaluation with an aim, conscious or not, to provide ideological orientation.

In the following I will highlight four such counter-strategies. Since this chapter deals with the guiding potential of the totalitarianism approach, my examples are all connected to the anti-communist theme and different ways of questioning this as a rational position. However, it may be argued that the different strategies used are more or less generally applicable, since they are all connected to different contexts that always surround the historical agent. The two quotes that will emerge in the following are originally published in Swedish and have been translated by me.

My first example touches upon one of the core questions of scholarly history: structure versus agency. An important dynamic when discussing the moral use of history is that a focus on agency also tends to be a focus on ideological intention, whereas emphasizing structural aspects tend to turn the agent, "the perpetrator," into a victim of this structure. When Courtois identified Lenin's ideas as the starting point of Soviet repression, one common objection followed this path. Firstly, Lenin was regarded as a product of a brutalized czarist Russia. Secondly, a great emphasis was laid on the civil war that in turn was regarded as a product of foreign aggression from former allies and supporters of "the reaction." The brutality of the czarist society and the violence of the civil war formed important cultural and historical contexts, which became vital when describing Lenin as the victim of a structure rather than a perpetrator of ideologically motivated terror. One historian characterized this repressive structure as a "cocktail of violence," including capitalist violence within the industries, traditional violence among the peasantry, and modern violence exemplified by the First World War.[20] The same historian uses this structural strategy also when discussing crimes committed by other communist regimes:

> How shall the brutality of Russian bolshevism be understood separate from the hurricane of violence during the First World War, or the firmly rooted despotism and everyday violence of the czarist regime? How can the violence, the dictatorship, and the nationalism of the Chinese revolution be grasped, without mentioning western imperialism and the Japanese occupation? Who can understand the almost incomprehensible brutality of the Khmer Rouge regime in Cambodia, not being aware of the most extensive bombings of civilians ever?[21]

The "extensive bombings" are the bombings made by the United States in 1973. This quote illustrates well the function of a moral counter-strategy, focusing on structures or functionalist modes of explaining repression in communist states rather than ideological intention.

The second counter-strategy, which situates the repression of the Soviet system in a wider context, is to focus on emancipation or welfare. This means that we have now changed our perspective from intentions to consequences, or, to be more precise, from the distinction between intention and structure to the distinction between intention and consequence. It may be noted that focusing on welfare, or emancipatory consequences of political actions, not just acknowledges that there may be repressive consequences of the same political actions—the repression may also be regarded as a necessity to reach this emancipation. A lesser evil is counterbalanced by a greater good. When speaking of communist regimes, a striking example of this dynamic may be the words by Mao Zedong who, when characterizing his fellow communist leader Stalin, characterized him as 30 percent "bad" but 70 percent "good," leaving a "surplus of goodness" by 40 "units."

Courtois's critics did not put a lot of focus on the emancipation within the Soviet system, even though some remarks about "reforms after the revolution" or the Stalinist campaigns of fighting illiteracy were made.[22] There was, however, one important emancipatory consequence outside the Soviet system which was frequently mentioned: the defeat of Hitler and German Nazism in the Second World War. As when speaking of the dystopian trilemma, it is clear that the anti-fascism of Communism provides the communist perspective with a great credibility. The great emancipatory achievement of Soviet Communism lies in saving Europe from fascism. This idea is to some extent similar to the argument presented by the late British historian Eric Hobsbawm who, in his book *The Age of Extremes,* argues that the Soviet Union served as a threat to the Western European bourgeoisie and their governments, a threat that made them willing to accept democracy and social welfare systems to avoid further radicalization of the social democracy, or even revolution.[23] This perspective, in sum, means that the emancipatory consequences of Soviet Communism are important, but that they to a great extent were situated outside the system's own territory, in the welfare states of Western Europe. Yet another example of this second counter-strategy, emphasizing welfare, is to frame a category of "beneficiaries of the purges," as has been done in the field of Soviet studies, perhaps most prominently by Sheila Fitzpatrick.[24]

The third counter-strategy that comes naturally, especially when discussing *The Black Book of Communism,* is different ways of counting casualties. This means that we have now turned away from emancipation back to the repression of the Soviet system and different ways of dealing with it. "Body count" is a term usually associated with the political scientist Rudolf J. Rummel, as well as the term democide used by him as a definition of "the murder of any person or people by a government." Rummel suggests that about one hundred million people were killed by communist regimes during the twentieth century, among them almost sixty-two million in the Soviet Union in the period 1917–1987.[25] In the introduction to the *Black Book of Communism,* Courtois also mentions about one hundred million victims, but only twenty million in the Soviet Union. In a book published as an answer to the Black Book, the estimations made by Courtois and Rummel as well as Robert Conquest are all questioned. When Conquest declares that there were at least nine million prisoners in the Gulag camps in the beginning of the Second World War, the author of this book states that there were never more than 2.5 million prisoners in these camps. Seemingly unprovoked, he also adds that this number was equivalent to 1 percent of the Soviet population, which may be compared to the 2.8 percent of the U.S. population being imprisoned in 1997.[26]

This example reveals a common strategy of keeping the death tolls and number of people exposed to the repression of the system, the victims, on a low level. At the same time as excessive death tolls in communist states are kept to a minimum, casualties in other systems are often exaggerated. The best example of this is probably *The Black Book of Capitalism*, written as an answer to Courtois by a number of French sociologists. In answer to Courtois and the one hundred million victims of Communism that he suggests, the French sociologists state that there have been at least one hundred million victims of capitalism between 1900 and 1997. In addition to this, the victims of colonialism during the eighteenth and nineteenth centuries may also be counted as victims of capitalism. In sum, this means that capitalism has caused mankind more harm than Communism.[27] This reveals a pattern of extreme importance: in the same way as repression may be counterbalanced by welfare in the examples previously mentioned, the number of victims in one system may be counterbalanced by an even larger number of victims in another system. In both cases, consequentialism is the guiding moral principle, and a lesser evil may be regarded as "lesser" when compared to a greater good *within* the system as well as to a greater evil *outside* the system.

This argumentation also exposes some of the traits of the fourth moral counter-strategy: the dystopian trilemma as such. This moral strategy can be understood as a basically *a*moralist strategy in the sense that moral judgments are always made with reference to the political opponent, and more seldom about your own ideological position and the historical experiences associated with it. As mentioned above when elaborating the trilemma, the totalitarianism approach tends to have a mobilizing function in advantage of liberalism. This fourth counter-strategy turns this pattern upside down, associating liberalism, or rather liberal capitalism, with other kinds of repression such as the "structural violence" of the capitalist system or even imperialism and colonialism. As said, most prominently by Lenin himself, imperialism may be regarded as the highest stage of capitalism. This means that in the same way as anti-Communism tends to have a mobilizing function in favor of liberalism, anti-capitalism tends to have a mobilizing function in advantage of Communism. In both cases, one's own ideological position is negatively defined, and this negativism is what is most important when using this strategy.

The dynamic of this strategy has already been shown, for example when repression of communist regimes is regarded as a structural response to the history of colonialism and imperialism. A striking example is also, once again, the fact that no "white" book of Communism was published in response to Courtois, but instead two other "black" books were written. The idea that western crimes also somehow need to be taken into account when discussing Communism becomes clear from the following quote from a review article of another book dealing with the Nazi-Communist nexus, Timothy Snyder's *Bloodlands*:

> Choosing to write just about the areas affected by Nazi and Stalinist destructiveness implicate a dubious political tendency. Writing careful-ly and in detail about German and Soviet atrocities (without mention-ing the rapes and terror bombings by the Western allies), as well as the Soviet control of the satellite states in the Eastern Bloc (without men-tioning the British and American intervention in Greece), have far-reaching consequences for our understanding of the Cold War.[28]

CONCLUDING REMARKS

My ambition in this chapter has been twofold. The first aim has been to extract one comprehensive analytical perspective on the ideological de-velopments during the twentieth century, based on two postulations. The first is that Nazism, Communism, and liberalism have been the most influential ideologies during the twentieth century. In principle, an ideo-logical position in this spectrum may be defined either by what you want to achieve or by what you want to avoid. The second postulation is that negative, dystopian experiences have become increasingly ideologically significant, almost universally prevailing. Based on this, it has been sug-gested that the ideological alterations during the century may be de-scribed as a process from utopian expectations to dystopian experiences. The dystopian trilemma embraces the negative ideological definitions as well as the ideological development from "utopianism" to "dystopian-ism."

The second aim has been to extract a number of strategies when ques-tioning this way of ideologically using dystopian historical experiences. One way of dealing with the Nazism-Communism comparison is to adopt the idea of totalitarianism, stating that there is a straight line be-tween ideological intention and repression. Based on such a retrospective moralization, anti-Communism seems to be a rational position with a guiding potential for the future, based on experiences of the past. There are, however, ways of questioning this argument. The first moral coun-ter-strategy is to emphasize structural instead of ideological aspects, turning the agent, or "the perpetrator," into a victim of this structure. The second way is to focus on emancipatory consequences or welfare, by which the repression may be counterbalanced. The third way is to ques-tion death tolls, or the number of people exposed to repression, with the underlying ambition to extract a revised moral quality from a revised quantity of victims. The fourth counter-strategy, finally, is to focus on crimes committed by or associated with someone else, most likely Western capitalism and imperialism. This fourth strategy reveals the logic of the dystopian trilemma itself.

It may be noted that these four different strategies are not mutually exclusive. Rather, they intersect. It may also be noted that in principle, the different contexts highlighted by the different strategies are all valid on an intra-scholarly level. Structural aspects always need to be taken into account when understanding historical events. It is fair to assume that there is a wider spectrum of consequences of a political system than merely repression. Death tolls are always hard to fix. There have been a lot of victims in, for instance, the former European colonies. The problem that remains unsolved is how these different contexts should be regarded: as historical contextualizations, legitimate and eligible from a scholarly point of view, or as moral trivializations, usually regarded as scholarly illegitimate. Is it even possible to draw a distinct line between intra-scholarly contextualization and trivialization? This final question will be left open.

NOTES

1. Francis Fukuyama, "The End of History?" *The National Interest* (Summer 1989): 3–18.
2. Stéphane Courtois et al., *The Black Book of Communism: Crimes, Terror, Repression* (Cambridge, MA and London: Harvard University Press, 1999), 9.
3. Marc Ferro, ed., *Le livre noir du colonialisme* (Paris: Éditions Robert Laffont, 2003), and Gilles Perrault, *Le livre noir du capitalisme* (Paris: Le Temps des Cerises, 1998).
4. Cf Johan Stenfeldt, *Dystopiernas seger. Totalitarism som orienteringspunkt i efterkrigstidens svenska idédebatt* (Höör: Agerings Bokförlag, 2013).
5. Carl J. Friedrich and Zbigniew Brzezinski, *Totalitarian Dictatorship and Autocracy* (Cambridge, MA: Harvard University Press, 1965), and Merle Fainsod, *How Russia is Ruled* (Cambridge, MA: Harvard University Press, 1953).
6. Concerning the concept "piecemeal engineering," see Karl Popper, *The Open Society and its Enemies. Volume One: The Spell of Plato* (London and New York: Routledge, 2010), 166–168.
7. Abbot Gleason, *Totalitarianism. The Inner History of the Cold War* (New York and Oxford: Oxford University Press, 1995), 71.
8. Jane Caplan, "The Historiography of National Socialism," in *Companion to Historiography*, ed. Michael Bentley (London and New York: Routledge, 2006), 550, and Wolfgang Wippermann, *Fascismustheorien. Die Entwicklung der Diskussion von den Anfängen bis heute* (Darmstadt: Primus Verlag, 1997), 58.
9. Karl Marx and Friedrich Engels, *The Communist Manifesto* (Rendlesham: The Merlin Press, 1998), 4; Vladimir Lenin, *Imperialism, the Highest State of Capitalism: A Popular Outline* (Beijing: Foreign Languages Press, 1969).
10. Ferro, *Le livre noir du colonialisme*.
11. Hannah Arendt, *The Origins of Totalitarianism* (New York: Harvest, 1979).
12. Adolf Hitler, *Mein Kampf* (New York: Reynal and Hitchcock, 1941), 289.
13. Friedrich and Brzezinski, *Totalitarian Dictatorship*, 90.
14. Isaiah Berlin, *Two Concepts of Liberty. An Inaugural Lecture, Delivered Before the University of Oxford on 31 October 1958* (Oxford: Clarendon Press, 1958).
15. Wippermann, *Fascismustheorien*, 17–19.

16. Arendt, *Totaliarianism*, 258–60.

17. Mark Mazower, *Dark Continent: Europe's Twentieth Century* (London: Penguin Books, 1998), x.

18. Hans-Georg Gadamer, *Truth and Method* (New York: Continuum, 2006), Reinhart Koselleck, *Futures Past: On the Semantics of Historical Time* (New York: Columbia University Press, 2004).

19. Gadamer, *Truth and Method*, 347, 350.

20. Daniel Bensaid and Håkan Blomqvist, *Lenin: Massmördare?* (Stockholm: Moteld, 1999), 10–20, 23–33.

21. Håkan Blomqvist, "Forum för statlig propaganda," *Aftonbladet*, April 2, 2008 (my translation).

22. Bensaid and Blomqvist, *Lenin*, 45, 50–52, 66.

23. Eric Hobsbawm, *Age of Extremes: The Short Twentieth Century 1914–1991* (London: Michael Joseph, 1994), 7–8.

24. Sheila Fitzpatrick, *The Cultural Front. Power and Culture in Revolutionary Russia* (Ithaca and London: Cornell University Press, 1992), 177.

25. Rudolf J. Rummel, *Lethal Politics: Soviet Genocide and Mass Murder since 1917* (New Brunswick and London: Transaction Publishers, 1996).

26. Stefan Lindgren, "*Kommunismens svarta bok*—slutet på 'body-count,'" in *Utan heder. En bok om ohederliga debattörer och högerns rädsla för förändring*, ed. Aron Etzler (Stockholm: Röd Press Förlag, 1999), 39.

27. Perrault, *Le livre noir du capitalisme*, 423–25.

28. Fredrik Persson, "Den blodiga jorden," *Sydsvenska Dagbladet*, June 1, 2011 (my translation).

FOUR

The Intertwined History of Political Violence in the Soviet Union and Nazi Germany

The Case Study of Helmut Weiss

Anton Weiss-Wendt

INTRODUCTION

Comparison may assume different forms. One can study mass violence, or any other aspect of human existence for that matter, on both macro and micro levels. One can choose, as Norman Naimark has done, to focus on a particular form of mass violence or, as Steven Wheatcroft attempted, to advance a statistical analysis.[1] One can draw a comparison between two or more institutions or key individuals, to approach comparison from the perspective of perpetrators or victims. In the case of Nazi Germany and the Soviet Union, it makes sense comparing, for example, the Gulag and the Nazi camp system, the NKVD and the RSHA, Nikolai Ezhov and Heinrich Himmler.[2] Among specific elements of mass terror, scholars have been particularly keen on studying the practice of denunciation.[3] It can be a comparative study of particular concentration camps, prisons, execution sites, methods of incarceration, agency (say, concentration camp guards), or ideology versus expediency. It can also be a comparison of survivors' experiences, literary representations, memory culture, and so on.[4]

The problem with this kind of comparison is that very often it amounts to parallelism. In other words, there are two separate stories with only insignificant overlap.[5] Simultaneously, taking cues from sociology, historians engaged in comparative analysis tend to focus on commonalities rather than differences between cases under consideration. Obviously, the larger the scope of a comparison, the larger is the margin of error. Whatever contributes to that margin of error, however, is usually dismissed as exception. So far, the most successful attempt at comparison constitutes a chapter by Christian Gerlach and Nicolas Werth in the edited collection of essays *Beyond Totalitarianism: Stalinism and Nazism Compared*. Gerlach and Werth vouch for detailed case studies rather than an overarching comparison between the Soviet and Nazi systems of terror. The mistreatment of so-called asocial elements, ethnic minorities, and prisoners of war in both countries perfectly illustrate their point.[6]

In order to avoid the pitfalls mentioned above, I advance a bottom-up approach to the comparative study of political violence. Rather than direct comparison, I prefer talking about intertwined history—a critical mass of interconnections that may help to establish a pattern and/or to probe broader questions. Needless to say, micro-level studies pose as many challenges as macro-level studies. First, studying mass violence on an individual or group level requires digging through a tremendous amount of archival material. Second, it has to make up big enough a sample. Third, conclusions may have only limited applicability, that is to say, one has to be cautious generalizing from the particular.

Keeping this in mind, I deliberately avoid making far-reaching conclusions in this chapter. Rather, I make several propositions, pinpointing specific research questions and identifying prospective avenues of inquiry. The fact that the subject of this chapter, Helmut Weiss, is my paternal grandfather makes my task simultaneously easier and more difficult. On the one hand, I have access to certain personal information, which I would not have been able to acquire otherwise. On the other, as long as I want to claim impartiality, I have to keep emotional distance. Effectively, this chapter probes the following three questions: what issues arise from Weiss's double victimization by the Nazi and Soviet regimes; what historians can learn about the respective systems of institutionalized terror from this particular case; and finally, to what extent Weiss's experience is archetypical when it comes to political mass violence. Before I proceed, however, I want to situate the case of Helmut Weiss in the existing scholarship on Soviet and Nazi terror.

DOUBLE VICTIMIZATION: GERMAN COMMUNISTS AND THE 1930S PURGES IN THE COMINTERN

Helmut Weiss belonged to a group of idealistic, ideological German youth who saw the Bolshevik experiment as a beacon of hope for humanity, who made a conscious choice to move to the Soviet Union in the

1930s fleeing Nazi persecution at home, and who fell victim to the Stalinist Great Terror. In order to better understand the mechanisms of political violence, it may be helpful thinking in terms of groups targeted by both Nazi and Soviet regimes. One such group comprised Jewish refugees from Germany and Austria, particularly since 1938. Yet the total number of refugees barely exceeded several thousand, mainly due to restrictions on emigration. Furthermore, most of them traveled to the then independent Lithuania, Latvia, and Estonia, not so much to Soviet Russia. Some of those refugees were arrested during the Soviet mass deportation of June 1941.[7]

A much more prominent group was made up of German communists or German communist sympathizers. The former were almost exclusively members of the Comintern, or else they simply would not have been allowed into the Soviet Union. Many of the foreign-born communists who moved to the Soviet Union in the 1930s had previously been arrested, interrogated, and incarcerated by the police in their home countries. The predominant explanation of their victimization by the Stalinist regime can be described as functionalist. By having immigrated to the Soviet Union, foreign communists, including German nationals, ceased to be part of an underground movement that provided the sense of common purpose. This led to fracturing of the national sections of the Comintern, undoing of internal cohesiveness, and eventually score-settling, typically by means of denunciations. The ultimate cause of their demise, however, was the war scare, xenophobia, and ill-conceived Stalinist policies fueling suspicion of foreign communists. Ironically, the fact of arrest (and eventual release) of any given German communist by the Gestapo prior to emigrating to the Soviet Union worked against him or her in the eyes of the Soviet officials. Those foreign communists who had acquired membership in the Soviet Communist Party were viewed with an even greater suspicion. The Communist Party suspicion of foreigners intensified in 1935. The vigilance campaign prompted a political review of all foreign communists in the Soviet Union a year later.[8] What happened next is well known: the first show trial in Moscow in August 1936; the appointment of Nikolai Ezhov as new head of the NKVD in September 1936; and the growing hysteria culminating in an unprecedented campaign of political violence typically referred to as the Great Terror, which lasted roughly from June 1937 until December 1938. A majority of German communist victims were swept by Stalinist terror during that period.

A string of decrees from August 1936 onward proved ominous for political émigrés from Germany. Remarkably, among the sixteen defendants who stood the first Moscow show trial that month, five were German-Jewish émigrés. In the wake of trial, the Central Committee instructed local party cells to increase vigilance and to better learn identifying the enemy within: Supporters of Leo Trotsky and Grigory Zinoviev were supposedly plotting to assassinate Stalin and other members of the Politburo. In his January 1937 letter to Stalin, the Secretary of the Saratov Region Communist Party singled out as "Trotskyites" German émigrés who had gone through Nazi concentration camps. On July 20, 1937 the Politburo ordered NKVD to arrest all ethnic Germans working in defense industries. Five days later NKVD launched the operation against the German nationals suspected of espionage against the USSR, which was effectively extended to all Germans regardless their citizenship. Finally, the notorious order No. 00447 of July 30, 1937, which lashed out against "former kulaks, criminals, and anti-Soviet elements," targeted specifically "members of fascist, terrorist, and spy-sabotage counterrevolutionary groups." The operation should be completed within four months.[9]

In order to establish, at least approximately, the percentage of German communists swapped by the Great Terror, a brief overview of German immigration to Soviet Russia in the 1920s and 1930s is due. On the eve of Nazi takeover close to twenty thousand foreign workers and professionals (forty thousand together with family members) resided in the Soviet Union. About eleven thousand (seventeen thousand) of economic émigrés were Germans, whereas 95 percent of them had arrived between 1930 and 1932. Political emigration from Germany began in earnest in 1933. In that year 688 Germans received the status of a political émigré. In 1934 and 1935 some 2,045 Germans received political asylum in the Soviet Union. The following year, however, only seventy-seven political émigrés from Nazi Germany were allowed into the country. All but one indicated the threat of imprisonment as the reason for emigration. The numbers of foreign arrivals would have been much higher had it not been for restriction on immigration imposed in the Soviet Union in the wake of Sergei Kirov's assassination. While continuously publicizing its support for the "antifascists," the Soviet authorities effectively turned the inflow of political émigrés to a trickle. According to Oleg Dal', among the main reasons were general suspicion of immigrants and their possible collaboration with the Gestapo; the eagerness to use foreign communists to foment revolutions abroad; limited resources to accommodate the new arrivals; and the need to maintain good diplomatic relations with Germany in order to secure the technologies and equipment for industrialization. As of January 1937, an estimated four thousand German communists lived in the Soviet Union.[10]

As political refugees from Germany came streaming in, economic émigrés became increasingly dissatisfied with working conditions in the Soviet Union. Many of them opted for remigration. The onset of forced collectivization made some 4,500 German Mennonites congregate in Moscow and apply for exit visas in the fall of 1929. If this was a sign of things to come, the flight from Moscow of the prominent German communist Erich Wollenberg in 1934 sounded full alarm with the Soviet authorities. Consequently, the distinction between economic and political émigrés became hazier. Instead of extending Soviet influence in the border regions—as was originally envisaged—ethnic minorities appeared to undermine national security of the Socialist State. Soviet xenophobia and the omnipresent fear of foreign encirclement prepared the ground for comprehensive ethnic cleansing of the borderlands beginning in 1935, as Terry Martin has convincingly argued.[11]

In the period following Hitler's ascent to power, the Comintern had stipulated that any potential émigré should secure the permission of the German Communist Party prior to arrival in the Soviet Union. Otherwise, the arrivals were blamed for "avoiding the difficulties of the party work in the conditions of the increasing fascist and police terror, being effectively party deserters." Party oversight should also ensure that no hostile elements such as members of the Social-Democratic Party or the Nazi Party among the German workers could steal into Soviet factories. Simultaneously, in order to prevent foreign nationals from returning home, they had been pressured to take up Soviet citizenship and/or transfer to the Soviet Communist Party. Proposed by Wilhelm Florin, Secretary of the Comintern Executive Committee, in July 1932, this policy became commonplace from 1934 onward. During the Great Terror, those foreigners, including the Germans, who had failed to get Soviet nationality prior to 1937 risked a deportation to their home countries. Regardless, the freshly minted Soviet citizens were in 1937 and 1938 routinely dismissed from their positions because of their ethnicity.[12]

Typical for the Stalinist system as a whole, as William Chase has argued, Comintern was at the same time an agent, instrument, and victim of mass violence. The conspiratorial logic came to haunt Comintern. During the 1936 political reviews, the "true" Bolsheviks within the Comintern perpetuated terror by organizing meetings, demanding "vigilance," denouncing alleged enemies within their ranks, recommending their expulsion from the party, and occasionally suggesting the arrest. As postulated in official documents, the issue at stake was compromised party loyalty and a potential threat to national security.[13] The German Section of the Comintern was not only the most thoroughly purged—with 70 percent of the members arrested by the spring of 1938—but also the most willing to cooperate with the NKVD, as attested by the Cadres Department staff.[14] Once again, ethnic Poles, Germans, and Latvians were overrepresented among the Comintern staff apprehended by the NKVD.[15]

The earlier arrests among the German Communist Party members (126 in 1935 and 1936) targeted three categories of alleged offenders: "Trotskyites," persons incriminated in contacts with the Gestapo and the German Consulate in Moscow, and "other anti-Soviet elements." The Gestapo label applied to anyone who had been previously released or had escaped from a Nazi concentration camp.[16] According to the twisted logic of the NKVD, since a defendant could not have possibly been released from a German concentration camp without the connivance of the

Gestapo, he or she was collaborating with the former agency. During the Great terror, the "Nazi link" permanently entered the plethora of criminal charges in the NKVD repertoire. In mid-July 1937 the prominent German communist in exile Walter Ulbricht drew a parallel between "counterrevolutionary Trotskyism" and Nazi policies of Adolf Hitler and Herman Göring. Around the same time began circulating the rumor about the alleged meeting between Trotsky and Rudolf Hess arranged through the Comintern.[17] In early 1938 the Moscow NKVD uncovered the mythical terrorist organization called Hitlerjugend. The seventy individuals who had been arrested as part of the ensued police operation allegedly spread fascist propaganda and plotted acts of sabotage.[18] The only documented case in which the Nazis played their hand in the Great Terror relates to the decimation of the Red Army top brass in June 1937. Although the evidence is still inconclusive, historians have a consensus that Reinhard Heydrich's Security Service (*Sicherheitsdienst*) had indeed forged documents framing Marshall Mikhail Tukhachevsky as a German agent with the purpose of undermining the Soviet military. Whether Stalin actually needed it in order to send Tukhachevsky and eighteen other top military commanders to their death is a different question altogether.[19]

Among the total of 1,575,000 people who were arrested during the Great Terror, 70,000 claimed German origin. With the number of executions for 1937 and 1938 estimated at 681,692, the death toll among German political émigrés is difficult to establish.[20] According to Alexander Roginsky, out of four thousand German nationals residing in the Soviet Union, about eight hundred were arrested in 1937–1938; among some eight hundred individuals who had taken Soviet citizenship, or remained without citizenship, close to one-half.[21] Stéphane Courtois and Jean-Louis Panné operate with comparable figures based on the statistics produced by the German Communist Party in the 1950s. By analyzing the available data on 561 individuals—or about a half of the German victims of terror—they established that 82 of them were executed, 197 died in incarceration, 132 were expelled to Nazi Germany, and 150 survived their long sentences.[22]

The expulsion of German communists to Nazi Germany by the Soviet authorities constitutes perhaps the most counterintuitive aspect of political violence. Indeed, perhaps as many as one-third of the victims, not all of them communists, arrested by the NKVD were not executed or imprisoned but handed over to the Gestapo. Significantly, it was the Comintern that paved the way for deportation of select German communists to Nazi Germany. The forced repatriation of political refugees was framed as part of the campaign against "desertion from the battlefields of class struggle," including those in Nazi Germany. In December 1935 the Comintern Secretariat condemned the existing practice of recommendations issue on behalf of foreign communists willing to join the Soviet Communist Party.

Supposedly, a great many "spies, saboteurs, and class-alien elements" had sneaked into the party ranks. All those individuals automatically entered the "enemies of the people" lists.[23] The decree of March 7, 1936 prescribed expelling the individuals suspected of espionage and disloyalty to the Communist Party to the countries of their origin.[24] Wilhelm Pieck, Secretary General of the Comintern in waiting, estimated in August 1938 that anywhere between one-third and two-thirds of all political émigrés would eventually (be forced to) re-emigrate.[25]

Initially, Nazi authorities were not very enthusiastic about the return of German communists. Their hands were literally full after the Gestapo had arrested some eleven thousand communists in the wake of the Reichstag fire. Already in 1934, however, a special agency came into existence for the purpose of utilizing the experiences of German returnees as part of the anti-Bolshevik propaganda. Eventually, this agency came under Anti-Comintern, an umbrella organization established by the Reich Minister of Propaganda Joseph Goebbels in 1933. Through October 1936, the Gestapo processed 1,100 arrivals from the Soviet Union, 70 percent of whom it labeled sympathetic to Communism and thus politically unreliable. Jews and persons of mixed blood (Mischlinge) among the re-immigrants went straight into concentration camps while the rest spent half a year under the police surveillance. Between January 1937 and June 1939 the Gestapo received further 2,180 persons from the USSR. Roughly one-quarter, or 604 to be precise, of these individuals had been previously arrested by the NKVD. In parallel, from 1938 onward Hitler's regime forced Soviet citizens of Jewish origin to leave the country. Of an estimated five hundred to eight hundred such individuals, some two hundred fifty had departed by the summer of 1939, though mainly for the countries other than the Soviet Union (Soviet authorities did all possible to prevent their return).[26]

For the first time, the group of ten prisoners was handed over to the Germans in February 1937, that is, before the Great Terror had been instituted. Urged by the German Ambassador in Moscow Werner von der Schulenberg, in November and December 1937 Soviet authorities transferred 148 Germans under arrest, and yet another 297 the following year, usually via Poland. The practice of expulsion of German and Austrian refugees to Nazi Germany continued beyond 1938, especially after signing the Molotov-Ribbentrop Pact. According to estimates, some 350 communists had been delivered to the Nazis between November 1939 and May 1941.[27] Typically, the NKVD delivered the deportee lists to the German embassy, which then screened them in accordance with the Gestapo guidelines. Although the Embassy was specifically instructed to prevent the entry of Jews into the Third Reich, some of them ended up among the expellees and eventually in sites of Nazi terror such as Lublin ghetto and Majdanek death camp.[28]

HELMUT WEISS: THE IDEA OF CLASS STRUGGLE BETRAYED

Helmut Weiss was born in 1913 in Dresden, Germany, to a family of a small Jewish businessman. His father came from Austrian Galicia (nowadays Chervonohrad in Ukraine) and his mother from Leipzig. Weiss Senior worked as an accountant while his wife stayed at home with their only son. Despite financial problems, the parents enrolled their son in the King George Gymnasium and parallel in a music school. Not untypical for assimilated German Jews, Helmut Weiss rejected his roots, describing his parents later in life as "proletarians with petty bourgeois ideology."[29] At the age of sixteen he began pondering about big problems in life: his sympathy for the labor movement made him turn to Communism for answers. Despite objections of his parents, in 1929 he officially left the Jewish congregation and joined the German Communist Youth organization. A year later he became a member of the German Communist Party. He made his political sympathies known also at school. He chose to write his term papers, among other things, on religious philosophy of Tolstoy and Dostoyevsky and Hegel in the Light of Marxism; one of his writings had a straightforward title: "War to the Imperialist War!" Simultaneously, he started contributing short stories and sketches to local communist publications. One of his publications featured an aggressive polemics against some of the teachers at King Georg which resulted in his expulsion from gymnasium (he then was in the seventh grade). Subsequently, he became even more active in the communist press, publishing under the pennames *Chronos* and *Hans Wendt*. Whatever short employments he had had, he ended up indoctrinating his co-workers in communist ideology. Predictably, the fiery teenager found it increasingly difficult having a steady income. Otherwise, he found his calling as a leader of a communist propaganda unit.[30]

Weiss's first encounter with the German police occurred in 1930: he was arrested for the participation in an unsanctioned demonstration, spent a few hours under arrest but was released after having paid the twenty-five Reichsmark fine.[31] In order to get his articles published, he had to bring them illegally over the border to Czechoslovakia where the editorial board of *Arbeitersstimme*—the communist daily of the Saxon section of the German Communist Party—had relocated. On the way back, he brought banned communist literature. One time he nearly escaped the arrest and potential conviction when the German border guard searched his luggage at the crossing. An extra pack of cigarettes and the obvious ignorance of the guards—who took at face value the title of one of the communist-inspired books, *Bauernroman*—had saved his life.[32]

The second time Weiss came in the direct contact with the police was in 1933. According to Weiss, the police conducted search in his Dresden apartment on suspicion of his membership in the Communist Party. There are two different versions of this particular encounter. According to the first version, Weiss escaped arrest because the police found no illegal literature, which he had previously hidden in a friend's house.[33] According to the second version, the police did discover the literature and threatened Weiss with expulsion unless he stopped his illegal activities.[34]

As a Jew and a communist, Weiss had no chance to carry on in Germany. In March 1934 he severed his contacts with the comrades as not to endanger their lives. Eventually, Weiss lost all his contacts with the underground German Communist Party. At that point, emigration remained the only option. At the end of November 1934 he received from the Soviet Embassy in Berlin an official reply to his earlier request: He was granted Soviet citizenship. The fear of imminent arrest, his ideological convictions, and his genuine belief that the Soviet Union was a success story made Weiss decide in the instant to move to the state of peasants and workers. Beside ideological affinity, he had maintained literary connections to the Soviet Union: Since 1931 he had published in the Soviet German-language magazine *Sturmschritt* and in 1933 the Publishing House of National Minorities in Kharkov (the editorial board later relocated to Kiev) printed the Russian translation of one of his novels. On December 8, 1934, he boarded a train in Dresden, passing the border control as a Soviet citizen without any problem. Two days later he arrived in Kharkov, the then capital of the Ukrainian SSR.[35]

The disappointment arrived quickly: He had difficulties proving his credentials as a member of the German Communist Party. At the same time, as a newly minted Soviet citizen, he was not recognized as a political émigré. Even worse, he immigrated to the Soviet Union without the sanction of the German Communist Party. As a result, he could not claim protection of the International Red Cross or the International Red Aid (MOPR), had difficulties getting employment, accommodation, or even foodstuffs. Consequently, he managed to publish just a handful of short stories in 1935 and 1936.[36] Upon inquiry from his publisher, the Comintern Cadres Department in January 1936 reported that his documents were currently with the German Section. Weiss had failed to secure a recommendation in order to officially transfer from the German to the Soviet Communist Party due to the unverified circumstances of his departure from Nazi Germany.[37]

Finally, he managed to get an employment as a lab assistant at the Meteorological Institute in Kharkov, playing piano at the Club of Foreign Workers at night. Soon he married a fellow political émigré, Erna Asta Brandt (a German from Czechoslovakia, eleven years older than him), whom he met at the Worker's Club.[38] Yet he was eager to resume the party work that he had pursued previously in Germany. In April 1935 he approached the German Section of the Comintern in Moscow, suggesting that his fellow German émigrés in Kharkov should get in touch with the comrades elsewhere in order to collect data about the realities in Nazi

Germany. Unbeknownst to him, Helmut tapped into the Soviet spy-ma-
nia, which treated with suspicion any contacts of the political émigrés
with their homeland. Helmut sought to rectify his case through the Cadres Department of the Comintern German Section. Instead, the German
party officials refused in June 1936 to recognize his reasons for emigration and recommended against his admission into the Soviet Communist
Party. Simultaneously, the NKVD in Kharkov opened an inquiry into his
case.[39]

> H. M. Weiss, born in 1913 in Germany, German, member of the CPG
> [Communist Party of Germany], arrived in the USSR legally in 1934,
> without the sanction of the CPG, was not recognized as political refu-
> gee. Works as a lab assistant in the Aerometric Lab at the Ukrainian
> National Research Institute of Metrology, citizen of the USSR, city of
> Kharkov, 42 Kontorskaia St.
> We are investigating Weiss as a fairly suspicious [individual] in view of
> his counterrevolutionary links to espionage. In 1932, while in Germa-
> ny, Weiss collaborated with the German magazine *Sturmschritt*, which
> had been published in Kharkov as the organ of the German Branch [of
> the Communist Party] and of, by now closed down, literati organiza-
> tion *Pflug* ingrained in kulak-nationalist viewpoint. Along with Weiss,
> another contributor to the magazine was Kaltofen, who used to come to
> the USSR from Germany as foreign tourist, suspected of links to the
> German police.
> When working as a part-time correspondence of *Das Neues Dorf* news-
> paper, Weiss was closely linked to a number of senior employees of the
> Publishing House of National Minorities (Knorre, Fiestner, etc.) who
> had been arrested on charges of counterrevolutionary fascist activities.
> As the *DND* correspondent, Weiss was especially keen, suspiciously,
> ongoing on business trips in the border areas. Weiss is maintaining
> correspondence with his relatives in Germany. Weiss is the head of the
> [propaganda] brigade of the German Club and he is being investigated
> on suspicion of counterrevolutionary nationalist activities.
> As a lab assistant, Weiss is worthless, he is reserved and does not
> demonstrate any particular zeal at work.
> Regard as belonging to Category 1: expulsion [*vydvorit'*].[40]

Obviously, the NKVD was "building up" the case from the thin air, by
advancing several rather than one specific charge against Weiss. The reference to his legal status attests that the NKVD was taking cues from the
Comintern Cadres Department. He automatically fell in the category of a
suspect because some of his contacts had been arrested on counterrevolutionary charges. The use of the word *fascist* in the inquiry was purely
rhetoric; the NKVD might as well have chosen the generic *enemy*. Significantly, as the proposed punishment for his alleged offenses, the NKVD
initially suggested expelling Weiss from the Soviet Union.

In July 1936 Weiss and his wife traveled to Moscow, once again without having previously informed the Comintern (he cited low pay as the

main reason for leaving Kharkov). In Moscow he met the director of a cultural center in Engels, who offered him a position as a music instructor. When he arrived in the capital of the Autonomous Republic of Volga Germans a few days later, however, his appointment had been suddenly canceled. This is when Weiss learned that the German Section of the Comintern had an issue with him, effectively having black-listed him. For the same reason, a potential job at the German Service of the Radio Moscow also fell through. The only employment Weiss could get upon his return to Moscow was working as an accordion player in a jazz orchestra in one of Moscow's movie theaters. In the attempt to clear his name, on September 5, 1936 he wrote a letter to the German Section of the Comintern. Typical for the Communists under suspicion, he wondered if it was some sort of misunderstanding: He must have been confused with some other "Weiss."[41]

Unbeknownst to Weiss, at the exact same time his fellow communist German writers were looking into his "case." Two months earlier, the organization of German writers in exile launched an internal review of its members. Between September 4 and 9, nineteen well-known figures in the German political and literary circles attended the closed meetings in the editorial office of the *Internationale Literatur* magazine in Moscow. Party activists attacked each other over alleged connections to certain "counterrevolutionaries." Ernst Ottwalt appears to be the main target of the vicious criticism during the grueling five-day proceedings.[42] The name of Helmut Weiss, variously spelled, came out in the bitter exchange between Ernst Ottwalt and Ernst Fabri, with participation of Gustav von Wangenheim and Emma Dornberger. What they had to say about Weiss and his wife was a mixture of truth and fiction.

The way Fabri and Ottwalt described Weiss created the impression that they were talking about two different people. Fabri portrayed the imaginary Wolf (Helmut?) Weiss as a "piece of filth unsuitable for political work who was senselessly roaming the streets of Moscow." According to Ottwalt, after a stint at Comintern Radio, Weiss traveled to Leningrad where he was later arrested. Counter Ottwalt, Fabri claimed that after having committed "grave political excesses" in Leningrad Weiss actually returned to the capital city. In Moscow he reportedly shared the room with an exposed spy and provocateur and was eventually apprehended all the same. Ottwalt slammed this allegation as false, indeed harmful, driving the "proletarian youth" into the hands of class enemies. The common reference point was a manuscript that Weiss had submitted for publication in *Deutsche Zentral-Zeitung* (the organ of the German Communist Party in exile), unsuccessfully. Fabri insisted that the manuscript was unacceptable, coming from a "morally corrupt" individual. Ottwalt, however, said that the manuscript was not so bad and its author talented.[43]

The rest of information concerning Helmut Weiss effectively confirmed his own testimony during the NKVD interrogation a year later. Some of the details, especially concerning his wife Erna Brandt, emerged for the first time, however. Dornberger depicted Brandt as a good human being with no "counterrevolutionary" traits. A typist and a tailor, Brandt arrived in Moscow with her young writer of a husband from Kharkov. Obviously, finding a job proved challenging (here Dornberger recalled the piece of advice by Stalin not to change one's job). To help out, she arranged for Brandt doing sewing jobs for the Comintern people staying at Lux Hotel. Ottwalt explained that Weiss had exposed himself by having sent out several reports from Nazi Germany while in Communist underground. He related the story of how Weiss had nearly been apprehended carrying illegal literature over the border from Czechoslovakia. The promising young writer had published a few stories in *Arbeiter-Illustrierte-Zeitung* (*AIZ*) but failed to claim his honorarium from Prague. Then, he suddenly received Weiss's letter from Kharkov. Weiss told Ottwalt that he had emigrated without the explicit permission of the German Communist Party. Weiss's case was taken up by the Dresden party cell, of which Ottwalt had reportedly notified his junior comrade. Consequently, Ottwalt discontinued all contacts with Weiss.[44]

For once, Fabri confirmed Ottwalt's account. He had heard from someone about a comrade who had recently arrived from Germany. That individual had failed to reestablish the contact with the German Communist Party or any local affiliates; neither did he succeed while in Prague. Apparently he had received a Soviet passport from the Soviet Embassy in Berlin. Wangenheim told another anecdote about Weiss. The director of the Cultural Center in Engels had promised Weiss a job. However, the couple only spent a few days in the capital of the Autonomous Republic of Volga Germans, since Weiss's professional qualifications were pronounced not enough. Eventually, someone advised Weiss to approach the Party Control Committee and Karl Radek. The latter helped Weiss to secure the position as a musician in the Orion movie theater with an eight hundred ruble salary.[45]

Reverting to the question that Weiss had on his mind: Was it indeed a case of mistaken identity? For instance, the proceedings of the Comintern Cadres Department of September 1936 (subsequently forwarded to the NKVD) included the names of Ernst Ottwalt and Erich Wendt. A member of the German Communist Party, Wendt worked at the Publishing House of Foreign Workers.[46] Both were subsequently arrested and sentenced to forced labor, except that Ottwalt died in the Gulag in 1943 while Wendt managed in 1947 to return to East Germany where he later made a successful career.

THE PERVERTED LOGIC OF POLITICAL MASS VIOLENCE

For the very last time, Helmut Weiss was registered paying his party membership dues in September 1937.[47] On November 19, 1937, as usual, Weiss reported for work at the Orion. During the intermission, two men in plain-clothes approached him, asking him to follow them. Upon the question whether he should take his accordion with him, the men replied that he should not be worried for he would be back in no time.[48] He was only able to return twenty years later.

Eight days after his arrest, *Deutsche Zentral-Zeitung* printed a review of Weiss's book, *Heer im Dunkeln: Geschichten aus Hitlerdeutschland* (Army in the Dark: Stories from Hitler's Germany). The book comprised three short stories and was published under his penname, Hans Wendt. The book was released by the Publishing House of National Minorities in Kiev in January 1937. Effectively, it was Weiss's only German-language publication since he had arrived in the Soviet Union. The stories in the book were set up in Hitler's Germany. At least one of them, "Das Opfer" (which can be translated as "victim" or "sacrifice"), was clearly painted after himself. The story described a young communist activist who had transported illegal publications over the Czech border. The protagonist oscillated between elation and dejection, was captured by the Gestapo, and eventually died in prison. "Not an informer, but romantic. It's a pity," ended this particular story.[49]

The focus of the review, however, was on one other story in the book, "Das Werkzeug" ("the Tool"). The review, poignantly called "Denkmäler für Verräter?" ("Monuments to Traitors?"), blasted the author of the book for "rightist tendencies." The story went as follows. A certain Communist Party official, Franz Schulz, belonged to an underground cell that had been infiltrated by the Gestapo. The Gestapo framed Schulz as if it were he who had denounced his comrades. The Gestapo occasionally released him, then again paraded him in front of the inmates in the company of the police officers. Schulz failed to shed off the label of an informer. He attempted, but failed, to commit suicide in his prison cell. A fairly simple story at first glance, Weiss had actually described an extremely complex psychological situation. He emphasized that the story had been painted from facts, and that "Franz Schulz is one of many—an unfortunate tool of Fascism, a victim."[50]

The author of the review, who signed as Kurt Funk, accused Helmut Weiss/Hans Wendt of "retouching the objective reality." Weiss purportedly excused the behavior of the person who had been broken by the Gestapo, who stabbed his comrades in the back, and thus rendered a service to the "fascist bloodhounds." Effectively, argued the reviewer, the author of the book had built a monument to the traitor. Funk finished his review ominously, inquiring why the Publishing House of National Minorities had released such a harmful book. As for Weiss/Wendt, he suggested his case to be considered by "appropriate authorities," which in that particular context could only mean NKVD.[51]

As far as the publishing house in Kiev is concerned, there is no information as to what ultimately happened to its employees. Most likely, they paid dearly for their alleged oversight. Indeed, the men and women operating the printing press had been a conventional scapegoat for any allegations of political disloyalty from early on. The Publishing House of Foreign Workers had been decimated already by the summer of 1937. A staff member in charge of Marxism-Leninism, for example, "confessed" of collaboration with the German and two other intelligence services. She was executed on November 1, 1937.[52] The Editor-in-Chief of *Deutsche Zentral-Zeitung* had been arrested not once but twice. His second arrest in December 1937 led to capital punishment the following month. Several others in the newspaper staff were charged with creating a "counterrevolutionary fascist organization"; one of them had subsequently been deported from the Soviet Union.[53]

Coming back to the circumstances of Weiss's arrest, the essential question is who was Kurt Funk and what possibly made him discredit a fellow communist. Like Hans Wendt, Kurt Funk was a penname that belonged to one of the leaders of the German Communist Party in exile, member of the Central Committee Herbert Wehner. Seven years older than Weiss, coincidentally, Wehner also came from Dresden. In fact he grew up in the same neighborhood as Helmut, just a few blocks away. As the deputy secretary of the Communist Party in Saxony between 1930 and 1931 he might or might not have personally known Helmut Weiss. An earlier encounter between the two is possible, though unlikely: Weiss played no major role in the Communist Party while Wehner was an established functionary.[54]

The internal review of Comintern members extended into all quarters, including literary. Shortly before Wehner's arrival in Moscow in January 1937, the press section of the Comintern had received the instructions to weed out "Trotskyite double-dealers" among the affiliated authors. Embracing the genre of book review as a weapon of self-defense, Wehner jumped on the bandwagon. Within one year, he sank several writers among the political émigrés. Reinhard Müller has speculated as to Whener's motivation in the section of his 2004 book called "Review as Destruction." In his reviews Wehner weaved ideological conformism into the Manichean logic of Stalinist terror. By resorting to devastating critique, he also compensated for his inferiority complex vis-à-vis the other German Communist greats Pieck and Ulbricht. More than anything else, however, he sought to shift attention away from the accusations leveled against him. To put it bluntly: Wehner wanted to save his own skin.[55]

In a sense, Herbert Wehner exemplifies the mechanisms of Stalinist terror. Wehner was one of the few German Communist Party leaders who had escaped from the Third Reich. The ultimate irony is that Wehner himself became a subject of investigation in early 1937. Wehner managed to fend off the allegations of collaboration with the Gestapo by testifying against other members of the German Communist Party. By authoring an extensive report on "subversive activities of Trotskyites in the German antifascist movement," he perpetuated a conspiracy theory and reignited the persecution of German émigrés in Stalinist Russia.[56] In late September 1937 the Comintern Cadres Department launched yet another investigation, charging Wehner with the breach of conspiratorial practices.[57]

Wehner's book review served as a catalyst rather than an immediate cause of Weiss's arrest. Since all articles appearing in *Deutsche Zentral-Zeitung*, or any other newspaper for that matter, had been vetted by censorship, it can be that the NKVD had read the book review before it went to print.[58] One way or another, the NKVD arrest warrant of November 16, 1937 said nothing about Weiss's literary activities. Instead, it questioned the circumstances of his arrival in the Soviet Union—the information passed down to the NKVD definitely by the Comintern German Section. The investigation was initiated on notorious Article 58, Paragraph 6, that is, "counterrevolutionary crimes" and espionage.[59]

Helmut's interrogation records from November 21 hark back to his last years in Germany. It turned out that until 1931 he had no citizenship and that the German police pressured him to get one. He opted for and got the Polish citizenship. Then and again, Helmut explained that many members of his cell had been arrested while he survived. One can see why Helmut was so preoccupied with the issues of duty, loyalty, and betrayal, which found its way into his writings. The NKVD took for granted that Helmut Weiss had conspired against the Soviet Union. In the course of the interrogation came the painful reality—something that Helmut had psychologically suppressed—he was persecuted in Nazi Germany not only as communist but also as a Jew. Obviously he had difficulties spelling it out, referring to himself as "non-Aryan" (*ne ariiskogo proizkhozhdenia*, as the records have it). Apparently, his interrogator was also non-Aryan, though not necessarily Jewish.[60]

Perhaps most heartbreaking to read are the few surviving letters that Weiss had received from his parents in Germany in 1936 and 1937. At some point, in a very convoluted language (presumably due to potential Nazi censorship and own anxiety) Ella and Markus Weiss beg their son to bring them over to the Soviet Union. They hinted at persecution that they endured at the hands of the Nazis when stating that, despite the fact that they still had food and roof above their head, they could no longer exist in Germany as human beings.[61] What they meant, obviously, was the systematic persecution of Jews by the Nazis. In Dresden, in May 1933, students of the Technical University staged a public burning of books of Jewish authors. The infamous exhibitions the "Degenerate Art" (*Entartete Kunst*) and the "Eternal Jew" (*der ewige Jude*) came to tour the city. Jewish professionals were sacked, their real estate confiscated, and entire neigh-borhoods proclaimed *judenrein*. On March 1, 1938, a four-hour-long carni-val procession under the banner "Exodus of the Children of Israel" passed through the streets of Dresden.[62]

Tragically, Ella and Marcus Weiss believed that, in the face of the Nazi brutality and despite their earlier opposition to their son's political credo, Helmut had established himself in the Soviet Union, perhaps occupying a position of authority: How could it have been otherwise in the case of a political opponent of the Nazis who sincerely subscribed to the Soviet cause! Obviously, Weiss Jr. was in no position to explain to them that it was not the case. Naturally, he could not have taken their case to the German authorities, but neither could he approach the Soviet officials due to his own rather insecure situation. He made it to the Polish Embas-sy in Moscow, the only other place he knew to go.[63] The Poles, however, who had been planning for the Final Solution of the Jewish Question and the Madagascar Plan of their own at that time, were certainly not in the mood to help.

The interrogations, held in the infamous Taganka Prison in Moscow, continued through early December 1937. The NKVD twisted Weiss's arm by implicating him in illicit contacts with the suspects inside the USSR and individuals abroad, insinuating that he had attempted to acquire strategically important information, and claiming that he intended to get into the Kremlin and that he received financial assistance from foreign countries. This is probably the most violent and abhorrent part of the Soviet sham justice that made it onto the paper in this particular case: That is when the interrogator consistently accused Weiss of lying. It might as well be accompanied by intimidation, verbal and/or physical abuse, off the record so to say.[64] The Bill of Indictment the next day summed up the fabricated charges as follows:

> Having arrived from Germany, he had led a suspicious lifestyle, estab-lished contacts with the [ethnic] Germans who worked at most impor-tant state institutions, received certain information from them, ex-pressed his dissatisfaction [with the life in the Soviet Union], attempted to sneak into a defense factory, had an intention to sneak into the Kremlin, [and is] suspected of espionage and terrorism. The accused Weiss has confirmed that he had contacts with the Germans and that he received certain information from them.[65]

On December 29, 1937, NKVD's Special Conference sentenced Helmut Weiss to ten years of corrective labor on charges of counterrevolutionary activities.[66]

Most extraordinarily, Erna Brandt pleaded in December 1938 on be-half of her husband before Lavrenti Beria, the newly appointed head of the NKVD. She was both a courageous and desperate woman who used strong language to make the case for Weiss. Remarkably, she did it not once but twice, before different Soviet agencies. Her emotional plea is also the last that we know about her. To paraphrase Eugenia Ginsburg, she vanished into the whirlwind. Weiss had never heard from her either. Officially, he remained married to Brandt.

She read the devastating review of Weiss's book. Whether she read *Deutsche Zentral-Zeitung* on a regular basis or if someone alerted her to the book review, one way or another Brandt learned of the indirect cause of her husband's arrest. She was not afraid calling names: Indeed, Gerhard Wehner—whose personality behind the penname she did not know—was an informer in the direct meaning of the word.[67] Neither did she know that in May 1938 Wehner, along with Pieck, Ulbricht, and Florin, approved the exclusion of Weiss—along with 157 other communists—from the ranks of the German Communist Party, a standard procedure applied to the arrested German communists.[68] She was direct about the personality of Weiss, pinpointing the obvious contradiction embedded in the fact that he was Jewish and thus could not possibly be a Nazi (she used the word *fascist*, as was common in the Soviet Union). She implied that, even though he was Jewish, despite the general persecution of Jews in Germany, Weiss stayed put, continuing his important underground work as a communist. Brandt emphasized this point by referring to the brutal treatment of Jews by the Nazis, and specifically the ordeal of Weiss's parents in Dresden in the wake of the Kristallnacht pogrom. Obviously, she continuously stayed in contact with her husband's parents since she knew that Ella Weiss had sought refuge in Krakow, Poland. Significantly, she wrote to Beria that Weiss's father was severely beaten because his son was a communist who had immigrated into the Soviet Union.[69] The situation of Jews in Nazi Germany was even more precarious than Brandt had described it. Most likely, Ella Weiss found herself among the 724 Jews with Polish citizenship who had been collected by the police in Dresden on October 27, 1938 and dumped over the Polish border. Further 151 Dresden Jews were dispatched to Buchenwald concentration camp following the November 9–10 pogrom.[70]

Unfortunately, as well as predictably, Brandt's appeal had been rejected. The NKVD's final decision of July 25, 1940 is a grotesque document. The NKVD added further nebulous details attesting to Weiss's subversive activities. The remark of an NKVD investigator to the effect that Weiss's parents worshipped Hitler comes across as insulting in the context of the escalating violence against the Jews in Nazi Germany:

> The review of secret materials [*agenturnye materialy*] and personal letters of H. M. Weiss revealed that in 1932 Weiss has published in Kharkov-based *Sturmschritt*, the journal that espoused kulak-nationalist views; has been in close contact with a number of executive employees of the Publishing House of National Minorities [*Natsmenizdat*] (Knorre, Fichtner and others) who had been arrested as counterrevolutionary spies; maintained written correspondence and met in person [*imel och-*

nuiu sviaz'] with the former cadet of the Coastal Defense College in
Sevastopol, M. Sh. Poliak who had been subsequently arrested on suspicion of espionage for the benefit of Germany. Moreover, Weiss has
persistently requested in his letters to Poliak to tell him in detail about
the latter's life and studies. When working in a political propaganda
group in the German Club, he made a strenuous effort to present on
stage the ideology [*ideii*] of fascist Germany, tried to surround himself
exclusively by Germans-citizens of Germany, and squeezed out Soviet
citizens.

That entire political propaganda group had connections with foreign
countries and the German Embassy; he maintained frequent correspondence with foreign countries. The most typical [*naibolee kharakternoe*]
letter, which included a newspaper clip, was sent to H. M. Weiss by his
parents. The contents of the newspaper excerpt can be formulated as
follows: Hitler has brought happiness to the German people.

On the basis of above, I see no [valid] grounds why the decision of the
Special Conference regarding H. M. Weiss should be reconsidered.[71]

DAS LEBEN DANACH

The following ten years Weiss spent in Dolinka, Karlag, in Kazakhstan.
During the first seven years of his imprisonment he performed physical
labor, anything from carting stones and digging earth to casting iron and
carrying goods. In 1944, however, his situation improved as he was selected to join the camp musical brigade, first as a piano player and later
as a concertmaster. Staging, no more and no less, Kalman's "Countess
Maritza" operetta before the camp personnel, the Dolinka brigade
needed extras. That's how Helmut met his second wife and my grandmother, Elisabeth Luigas.[72]

How Luigas ended up in the Gulag is a story in its own right. Born in
1918 to an Estonian father and a Russian mother, she gravitated toward
the Russian culture. The year Weiss was arrested by the NKVD Luigas
joined the Russian Christian Youth Association (an equivalent of YMCA/
YWCA). As the name of the organization suggests, she and her fellow
members hoped for a religious revival in Soviet Russia. Following the
annexation of Estonia by the Soviet Union in 1940, the mere fact of the
membership in the kind of organization was interpreted by the new authorities as counterrevolutionary activity. Luigas was arrested on July 10,
1941 and a year later sentenced by NKVD's Special Conference to five
years of forced labor (other documents suggested a three-year and/or
eight-year term respectively).[73]

Eventually, Luigas's mother back in Estonia was able to establish the
whereabouts of her daughter. In reply to her request, in May 1945 the
NKVD informed Iraida Luigas that her daughter was serving a term in
the Dolinka camp.[74] Both of Weiss's parents were dead by then. His

father died his own death in August 1939 and was buried in a Jewish cemetery in Dresden. Ella Weiss vanished without a trace; most likely she was murdered by Nazis in the occupied Poland.[75] As soon as Weiss finished serving his term—Luigas had finished hers the previous year—they got married, on Christmas day 1947. Courtesy of the NKVD, from then onward they featured on official documents as Weiss-Wendt. In November 1948 their son, Yuri, was born. Until the age of nine, Yuri spent his childhood in the Gulag, officially designated as "the son of the enemies of the people" and sometimes scoffed by his schoolmates as "fascist."

Like hundreds of thousands of other victims of Stalinist terror, Weiss was rehabilitated following the famous Khrushchev's speech, yet not until he has officially requested it from the Presidium of the Supreme Council of the USSR in September 1955.[76] After their release from the Gulag, they came to the only place where they had any personal connections at all, the city of Narva in Estonia. They lived through the disintegration of the Soviet Union. Weiss renounced his Communist Party membership in early 1991, even though he continued believing in the ideal of Communism—the phenomenon that Nancy Adler has comprehensively analyzed in her recent book.[77] They outlived most of their jailers: Elisabeth Luigas died in September 1999 and Helmut Weiss, nearly blind and deaf by then, a year later. He made no mistake: He lived most of his life and died in exile.

CONCLUSION

The NKVD interrogation records clearly followed a certain script that had been passed down with the ultimate goal of securing conviction. Incriminating evidence was drawn almost exclusively from hearsay, botched confessions, and twisting the words of the defendants. Helmut Weiss, his political and literary career as a German communist, offered rich material for the "enemy within" mythology. As if it were a checkbook, NKVD officials diligently listed the alleged offenses that the respective Soviet decrees kept turning out: compromised lifestyle, breach of procedure, unauthorized traveling, moving jobs, ethnic nationalism, lax party vigilance, ideological immaturity, correspondence with relatives abroad, links to the Gestapo, fascist propaganda, espionage, sabotage, terrorism, and counterrevolutionary activities in general. Thus, within the larger context of Stalinist mass violence, his case was not untypical. The only common charge that did not stick to Weiss was "Trotskyism"; as a variation of the above allegation, he was accused of plotting to assassinate members of the Soviet government. What the investigation file does not reveal is the original source of Weiss's arrest. This information, however, can be found in the Comintern Cadres Department files, known in German historiography as *Kaderakte*. In combination, these two kinds of document paint a fairly complete picture of the Stalinist political violence directed against foreign communists.

Stalinist regime practiced expulsion alongside death sentences and longer labor-camp terms vis-à-vis foreign communists during the Great Terror. Remarkably, expulsion was also the punishment that the NKVD initially proposed in the case of Weiss. Counterintuitively, the Gestapo did not uniformly persecute the communists deported by the Soviets, unless they were Jewish, beyond police surveillance. Without hard data at hand, it can nevertheless be argued that the extent of political repression against German communists in the Soviet Union in 1937–1938 was at least as significant as the persecution of the communists who had been expelled to Germany from the Soviet Union all the way through 1940. It does not imply a linear relationship between Stalinist and Nazi terror, though. For example, there is nothing to suggest that the signing of the Anti-Comintern Pact by Nazi Germany and Imperial Japan in November 1936 had direct bearing on the purges within the Comintern ranks.[78] The latter campaign had a dynamics of its own; indeed, the "verification" campaign goes back to 1931 or even 1925, not to mention the broader context in which the Great Terror had emerged.

There is no indication that the NKVD had displayed any anti-Semitic tendencies in their handling of individual cases, including the decision to expel a number of German Jewish communists to Nazi Germany. When Erna Brandt emphasized that her husband was first and foremost communist, and only then a Jew, she was trying to dispel the notion of "deserting from the battlefields of class struggle" rather than to preemptively debase anti-Semitic clichés. Nor is there any evidence that the NKVD had paid any attention to the specific interests of the Gestapo when it came to deciding the fate of individual German émigrés. At the same time, the Soviet agencies displayed no concern whatsoever for the ultimate fate of these persons after they had been handed over to the Nazis.[79] I concur with Carola Tischler, who has argued that the fact of transfer of German communists to Nazi Germany should be viewed as an extension of the callous Soviet quota system rather than a Faustian bargain between Stalin and Hitler.[80]

It appears that one of the cornerstones of Nazi propaganda—the notion of "Judeo-Bolshevism"—had not been applied consistently when it comes to the genuine cases of German-Jewish communists. Either of the two identities, ethno-cultural or political, was enough to spark repression, though only the former had lethal consequences for the targeted individual. Significantly, the fifty-two-year-old Markus Weiss was physically mistreated during the November 1938 pogrom in Germany specifically because of his son's political affiliation and the fact that he had immigrated to the Soviet Union. Nevertheless, he died a free man in 1939. Many questions still remain unanswered. How did the fact of political emigration from Germany in the first half of the 1930s affect the parents and other closest relatives of the émigré, especially if he or she happened to be Jewish? Did the repression intensify, did it take a different form, or did the double identity of the designated enemy play any roles at all for the Nazis, despite the thrust of their propaganda?

Evidently, the Soviet authorities had relatively little, if any, knowledge about the nature of Nazi terror or, alternatively, displayed any interest in learning more about its peculiarities, despite the frequent, abstract references to the "fascist" connection of the purported enemies. German fascism, in the face of the Gestapo, was for the Soviets a kind of bogeyman, a conventional, abstract point of reference that served as an aggravated circumstance when it came to exercising political "justice." Even though, in the long run, the fascist threat and the fear of war were justified, for the Soviets, the mythical Trotskyite was the arch-enemy who acted as the agents of all enemies. Hence the talk of the Trotskyite-fascist conspiracy, which became so prominent during the Moscow show trials. And since that was pure fiction—an expression of Stalinist political paranoia—no additional proof was required or sought. In other words, due to ideological blindness, the NKVD did not bother substantiating yet another of its standard, bogus claims. Obviously, incriminating evidence was non-existent in the criminal cases whose ultimate purpose was to eradicate potential opposition to Stalin's regime. So deeply ran the sense of self-righteousness that the Chief Soviet Prosecutor Andrei Vyshinsky swore by the principles of Stalinist justice even ten years later, at the 1947 UN General Assembly. "We are not obliged to submit evidence of any kind beyond the undisputable fact that the past history of the individual in question speaks for itself," he declared.[81]

It is not clear at all that the Nazi security apparatus had any better knowledge about the Great Terror, the Gulag, or any other aspects of Stalinist terror either—contrary to the rhetorical statements by some authors, most recently Timothy Snyder.[82] A majority of Nazi publications on the Gulag were worthless propaganda treatises depicting the central government and the camp administration as Jewish institutions aiming to destroy a host of Russian people by means of forced labor.[83] At the same time, the Nazis traced the German communists who had immigrated to the Soviet Union in the 1930s. The German diplomats in Moscow closely followed the escalation of political violence with the purpose of getting "their men." Otherwise, the Gestapo simply could not keep up with the pace of political repression in the Soviet Union. For example, from a Polish archive comes a 1936 list of some seven hundred communists sought by the Gestapo: about 110 of these individuals fell victim to Stalinist terror.[84]

By early 1941 the Reich Security Main Office (*Reichsicherheitshauptamt*) had assembled so-called search lists USSR that contained some five thousand names. The lists included birth place and date, sometimes occupa-

tion and residence in the USSR of many political émigrés that the police
and the Gestapo had collected through interrogations of ethnic Germans
who had resettled to Germany proper from the fall 1939 onward.[85]
Whether the Nazis prioritized hunting down the individuals on these
lists following the invasion of the Soviet Union in 1941, especially after
the debacle at Moscow in December of that year, is questionable, however. Did the name of Helmut Weiss appear on those lists? I do not know.

NOTES

Acknowledgments: The story of Helmut Weiss would remain incomplete had not it
been for Wilhelm Mensing and his research on German communists who vanished in
the Gulag. I also want to thank Alexander Vatlin, who was instrumental in acquiring a
copy of Weiss's NKVD investigation file.

1. Norman M. Naimark, *Fires of Hatred: Ethnic Cleansing in Twentieth-Century Europe* (Cambridge, MA and London: Harvard University Press, 2001), 57–107, Stephen
Wheatcroft, "The Scale and Nature of German and Soviet Repression and Mass Killings, 1930s–1945," *Europe-Asia Studies*, 48 (1996): 1319–53.

2. So far, comprehensive analysis has been advanced only in the case of the camp
system in both states. See *Lager, Zwangsarbeit, Deportation und Verfolgung: Dimensionen
der Massenverbrechen in der Sowjetunion und in Deutschland 1933 bis 1945*, ed. Ditmar
Dahlmann and Gerhard Hirschfeld (Essen: Klartext, 1999).

3. Some chapters on the Soviet Union and Nazi Germany in *Accusatory Practices:
Denunciation in Modern European History, 1789–1989*, ed. Sheila Fitzpatrick and Robert
Gellately (Chicago: University of Chicago Press, 1997), 85–221, are especially relevant,
namely Sheila Fitzpatrick, "Signals from Below: Soviet Letters of Denunciation of the
1930s," Vladimir Kozolov, "Denunciation and Its Functions in Soviet Governance: A
Study of Denunciations and Their Bureaucratic Handling from Soviet Police Archives,
1944–1953," John Connelly, "The Uses of Volksgemeinschaft: Letters to the NSDAP
Kreisleitung Eisenach, 1939–1940," and Robert Gellately, "Denunciations in Twentieth-Century Germany: Aspects of Self-Policing in the Third Reich and the German
Democratic Republic." The recent book of Wendy Z. Goldman deals specifically with
denunciation, *Inventing the Enemy: Denunciation and Terror in Stalin's Russia* (Cambridge: Cambridge University Press, 2011).

4. This subject list is essentially a desideratum. The only exception constitutes the
recent PhD Thesis by Nathaniel Golden, *Socialization, Survival and Witness: An Investigation of Gulag and Holocaust Literature* (Stoke-on-Trent: Keele University, 2007).

5. See chapters by Nicolas Werth and Philippe Burrin in *Stalinism and Nazism;
History and Memory Compared*, ed. Henry Rousso (Lincoln, Nebraska: University of
Nebraska Press, 2004), 73–107. The collection of essays edited by Ian Kershaw and
Moshe Lewin, *Stalinism and Nazism: Dictatorships in Comparison* (Cambridge: Cam-
bridge University Press, 1997), does not include a separate chapter on mass terror
altogether.

6. See Christian Gerlach's and Nicolas Werth's chapter "State Violence", in *Beyond
Totalitarianism: Stalinism and Nazism Compared*, ed. Michael Geyer and Sheila Fitzpatrick (Cambridge: Cambridge University Press, 2009), 133–79.

7. See, for example, Edith Sekules, *Surviving the Nazis, Exile and Siberia* (London:
Vallentine Mitchell, 2000).

8. William J. Chase, *Enemies within the Gates? The Comintern and the Stalinist Repression, 1934–1939* (New Haven, CT: Yale University Press, 2001), 4–5. For alternative
explanations, see Kevin McDermott, "Stalinist Terror in the Comintern: New Perspectives," *Journal of Contemporary History* 30, 1 (1995): 122–26.

9. Oleg Dal,' *Ot illiuzii k tragedii: Hemetskie emigranty v SSSR v 30-e gody* (Moscow: Neues Leben, 1997), 98–105; Carola Tischler, *Flucht in die Verfolgung: Deutsche Emigranten im sowjetischen Exil 1933 bis 1945* (Münster: LIT, 1996), 96–98, 105.

10. Dal,' *Ot illiuzii k tragedii*, 9–14, 70–77.

11. Terry Martin, "The Origins of Soviet Ethnic Cleansing," *The Journal of Modern History* 70 (1998): 813–61.

12. Dal,' *Ot illiuzii k tragedii*, 18, 48, 54–57.

13. Dal,' *Ot illiuzii k tragedii*, 67, 102, 109.

14. Alexander Vatlin, *Komintern: Ideii, resheniia, sud'by* (Moscow: Rosspen, 2009), 354–55, 370. See also his latest book *"Nu i nechest": Nemetskaia Operatsiia NKVD v Moskvei Moskovskoi Oblasti 1936–1941 99* (Moscow: Rosspe, 2012).

15. Mikhail Panteleev, "Repressii v Kominterne (1937–1938)," *Otechestvennaia istoria* 6 (1996): 162.

16. Alexander Vatlin, "Kaderpolitik und Säuberungen in der Komintern," in *Terror: Stalinistische Parteisäuberungen 1936–1953*, ed. Hermann Weber and Ulrich Mählert (Padeborn: Ferdinand Schöningh, 1998), 75; Reinhard Müller, "'Wir kommen alle dran': Säuberungen unter den deutschen Politemigranten in der Sowjetunion (1934–1938)," in *Terror: Stalinistische Parteisäuberungen 1936–1953*, ed. Hermann Weber and Ulrich Mählert (Padeborn: Ferdinand Schöningh, 1998), 144.

17. Vladimir Bobrenev, *Za otsutstviem sostava prestuplenia* (Moscow: Olimp, 1998), 80–81.

18. Tischler, *Flucht in die Verfolgung*, 105.

19. Robert Conquest, *The Great Terror: A Reassessment* (New York: Oxford University Press, 1990), 198, Robert C. Tucker, *Stalin in Power: The Revolution From Above, 1928–1941* (New York: W. W. Norton & Company 1992), 382, Robert W. Thurston, *Life and Terror in Stalin's Russia, 1934–1941* (New Haven: Yale University Press, 1996), 53–56, *The Road to Terror: Stalin and the Self-Destruction of the Bolsheviks, 1932–1939*, ed. Arch J. Getty and Oleg Naumov (New Haven: Yale University Press, 1999), 444–49, Simon S. Montefiore, *Stalin: The Court of the Red Tsar* (New York: Vintage Books, 2005), 226.

20. Nicolas Werth, "A State against Its People: Violence, Repression, and Terror in the Soviet Union," in *The Black Book of Communism: Crimes. Terror, Repression*, ed. Stéphane Courtois et al. (Cambridge, MA: Harvard University Press, 1999), 190.

21. Wilhelm Mensing, *Von der Ruhr in den GULag: Opfer des Stalinschen Massenterrors aus dem Ruhrgebiet* (Essen: Klartext, 2001), 85–86.

22. Stéphane Courtois and Jean-Louis Panné, "The Comintern in Action," in *The Black Book of Communism. Terror, Repression*, ed. Stéphane Courtois et al. (Cambridge, MA: Harvard University Press, 1999), 301.

23. Vatlin, *Komintern*, 342–45, 354.

24. Dal', *Ot illiuzii k tragedii*, 79.

25. Tischler, *Flucht in die Verfolgung*, 100.

26. Tischler, *Flucht in die Verfolgung*, 120–28. Hermann Göring originally intended to call the new police force the Secret Police Office (Geheimes Polizeiamt), but the German abbreviation GPA sounded too much like the Soviet GPU. See William L. Shirer, *The Rise and Fall of the Third Reich: A History of Nazi Germany* (New York: Simon & Schuster, 2011), 270. See also Lorna L. Waddington, "The Anti-Komintern and Nazi Anti-Bolshevik Propaganda in the 1930s," *Journal of Contemporary History* 42 (2007): 573–94.

27. Courtois and Panné, "The Comintern in Action," 301–2. Nicolas Werth writes about 570 German Communists who were delivered to the Gestapo at Brest-Litovsk in February 1940 (Cf. Werth, "A State Against Its People," 195). For individual stories of the Germans deported to the Third Reich, see Mensing, *Von der Ruhr in den GULag*, 93, 98, 106, 167. Perhaps the best-known among the individuals delivered to the Nazis was Margarete Buber-Neumann, who described her ordeal in her autobiography, *Under Two Dictators: Prisoner of Stalin and Hitler* (London: Victor Gollancz, 1949).

28. Tischler, *Flucht in die Verfolgung*, 133–137.

29. Weiss was one among the 5,120 Jews who lived in Dresden according to the 1925 Census; by 1933 the number decreased to 4,397. For the tension between Jewish and Communist identity, see Bettina Völter, *Judentum und Kommunismus: Deutsche Familiengeschichte in drei Generationen* (Leverkusen: Leske & Budrich, 2003).

30. Wilhelm Mensing, "Einem deutschen Sowjetbürger wird bei Stalin das Schreiben abgewöhnt: Aus dem Leben des Dresdner jüdischen Schriftstellers Helmut Weiss," *Exil: Forschung, Erkenntnisse, Ergebnisse* 23 (2003): 34–35.

31. Helmut Weiss NKVD file, interrogation records, 21 November 1937, State Archives of the Russian federation (hereafter: GARF), 10035/1/M-23290.

32. Anton Weiss-Wendt, *Small-Town Russia: Childhood Memories of the Final Soviet Decade* (Gainesville, FL: Florida Academic Press, 2010), 15–16.

33. Mensing, "Einem deutschen Sowjetbürger," 38.

34. Weiss NKVD file, interrogation records, 21 November 1937, GARF, 10035/1/M-23290.

35. Ibid. Weiss arrived in Ukraine just one year after the horrendous man-made famine, which killed 120,000 people in Kharkov alone. When recollecting his early years in the Soviet Union, he never ever mentioned the 1932–1933 famine.

36. Mensing, "Einem deutschen Sowjetbürger," 39.

37. Weiss Comintern file, Comintern Cadres Department to the Commission for the Transfer of Members of the Brotherly Communist Parties, 23 January 1936, Russian State Archives of Social-Political History (hereafter: RGASPI), 17/98/2320.

38. Born in Danzig, in 1923 Brandt joined the Communist Party of Czechoslovakia where she had moved with her first husband Gustav. The Brandts arrived in the USSR in August 1926, settling in Konstantinovka, Ukraine. Their subsequent request regarding the transfer to the Soviet Communist Party had been rejected. Gustav and Erna Brandt Comintern file, RGASPI, 17/98/10361.

39. Mensing, "Einem deutschen Sowjetbürger," 40–41; Weiss NKVD interrogation file, German Section of the Comintern to Weiss, 17 May 1935, GARF, 10035/1/M-23290.

40. Weiss NKVD file, Inquiry into the case of H. M. Weiss, 10 June 1936, GARF, 10035/1/M-23290.

41. Weiss NKVD file, Weiss to the German Section of the Comintern, 5 September 1936, GARF, 10035/1/M-23290.

42. Doris Danzer, *Zwischen Vertrauen und Verrat: Deutschsprachige kommunistische Intellektuelle und ihre sozialen Beziehungen (1918–1960)* (Göttingen: V & R Unipress, 2012), 302–6. Especially strong criticism of Ottwalt came from Willi Bredel, who had spent a year in Fuhlsbüttel concentration camp. Otherwise, occasionally, Ottwalt did as well resort to denunciation.

43. Proceedings of the closed party meeting of the German Commission of the Soviet Writers Union, 7 September 1936, RGASPI, 541/01/102b/30-30a. See also Reinhard Müller, ed., *Die Säuberung, Moskau 1936: Stenogramm einer geschlossenen Parteiversammlung* (Reinbek: Rowohlt 1991).

44. Ibid. Both Dornberger and Fabri mistakenly referred to Weiss's wife as "Maria" Brandt. Political émigrés were discouraged from staying in Moscow. Due to the lack of accommodation, Hotel Lux effectively became a permanent residence for many of them. See, for example, Ruth von Mayenburg, *Hotel Lux* (Bielefeld: W. Bertelsmann Verlag, 1978).

45. Ibid., 8 September 1936.

46. Müller, "'Wir kommen alle dran,'" 140–43.

47. Due payments of the German Communist Party members, 29 December 1937, RGASPI, 495/292/94.

48. Weiss-Wendt, *Small-Town Russia*, 17.

49. Mensing, "Einem deutschen Sowjetbürger," 41–42.

50. Mensing, "Einem deutschen Sowjetbürger," 42–43.

51. Mensing, "Einem deutschen Sowjetbürger," 43–44.

52. Bobrenev, *Za otsutstviem*, 255–56.

53. Müller, "'Wir kommen alle dran,'" 131. Alongside Leningrad-based *Rote Zeitung, Deutsche Zentral-Zeitung (DDZ)* was the most important newspaper catering to German émigrés in the Soviet Union. The newspaper featured lengthy publications by German antifascist writers, who were expected to uplift the morale of the local German workers. As of 1932, *DDZ* boasted 170 full-time correspondents and 5,000 readers (Dal,' *Ot illiuzii k tragedii*, 39–42).

54. Communication from Wilhelm Mensing, 2 December 2012.

55. Reinhard Müller, *Herbert Wehner: Moskau 1937* (Hamburg: Hamburger Edition, 2004), 132–45.

56. Vatlin, "Kaderpolitik und Säuberungen," 361–62; Tischler, *Flucht in die Verfolgung*, 113; Reinhard Müller, *Die Akte Wehner: Moskau 1937 bis 1941* (Berlin: Rowohlt, 1993), 106, 113, 120–21, 137, 142–43. Needless to say, in his 1982 memoir, *Zeugnis: Persönliche Notizen 1929–1942* (Halle: Mitteldeutsher Verlag), Herbert Wehner denied any personal responsibility for perpetuating the Great Terror.

57. Müller, "'Wir kommen alle dran,'" 142. When Wehner has ex post facto described the atmosphere of fear and subservience in Comintern HQ during the mass arrests, he deliberately spoke in the abstract (Wehner, *Zeugnis*, 217–218).

58. Müller, *Herbert Wehner*, 140.

59. Weiss NKVD file, arrest warrant, 18 November 1937, GARF, 10035/1/M-23290.

60. Weiss NKVD file, interrogation records, 21 November 1937, GARF, 10035/1/M-23290.

61. Weiss NKVD file, Ella and Marcus Weiss to Helmut Weiss and Erna Brandt, 19 October 1936 and 27 May 1937, GARF, 10035/1/M-23290.

62. Lilli Ulbrich, ed., *Buch der Erinerrung. Juden in Dresden: Deportiert, ermodet, verschollen 1933–1945* (Dresden: Eckhard Richter & Co., 2006), 10–12.

63. Weiss NKVD file, Ella and Marcus Weiss to Helmut Weiss and Erna Brandt, 19 October 1936 and 27 May 1937, GARF, 10035/1/M-23290.

64. Weiss NKVD file, interrogation records, 3 December 1937, GARF, 10035/1/M-23290.

65. Weiss NKVD file, bill of indictment, 4 December 1937, GARF, 10035/1/M-23290.

66. Weiss NKVD file, extract from the minutes of the NKVD's Special Conference from 29 December 1937, GARF, 10035/1/M-23290.

67. Weiss NKVD file, Brandt to Beria, 28 December 1938, GARF, 10035/1/M-23290.

68. Mensing, "Einem deutschen Sowjetbürger," 45.

69. Weiss NKVD file, Brandt to Beria, 28 December 1938, GARF, 10035/1/M-23290.

70. Ulbrich, *Buch der Erinerrung*, 14.

71. Weiss NKVD file, final decision, 25 July 1940, GARF, 10035/1/M-23290. Following the Nazi seizure of power, any correspondence with relatives in Nazi Germany was regarded a crime. Herbert Wehner expressed a similar opinion at a Comintern party meeting on August 17, 1937 (Vatlin, *Komintern*, 351–52). Soviet authorities were afraid that private letters may contain negative commentaries on the life in the Soviet Union, grist to the enemies' mill. Indeed, some German newspapers used such letters as part of the propaganda campaign against the USSR (Dal', *Ot illiuzii k tragedii*, 58).

72. Weiss-Wendt, *Small-Town Russia*, 18–19.

73. Elisabeth Luigas NKVD file, Estonian State Branch Archives, 130/4728.

74. Karlag NKVD to Iraida Luigas, 5 May 1945, in the author's possession.

75. Ulbrich, *Buch der Erinerrung*, 381. A Jewish cemetery in Dresden where he was buried had not been vandalized during the Nazi years; his tomb is still standing.

76. Weiss NKVD file, Moscow Military Prosecutor's Office, objection re. Prosecution of Helmut Weiss-Wendt, 25 April 1956, GARF, 10035/1/M-23290.

77. Nanci Adler, *Keeping Faith with the Party: Communist Believers Return from the Gulag* (Bloomington: Indiana University Press, 2012). See also Nanci Adler's chapter in this volume.

78. Cf. Bobrenev, *Za otsutstviem*, 437.

79. Mensing, *Von der Ruhr*, 105–6.

80. Tischler, *Flucht in die Verfolgung*, 137.

81. Vyshinky's statement during the debates on extradition of war criminals, *UN Official Records of the Second Session of the General Assembly, 102nd Plenary Meeting (31 October 1947)*, 529.

82. Timothy Snyder, *Bloodlands: Europe between Hitler and Stalin* (London: The Bodley Head, 2010), 177, 196.

83. David J. Dallin and Boris Nikolaevsky, *Forced Labor in Soviet Russia* (New Haven: Yale University Press, 1947), 313–14.

84. Friedrich Firsow, "Die Komintern und die 'Grosse Säuberung,'" in *Biographisches Handbuch zur Geschichte der Kommunistischen Internationale. Ein deutsch-russisches Forschungsprojekt*, ed. Michael Buckmiller and Klaus Meschkat (Berlin: Akademie Verlag, 2007).

85. Mensing, *Von der Ruhr*, 21. See also Werner Röder, *Souderfahn-dungsliste UdSSR* (Erlangen: DTE, 1977).

FIVE

Herbert Norkus and Pavel Morozov as Totalitarian Child Martyrs

A Study of Political Religion

Johan Dietsch

At dawn on January 24, 1932, six Hitler Youths moved through the Beus-selkietz district in Berlin, distributing flyers. The so-called propaganda blitz performed by the youths had been known to the opposing Red Front Fighters League in the district, which had put communist activists on alarm readiness. Soon the Hitler Youth Herbert Norkus, known by his nom-de-guerre Quex, was surrounded by communist pursuers, who stabbed and trampled him. Yet he managed to flee from his enemies, only to collapse in a nearby street. He was rushed by taxi to a hospital, where he died shortly thereafter. Soon after his death, Norkus became a central object of Joseph Goebbels's propaganda, underlining his heroic death, effectively turning him into a child hero of the Hitler Youth, and placing him at the center of the National Socialist pantheon of martyrs.[1]

Half a year later, thousands of kilometers from Berlin, young Pavel Morozov was murdered along with his brother Fyodor just outside the remote village Gerasimovka, some 350 kilometres east of Sverdlovsk (Yekaterinburg). The bodies were found on September 6, 1932, three days after the killings were supposedly committed. According to the most popular propaganda account of the story, Morozov was a dedicated communist who led the Young Pioneers at his school. He was a supporter of Stalin's collectivization drive, and in 1932, at the age of thirteen, Morozov reported his father to the political police. Supposedly, Pavel's father, the Chairman of the Village Soviet, had been "forging documents and selling

103

them to the bandits and enemies of the Soviet State," that is, to the kulaks. His family did not take kindly to his activities: his uncle, grandfather, grandmother, and a cousin murdered him, along with his younger brother. Just like Herbert Norkus, the story of little Pavlik was turned into myth, reflecting the attitudes children were supposed to learn about ethical values and revolutionary politics. In 1955 he was canonized as "Pioneer No. 001." By then he was already the subject of songs, plays, and even an opera.[2]

The propaganda figures of Pavel Morozov and Herbert Norkus seem, at a cursory glance, to be strikingly similar. This could of course be coincidental. Most countries have heroes, and there are martyrs for every religion and nation in the world. But the two narratives to be explored here seem to share so many characteristics that it is unlikely that propagandists in the Soviet Union and Nazi Germany would construct them by chance, independent of each other. Direct influence cannot be ruled out, but is very difficult to establish. It is known, for example, that the staff of *Pioneer Pravda*, which was the first national newspaper to report about Pavlik's death and instrumental in creating the myth surrounding him, was passionately internationalist, and frequently reported on youth movements abroad.[3] They could have learned about Herbert Norkus and set out to create a Soviet socialist equivalent. However, it is extremely unlikely that anyone would confess to such plagiarism, leaving any trace for the latter-day historian to find. The similarities may, on the other hand, not necessarily be the result of any conscious act of imitation or plagiarism, rendering the relation between the myths even more complex.

In order to explore the similarities and differences, as well as their respective causes and consequences, it is necessary to shift the attention away from the contents of the event, that is to say the actual history of Herbert Norkus and Pavel Morozov, and turn the attention to the simple premise: cults are made, not born. Both the Bolshevik Party in Russia and their Nazi counterpart in Germany were revolutionary movements, striving to recreate their human subjects. Like every revolutionary movement, they attempted to capture the new, younger generation and rally it to their cause. Both regimes stressed youth, at the expense of the older generation, and sought to create an improved version of the human race. In a striking metaphor, Joseph Stalin issued a call to arms in the Soviet Union, declaring educational institutions to be a pivotal citadel that had to be captured at any prize by the youth, "if they wish to take the place of the old guard."[4] Hitler, on the other hand, proclaimed that "German youth is truest to its people when it finds itself in greatest danger. German youth, what you glorify in your epic tales and songs, you yourselves must strive to become, so that one day your people will be worthy of a song of heroism."[5] In both societies role models, heroes, and martyrs were used to inspire the young.

Reviewing the literature on Nazi and Stalinist heroes, it is easy to be struck by the relative dearth. There are of course studies devoted to the "Hitler Myth" or "Cult of Stalin," that hardly exhaust the subject matter. Two works on National Socialist heroes in Germany stand out: Jay W. Baird's path-breaking study, published in 1990, of the Nazi pantheon of heroes, and Sabine Behrenbeck's similarly conceived, however more critical and nuanced, exploration of the Nazis cult of the dead.[6] Both works are essentially concerned with two related aspects of Nazi hero worship, namely cultic celebrations of Nazis who had themselves displayed "heroic" characteristics, and the fact that an essential attribute those heroes shared was that they were dead, fallen in the service of the movement.

Two works on Pavel Morozov also stand out. Catriona Kelly's documented work, published in 2005, aims to destabilize and deconstruct every aspect of the story, seeking to uncover Morozov's "real life" and to trace the creation, transmission, reception, mutation, and eventual eclipse of the Pavlik legend.[7] Thus Kelly's work follows closely Yuri Druzhnikov's investigation from the mid-1980s, which was published as a documentary book about Pavel Morozov, originally circulated in Samizdat. The first English translation appeared in 1996.[8]

Unlike the mentioned studies, this paper explores the myth of Herbert Norkus, later known as *Hitlerjunge Quex*, and his Soviet counterpart, Pavel Morozov, often simply known as Pavlik, in conjunction. The aim is to explore heroization in the context of the Third Reich and the Soviet Union, two states governed by regimes with totalitarian ambitions. A systematic scholarly comparison can yield new and important knowledge and an understanding of how the two regimes worked and molded their subjects by promoting exemplary myths of child heroes. Did they produce a new type of child hero? What function did it perform? How are these child heroes possible to explain?

Heroes might seem an unpromising subject for scholarship. However, the study of heroes of the past offers an effective topic for historical research by locating heroic reputations in a historical context, and analyzing them rather as sites within which a scholar can find evidence of the cultural beliefs, social practices, and political structures of the past. Of course, a historian can examine a range of "indicators" to gauge the level of collective emotional investment in an individual hero. Most importantly, however, any study must be sensitive to the variety of messages, sometimes contradictory, which could be projected onto any single individual hero.[9]

NATIONAL SOCIALISM, STALINISM, AND POLITICAL RELIGION

For many contemporary as well as latter-day observers, the National Socialist and Stalinist regimes have appeared surprisingly alike, not least in their power-centered politics.[10] This has not least been the case for those who observed the ideological fanaticism that seemed to permeate Germany and the Soviet Union around the time of the Second World War. "The new ideologies . . . have, indeed, assumed the place of the Bible or other sacred writ, and have engendered a type of fanaticism always associated in the past with deeply profound but intolerant religious convictions . . .", wrote Isaac Kandel, a pioneer in comparative educational studies, in 1935.[11]

Both the Bolshevik Party in the Soviet Union and its National Socialist counterpart in Germany strove to recreate their human subjects by capturing the new, younger generation and rallying it to the respective cause. In such a process, history fulfils a very similar function to myth when it comes to providing guidance for actions, and in particular when it comes to attempts aimed at constructing national identities and solidarities.[12]

In order to grasp the heroic, mythic stories of Herbert Norkus and Pavel Morozov, and to understand how they were put to work in order to influence and mold the young, it is necessary to keep in mind that they appeared at decisive turning points in both Germany and in the Soviet Union. 1932 marked the last year of the first five-year plan in the Soviet Union. In January 1933 Adolf Hitler was installed as chancellor in Germany, thus the Nazis took over power in the young democratic republic. 1934 was the important year when Stalin's regime did away with the progressive education introduced in the immediate aftermath of the revolution, and replaced it with more traditional schooling, aimed at educating builders of a classless socialist society through popularization of history. Previous history teaching was thought to have been too abstract and the textbooks "without tsars and kings." "Only 'class struggle' and nothing else!" was Stalin's message.[13]

The same year, Bernhard Rust was named the first Reich Minister of Science, Education, and Popular Culture in Germany, which marked the beginning of a concerted drive of Nazification in all spheres of education, and an attempt at unifying the decentralized educational system in the federation. Here too, the regime abolished an earlier tradition of progressive education, not least by burning all of the older textbooks, in favor of a more traditional and popularized version of history.[14]

It seems that the two regimes pursued similar and parallel strategies in the sphere of education in general. According to traditional totalitarianism theory, education was a means by which the state, the party, or simply the leader could channel authority and propaganda to the young when the totalitarian subject was created. One contemporary observer of Nazi German education described the goal in the following way: "all the citizens can be controlled to its last and finest expression, thus wiping out all remnants of individual freedom, of meaning of the individual."[15] In both societies, history was employed to fashion the subjects. In these turbulent years Herbert Norkus and Pavel Morozov, as mythical characters, became ideological beacons that could guide the young with their bright shining lights. They were mythical martyrs who could provide good examples for the youth of Germany and the Soviet Union.

One definition of myth holds that it is "a widely accepted belief that gives meaning to events and that is socially cued, whether or not it is verifiable."[16] Humans need myths to help us understand ourselves and our place in the world. Many of these are political myths, tales which help us make sense of our political past, present, and future. They can also persuade us to act in certain ways and can, for this reason, be powerful aids in the imposition of social control on a population.[17] Carl Friedrich and Zbigniew Brzezinski noted years ago that myths "play a vital role in totalitarian dictatorships."[18]

However, "in totalitarian dictatorships," myths are not simply constructed *ex nihilo* to control the population. As Peter Lambert has noticed, the Nazi cults and hero worship did not dramatically change the nature of heroization in German political culture.[19] Similarly, with regards to the Soviet Union, Carol Barner-Barry and Cynthia Hody have remarked that inculcating a new mythic and religious system is not the work of a few decades. The Soviet leadership tried to displace an older set of mythologies and replace them with a new one, but ultimately failed.[20] But when all is said and done, the new mythical stories of Herbert Norkus and Pavel Morozov became extremely popular. How is it possible to explain?

After the fall of the communist regimes in Central and Eastern Europe, a renewed interest arose in comparing the National socialist and Soviet communist dictatorships. If one considers the violent politics, represented by Italian fascism, German National Socialism, and Soviet Communism, and the historical role played by these regimes in the twentieth century, the question arises whether they shared common traits, despite their obvious differences. In order to grasp the essentially new and common features of these modern dictatorships, as has been noted earlier in this book, one has, in recent years, re-activated the concepts of "totalitarianism" and "political religion." The concept of totalitarianism had been in eclipse before 1989, especially in the 1970s, because of political and ideological reasons, but is now being used again with less restraint in numerous publications and research projects. The concept of political religion has never had common acclaim in the past. Only in recent years there has been growing interest in this concept.

Scholars who subscribe to the analytical value of the concept of "political religion" commonly use it in order to capture the characteristics of totalitarian political movements that went beyond the analytical reach of traditional concepts, such as despotism. Political religion has been used to capture the essential meaning of "totalitarian," namely the claim of these regimes to dominate and control not only the political and social sphere, but all aspects of human existence.[21] Nazism and Stalinism shared the notion of apocalyptic palingenesis.[22] And, as Tzvetan Todorov has argued, totalitarianism demands the conjunction of scientism, millennialism, and violence.[23]

The concept of political religion has been used in a number of ways, but there is a substantial body of publications that share a family of conceptions. Fundamental is the idea that politics and religion are not essentially separate, different, or incommensurable. Politics, fundamentally a secular phenomenon in modern society, can be sanctified, while religion, essentially a sacred phenomenon, can be secularized.[24] One of the most thorough attempts at explaining sacralization comes from Emilio Gentile. He argues that sacralization of politics takes place when a political movement consecrates the primacy of a collective entity, placing it at the center of a system of beliefs and myths that define the meaning and goal of social existence. Secondly, sacralization takes place when this conception is incorporated into a code of ethical and social commandments, compelling the individual to loyalty and dedication to it. Thirdly, the political movement considers its members to be an elect community and interprets political action as a messianic function aimed toward the fulfillment of a mission. Fourth, the political movement develops a political liturgy in order to worship the sacralized collective entity by way of an institutionalized cult.[25]

Viewing Herbert Norkus and Pavel Morozov from the perspective of political religion helps to explain their presence in Nazi Germany and the Soviet Union, and their apparent similarities. Both stories about the young boy heroes fit well with Gentile's argument about the development of political liturgy to worship a sacralized collective entity. In fact, Jesús Casquete has even argued that the "insistence on forging martyrs is key to identifying a movement or a regime as a political religion." Martyrs are generally manufactured by the movements' entrepreneurs in order to have a community to eventually believe and follow this figure. Unless there is a retrospective social attribution, there will be no belief in a martyr, nor a conviction that the acts attributed to him or her merit any remembrance.[26]

QUEX AND PAVLIK: REDEEMERS, MARTYRS, AND DENOUNCERS

Some kinds of heroization common in the Third Reich and the Soviet Union were plainly not peculiar to them. Sporting heroes as well as war heroes, for instance, did not single them out from pretty ubiquitous patterns. In addition, the obsession with martyrdom and death cults was by no means unique to Nazism or Stalinism. Often labor movements and left-wing parties, such as the German Communist Party, had a habit of wallowing in the blood of their dead. Both Pavlik and Quex can be derived from such a heroic standard figure in the late 1920s and 1930s.

However, to explore if the Nazi and Soviet regime did generate a new type of hero, or a peculiar intense engagement in heroization, it seems reasonable and necessary to start in the myths themselves.[27]

The epic saga of Herbert Norkus celebrated the achievements and exploits of a model Hitler Youth, and came to inspire millions of young Germans during the National Socialist period. So did the story of Pavel Morozov in the Soviet Union. It is possible to distill a number of common components, tropes, or themes in the propaganda stories. Both boys were presented as Christ-like martyrs, redeemers, undergoing transformation, and as outstanding pupils. The two stories also clearly pinpointed the evil villains, not only in a narrative sense, but as a real existing threat in the world of the young of Germany and the Soviet Union. The mythical stories were employed to promote denunciation of unwanted elements, that is, kulaks and Communists.

Herbert Norkus's behavior and actions were seen as an exemplary fulfilment of the central tenant of the Hitler Youth organization, and partly of Nazi ideology in general—life is but a preparation for a noble warrior's death. Among the Hitler Youth who laid down their lives in sacrifice to the Führer, Herbert Norkus became the standard-bearer, and his blood drained the mystical Blood Flag of the Hitler Youth.[28] The appalling death of Norkus, butchered by a gang of communists, lent credibility to Hitler's and Goebbels's demagogic claim that "Bolshevik sub humanity" was loose on German soil. "Jewish-Bolshevik beastliness" would not even waver at murder of a proletarian boy from the poor industrial north Berlin. The child martyr Norkus became the central theme of Hitler Youth propaganda. In the words of Reich Youth Leader Baldur von Schirach:

> This little comrade has become the myth of the young nation, symbol of the self-sacrificial spirit of all the young who bear Hitler's name Many died in the battle of the young for the Reich; the name "Norkus" embraces all of them in the eternal comradeship of the Hitler Youth. Nothing binds us Hitler Youths together more closely than the knowledge of our brotherly link to this dead boy, nothing is more alive than this murdered one, nothing is more immortal than he who passes away . . ."[29]

The apotheosis of Norkus was only partly a result of Goebbels's creation, propagated in newspaper articles and speeches, but foremost an outcome of the enormously popular novel *Der Hitlerjunge Quex*, published by Karl Aloys Schenzinger in December 1932, which later provided the basis for the screenplay of *Hitlerjunge Quex*.[30] Schenzinger treated Herbert Norkus, whom he renamed Heini Völker, as a modern child-redeemer. Forced by his drunken father to attend a weekend communist youth camp, Heini was disturbed and appalled by the group's disorderly behavior, which is presented as but an outward sign of inner degeneration—a stark contrast to the orderly and uniform Hitler Youths. Heini felt out of place and escaped the first night. Creeping through the woods he stumbled upon a Hitler Youth camp, where he heard songs of nation and glory and saw German boys and girls in uniform, singing German songs in a German forest. Henceforth he knew that his home had to be with these brave comrades.[31]

Less than a year after the novel was published, the film *Hitler Youth Quex* premiered in Munich Ufa-Phoebus-Palast on September 11, 1933, accompanied by a gala performance of Anton Bruckner's Fourth Symphony by the Reich Symphony Orchestra.[32] It contains all the elements of a passion play and family drama: an innocent blond child; a desperate mother who attempts a joint suicide with her son; a drunken father drawn to Communism; the dark slums of Berlin; German communists as tools of foreign power; idealistic and heroic Hitler Youth; the redemptive death of a lamb of the people (*Volk*). Interestingly, the father of Quex is portrayed as a brutal man and a communist, a character caused by the miseries of the economic and social system. The father wants the young boy to sign on for the communists but the latter feels that this political solution is completely wrong. True to himself, he declares himself loyal to the Hitler Youth. According to the Nazis, loyalty to parents must give way to loyalty to the larger Nazi family in the case of a conflict.[33]

Baldur von Schirach, the honorary director, found the film a noble chapter in German history, placing it alongside Goethe's Faust and Beethoven's ninth symphony.[34] The film, produced on the heroic theme of National Socialism, was at once propaganda and an aesthetic success. It seemed to have had a remarkable appeal for young people in Germany. As late as in 1942, it was still shown in the youth film hours of the Hitler Youth, an important propaganda activity of the organization.[35] *Hitler Youth Quex* schooled a generation of young Germans to prepare for a sacrificial death for their country.

Goebbels had previously stressed that film in general should emanate from political life and find its way into the depths of the German soul, transcend the everyday, and "intensify life."[36] He found *Hitler Youth Quex* to be a full-fledged successful first large-scale attempt to depict the ideas and world of National Socialism within the art of cinema.[37] Cinema was an important tool and quickly found its way into state institutions of discipline and education. Bernhard Rust spoke on the topic in 1934:

> [Film] is particularly important for our youngest citizens—the school children. Film must not only help them grasp contemporary political problems, it must also provide children knowledge about Germany's great past, and profound understanding regarding the future development of the Third Reich. The Nationalist Socialist State definitely and deliberately makes film the transmitter of its ideology.[38]

Hitler Youth Quex is striking in its focus on international Communism. More than any other film made in the Third Reich, the stereotype of the "Jewish Bolshevik" is devastating. The German Communist Party is viewed as a pack of marauding wolves with but one goal in mind—to destroy everything that they cannot control. As traitors and agents of the Soviet Union, they dispatch their *Kommandos* to carry out their evil deeds. Their only goal is to work for the welfare of the Soviet Union, never for the German nation.[39] This was noted already during the Second World War by prominent ethnographer Gregory Bateson, who undertook a close study of *Hitler Youth Quex* as part of a larger endeavor to comprehend National Socialism through its cinematic self-depictions. By employing the same kind of analysis "that the anthropologist applies to the mythology of a primitive or modern people" he showed how the film systematically structured the Nationalist Socialist Party and the Communist Party as absolute opposites. In Bateson's conclusion, this illustrated the projective workings of Nazi subjectivity. The Communists and the Communist Party become the unbearable images of the other.[40]

It is possible to argue that the story of Herbert Norkus, or rather Hitler Youth Quex, not only presents a role model, a person to glorify and with which to identify. It also "mediates the myth of a martyr in order to mobilize emotions."[41] Most importantly, the hero's death also clearly points out the villains, those with which not to identify, the enemy of the German nation and the German people. Looking closer at the myth of Pavel Morozov reveals the presence of this dual function as well.

The propaganda myth of little Pavel Morozov did not take off in such a straight trajectory as the story of Herbert Norkus. It took almost a month for the murder case to reach the national press, which might be explained by the need of the authorities to control matters. It did not get front-page space; it was consigned to a short note about a "characteristic" act of kulak aggression. It was described in the local press how Pavel and his younger brother Fyodor had been murdered because of their tireless efforts to expose the evil-doings of the kulaks in their village.[42]

When the story finally reached the national press, *Pioneer Pravda* mentioned that both brothers denounced their father as a counter-revolutionary, and that they had unmasked a kulak band that was carrying out wrecking work in the district. Subsequently Pavel Morozov the activist was underlined, a boy so dedicated to the cause that he would stop at nothing.[43] The two brothers were not simply murdered activists—they were martyrs. However, Fyodor Morozov soon faded into the background, while Pavel was raised to apotheosis.

"The memory of Pavel Morozov must never fade," wrote Maksim Gorky. Little Pavlik was an ideal figure, the archetype of the new Soviet Man, and Gorky joined in the demands for a statue to be erected in Moscow in the boy's honor. His example was of great social and educational value and taught children that "a close relative can easily be your enemy in his inner convictions" and that "such a person should be given no quarter."[44] In a short period of time, several books about little Pavlik or loosely based on the story of him, were published. Vitaly Gubarev, the author of *Pavel Morozov*, had himself taken part in the inquiry into Morozov's murder. In his book, which was re-issued in the 1970s, little Pavlik is presented as a model pupil in the village school and a social activist, inspired by reading Gorky's *Mother*. Set against Pavlik are the enemies of the Soviet state, who exploit the employees and refuse to pay for the upkeep of the school. The enemies also dream of a war breaking out, so that foreign enemies can arrive to hang the Young Pioneers by their red scarves. Similarly, in 1936 Aleksandr Yakovlev wrote the book *The Young Pioneer Pavel Morozov*, which was later adapted to a play version shown at the Moscow Theatre for Young Spectators in 1940. Sergei Mikhalkov wrote *The Song of Pavlik Morozov* in 1934, designed to be performed by a children's choir. Pavlik was the best communist, an example for all Young Pioneers, and his memory should never be forgotten, Mikhalkov exclaimed.[45]

The mythic story of little Pavlik evolved in several ways. First, he became an ideal Pioneer hero, exemplifying the fashionable virtues of the day, that is to say diligence in the schoolroom, concerns for his fellows, and modest participation in the political causes of the day. Secondly, his vigilant role as denouncer of his father was softened. In subsequent accounts, Pavlik became more and more hesitant and reluctant. It was seen as an unpleasant and extreme civic act, rather than a glorious feat of revolutionary zeal.[46]

In the middle of 1935, Sergei Eisenstein started working on his first film in more than three years' time, *Bezhin Meadow* (*Bezhin Lug*).[47] It was commissioned by the Komsomol, the Communist Youth League, to highlight the contribution of the Young Pioneers to collective farm work. It was a story about the martyrdom of a young peasant boy, Styopok, a member of the Young Pioneers, in a successful fight against sabotage by the village's kulaks, led by his own father. Eisenstein claimed that the film was directly based on the Morozov story. However, Eisenstein was stricken by illness and was unable to finalize the film. Ultimately, the unfinished original was destroyed in a bombing raid in 1941.

Since the 1920s, the Soviet regime had explicitly asked for "revolutionary spectacles." A few years prior to the Second World War this changed into a desire to portray heroes in order to encourage Soviet patriotism. Films about great individuals, such as Peter the Great, Kutuzov, and Suvorov were made by different directors. Eisenstein responded to the regime's demands by making *Bezhin Meadow*, *Aleksandr Nevsky*, and *Ivan Groznyi* (Ivan the Terrible). Many of the films produced during this time in the Soviet Union implicitly justified terror as a political mean. The viewers were to understand that no one was to be trusted. The enemy could be your closest friend. Frequently, the hero was the denouncer who put the state's interest over any other relation.[48]

By the mid-1920s, the Soviet press had also shifted toward more pedagogical examples, in line with the practical need of education in the country. The Soviet people, in general, were treated a bit like children by their stern but loving teachers, the party and Stalin, who helped them eliminate any character traits associated with the pre-revolutionary order. The metaphor of the family became ever more present and Stalin played the role of lover, father, husband, and grandfather of the people. Stalin was at the head, and Pavel Morozov, the heroic pioneer and staunch builder of the collective farm, became his most faithful son. Svetlana Boym has argued that the propaganda story of the little child-martyr is "the Soviet version of the Oedipal myth par excellence."[49]

A distinct feature in Eisenstein's film about Pavel Morozov is the father-son conflict, here underlined by Stypok's father murdering his mother at the onset, thus further justifying his denunciation of him. The father continuously complains about his son's allegiance to the Soviet regime and even quotes the Bible: "If the son betrays his father, kill him like a dog!" After the father is arrested for arson, Stypok leaves the house with the kolkhoz chairwoman. The father's kulak co-criminals barricade themselves in a church, but are eventually arrested. Later they overpower their guards and escape. At night the father finds his son among those who guard the harvest, and shoots him. The criminals are again arrested and Stypok dies in the arms of the leader of the political department of the collective farm. As noted by Peter Kenez, there are plenty of biblical references in the film. Peasants worship icons, they portray themselves as saints. Frequently there appears to be a strange halo around Stypok's head. Later critics would point out the mixed ideological message of these scenes.[50]

Without the permission or even knowledge of the director of the film, after a screening for members of the Politburo, the unfinished work was subjected to heavy criticism. Eisenstein was attacked for being engaged in mythmaking instead of making a picture about a real Soviet village. The level of conflict in the film between father and son was raised to biblical proportions and turned into a fight between good and evil, light and darkness, the critics proclaimed. Instead they wanted to see a different film, and Eisenstein was compelled to make another film with a rewritten script. In the new version, there was no mention of the death of Stypok's mother. Consequently, the boy's motivation was exclusively political, which is indicated by the fact that the head of the political department was given a much more prominent role, and together with his wife presented as Stypok's real parents.[51]

Still, the bureaucrats failed to be impressed by Eisenstein's work. The new head of Soviet film production, Boris Shumyatsky, published a vicious denunciation, "The Errors of *Bezhin Meadow*," and ordered the production to be halted. In his statement, published in *Pravda* in March 1937, Shumyatsky, who had criticized Soviet films for lacking romantic interest, accused Eisenstein of "making *Bezhin Meadow* only because it offered him an opportunity to indulge in formalistic exercises. Instead of creating a strong, clear, direct work, Eisenstein detached his work from reality, from the colors and heroism of reality. He consciously reduced the work's ideological content."[52] Soon after, Eisenstein replied with a published self-denunciation in which he pledged to "rid myself of the last anarchistic traits of individualism in my outlook and creative method."[53] Nevertheless, the filming of *Bezhin Meadow* was not resumed. Thus, the Soviet boy hero, martyr and redeemer Pavlik never made it onto the silver screen as his German counterpart did.

As model pupils, Herbert Norkus and Pavel Morozov were hardly unique in the pantheon of child heroes. What set them apart was their blind faith in their political systems and their leaders, which led them to denounce members of their families; in Pavel's case his father and uncle, and in the case of *Hitler Junge Quex* his drunken communist father. However, Catriona Kelly has argued that Soviet citizens would have denounced each other energetically even without Pavel Morozov. Possibly, it could be argued that Pavlik Morozov may have made the perpetrators of such activities feel ennobled. But more often, his legend gave the more politically conscientious of his readers a pause for thought: would their own heroism ever measure up to such high ideals? And thus they experienced exactly the sense of insecurity and dissatisfaction with one's own achievements that stories of this kind were supposed to foster, nurturing in themselves two of the quintessential Stalinist emotions: totalitarian governance depended as much on people's readiness to blame *themselves* as it did on their readiness to blame *others* and report their misdeeds.[54]

This was also true in the German case. Rudolf Ramlow, a theatre critic, wrote in a book for young boys:

> for whatever he does or does not do, not only he himself but the whole community of his comrades is responsible, that the energies of his body and spirit belong to his companions as much as to himself. And even if ever he should fall into the temptation to look out for himself rather than for his comrades, his guilty conscience would give hem no rest, even if he was formally in the right.[55]

TOTALITARIAN CHILD MARTYRS AS SECULARISED BLOOD LIBELS?

Unlike National Socialism and Italian Fascism, Bolshevism never officially defined itself as a political religion. Furthermore, it did not officially proclaim that it wanted to exercise a religious type of influence over the masses, despite some initiatives taken by Anatoly Lunacharsky, which aimed to establish socialism as a religion of man. Despite this, many observers, such as Bertrand Russell and John Maynard Keynes, considered Bolshevism to be a new religion. [56]

Apart from celebrating the two different child martyrs' behavior, the stories about them identified the threats to the two societies. In this respect, the stories come very close to the traditional myth of the blood libel, albeit in secular versions. As Bill Ellis has argued, the identification of threat in the blood libel is predicated on anxieties over groups regarded as foreign and therefore dangerous. [57]

An anti-Jewish accusation, the blood libel emerged in the Middle Ages, following the massacres of the First Crusade in the twelfth century. When Jews were accused of ritual murder of Christians in the thirteenth century, ritual murder accusations turned into blood libel, possibly due to an increased focus on the blood imagery of Christian ritual and worship. In the pre-modern period, the accusation was tinged with religious rhetoric. Sometimes political and economic goals were religiously motivated. In the modern period, however, the blood libel acquired a more secular and even scientific meaning, often with racial connotations. Accusations against Jews were not void of political goals.

Consequently, accusations of and stories about blood libels were well known in both Germany and the Soviet Union in the interwar period. The National Socialist Party paper *Der Stürmer* published a special "Ritual murder issue" in 1934. [58] Certainly, the paper was known for its vehement anti-Semitism, but interestingly this issue featured Aryans predominantly as children. In Damon Barry's conclusion, the

> Aryan male can only be a child in the nationalist blood libel. He is helpless, unable to protect the women and children, or even himself. One can imagine that this absence of the protective masculine figure expresses the fear of what may befall the women and children in his absence. That reading is too simple . . . this assumed absence actually signals the presence of that very masculine figure in impotent form. [59]

Similarly, Elisabeth Bemborad has shown that the myth of the blood libel also resurfaced in Stalin's Soviet Union, despite the authorities' insistence on combating anti-Semitism. The belief in Jews using Christian blood for ritual purposes became a source of embarrassment for the authorities, and often explained by evil influence of reactionary religious leaders, accused of encouraging the political enemies of the Soviet regime. [60]

However, it is possible to claim that any object could be signified, instead of "the Jew," within the structure of the blood libel narrative as the offender or victimizer. Besides the historical roots of the blood libel and its use against peoples other than Jews, Ellis has noticed that the accusation played on the "anxieties and taboos of the existing majority rather than knowledge of the scapegoated group." [61] She argues that the accused were in each case "ethnic or religious minorities," but in fact, any minority can be made to fit as the offender, such as German Communists and kulaks discussed in this chapter.

Most importantly, through the story of the blood libel, the victim's group is provided with a legitimate reason to carry out repression on the victimizer's group. By transposing subject and object, through a projective inversion, the initial party is left free to hate his or her enemy, and furthermore to be totally absolved of feelings of guilt therefore.[62] Christian hatred of Jews is transformed into Jews hatred of Christians, or the National Socialist hatred of communists is transformed into the communist hatred of National Socialists.

The stories of, or rather propaganda myths surrounding Herbert Norkus and Pavel Morozov certainly fit the trope of a secularized blood libel. However, they do differ in their simultaneous insistence on the pedagogical value of their lives and their didactic function as role models and victims. Thus, they amalgamate two different stories of the hero and of the victim. Future studies will have to shed more light on their entangled faiths as part of institutionalized, re-sacralized political religions.

NOTES

1. Jay W. Baird, *To Die for Germany. Heroes in the Nazi Pantheon* (London: Routledge, 1990), 114–15.

2. Catriona Kelly, *Comrade Pavlik. The Rise and Fall of a Soviet Boy Hero* (London: Granta Books, 2005), 1–17.

3. Kelly, *Comrade Pavlik*, 122.

4. Stalin quoted in John Rodden, *Textbook Reds. Schoolbooks, Ideology, and Eastern German Identity* (University Park: Pennsylvania State Press, 2006), 3. On early Bolshevik ideology and youth, see Anne Gorsuch, "Soviet Youth and the Politics of Popular Culture during NEP," *Social History* 17 (1992): 189–201.

5. Max Domarus, *Hitler: Speeches and Proclamations 1932–1945. Vol. I* (London: Tauris, 1990), 137.

6. Baird, *To Die for Germany*, Sabine Behrenbeck, *Der Kult um die toten Helden. Nationalsozialistische Mythen, Riten und Symbole 1923 bis 1945* (Vierow bei Greifswald: SH-Verlag, 1996).

7. Catriona Kelly takes notice of the similarities between Norkus and Morozov and compares them briefly in her book.

8. Catriona Kelly, *Comrade Pavlik*, Yuri Druzhnikov, *Informer 001: The Myth of Pavlik Morozov* (New Brunswick: Transaction Publishers, 1996). Druzhnikov has accused Kelly of extensive plagiarism from his book, and also of "dependence on those who have admitted her to archives," that is, from employees of FSB. See Yuri Druzhnikov, "Katriona Kelli, Pavlik Morozov i Lyubianka," *Voprosy literatury* 3 (2006), accessed February 3, 2015, http://magazines.russ.ru/voplit/2006/3/dru12.html.

9. See Max Jones, "What Should Historians Do With Heroes? Reflections on Nineteenth- and Twentieth-Century Britain," *History Compass* 5 (2007): 439–54.

10. Abbot Gleason, *Totalitarianism. The Inner History of the Cold War* (New York and Oxford: Oxford University Press, 1995).

11. Isaac Kandel, "Education in Nazi Germany," *Annals of the American Academy of Political and Social Science* 182 (1935): 154. See also Isaac Kandel, *The Making of Nazis* (Connecticut: Greenwood Press, 1970).

12. Chris Lorentz, "Drawing the Line: 'Scientific History' Between Myth-Making and Myth Breaking," in *Narrating the Nation: Representations in History, Media and the Arts*, ed. Stefan Berger et al. (Oxford: Oxford University Press, 2008), 35–55.

13. *Pravda*, April 5, 1934.

14. See Kurt-Ingo Flessau, *Schule der Diktatur: Lehrpläne und Schulbücher des National-sozialismus* (Munich: Fischer-TB, 1984).

15. Fritz Karsen, "Some Remarks on the Nazi Philosophy of Education," *The German Quarterly* 14 (1941): 137.

16. Murray Edelman, *Political Language: Words that Succeed and Politics that Fail* (New York: New York Academic Press, 1977), 3.

17. See Dan Nimmo and James E. Combs, *Subliminal Politics: Myths and Mythmakers in America* (Englewood Cliffs: Prentice-Hall Inc. 1980).

18. Carl Friedrich and Zbigniew Brzezinski, *Totalitarian Dictatorship and Autocracy* (Cambridge, MA: Harvard University Press, 1965), 91.

19. Peter Lambert, "Heroisation and Demonisation in the Third Reich: The Consensus-building Value of a Nazi Pantheon of Heroes," *Totalitarian Movements and Political Religions* 8 (2007): 526.

20. Carol Barner-Barry and Cynthia Hody, "Soviet Marxism-Leninism as Mythology," *Political Psychology* 15 (1994): 626. See also Christel Lane, *The Rites of Rulers: Ritual and Industrial Society—the Soviet Case* (Cambridge: Cambridge University Press, 1981).

21. A good overview of the concept of political religion is found in Emilio Gentile, "Political Religion: A Concept and its Critics—A Critical Survey," *Totalitarian Movements and Political Religions* 6 (2005): 19–32.

22. See Michael Burleigh, "National Socialism as a Political Religion," *Totalitarian Movements and Political Religions* 1 (2000), 13.

23. Tzvetan Todorov, "Totalitarianism: Between Religion and Science," *Totalitarian Movements and Political Religion* 2 (2001): 36–37.

24. See for example Uriel Tal, "Aspects of Consecration of Politics in the Nazi Era," in *Judaism and Christianity under the Impact of National Socialism*, ed. Otto D. Kulka and Paul R. Mendes-Flohr (Jerusalem: Historical Society of Israel and Zalman Shazar Center for Jewish History, 1987).

25. Emilio Gentile, "The Sacralisation of Politics: Definitions, Interpretations and Reflections on the Question of Secular Religion and Totalitarianism," *Totalitarian Movements and Political Religions* 1 (2000): 22.

26. Jesús Casquete, "Martyr Construction and the Politics of Death in National Socialism," *Totalitarian Movements and Political Religions* 10 (2009): 265, 271–72.

27. It should be noted that the life span of these mythical propaganda stories varies. While Morozov lived, forever young, with the youth of the Soviet Union right up until its end in 1991, Norkus faded away quickly after the defeat of Nazi Germany in 1945. In order to carry out a fair comparison, this account will limit itself to the period 1932 to 1953, that is, the year of Stalin's death.

28. George L. Mosse, *Nazi Culture. Intellectual, Cultural and Social Life in the Third Reich* (Madison: The University of Wisconsin Press, 1966): 266.

29. Quoted in Arnold Littmann, *Herbert Norkus und die Hitlerjungen vom Beusselkietz* (Berlin: Steuben Verlag, 1934), 6.

30. The book had been pre-published in instalments in the newspaper *Völkischer Beobachter* prior to its release in December, yet it sold one hundred ninety thousand copies in less than two years.

31. Karl Aloys Schenzinger, *Der Hitlerjunge Quex* (Berlin: Zeitgeschichte-Verlag, 1932).

32. The guests in attendance included many of the elite of the Third Reich: Adolf Hitler, Hermann Göring, Ernst Röhm, high-ranking generals, and others.

33. An in-depth study of the film is Eric Rentschler's "Emotional Engineering: Hitler Youth Quex," *Modernism/Modernity* 2 (1995): 23–44.

34. Baldur von Schirach, *Die Hitler-Jugend. Idee und Gestalt* (Leipzig: Koehler & Umelang, 1934), 18–19.

35. David Welch, "Education, Film, Propaganda, and the Nazi Youth," in *Nazi Propaganda: The Power and the Limitations*, ed. David Welch (London: Croom Helm, 1983), 65–87.

36. See Gerd Albrecht, *Nationalsozialistische Filmpolitik* (Stuttgart: Enke, 1969), 442–44.

37. *Der Angriff*, 25 September 1933.

38. The Speech was reprinted in *Völkischer Beobachter*, 23 June, 1934.

39. Jay W. Baird, *To Die for Germany*, 123.

40. Margaret Mead and Rhoda Métraux, "An Analysis of the Nazi Film Hitlerjunge Quex: Gregory Bateson," in *The Study of Culture at a Distance*, ed. Margaret Mead and Rhoda Métraux (Chicago: Chicago University Press, 1953), 302–11.

41. Rentschler, *Emotional Engineering*, 34.

42. Kelly, *Comrade Pavlik*, 69, 112.

43. *Pionerskaya pravda*, 2 October 1932, *Pionerskaya pravda*, 15 October, 1932.

44. *Pravda*, 29 October 1933.

45. Ben Hellman, *Fairy Tales and True Stories: The History of Russian Literature for Children and Young People (1574–2010)* (Boston: Brill, 2013), 394.

46. Kelly, *Comrade Pavlik*, 165.

47. The film was also based in part on a story by Ivan Turgenev, whose original short fiction titled "Bezhin Meadow" was a story about peasant boys in the 1850s, in the Oryol region, discussing supernatural signs of death, while they spend the night in the Bezhin Meadow with a lost hunter. Eisenstein would later remove any direct references to Turgenev's fiction, aside from the title, from the film.

48. Peter Kenez, "Bezhin lug (Bezhin Meadow)," in *Enemies of the People: The Destruction of Soviet Literary, Theater, and Film Arts in the 1930s*, ed. Katherine Bliss Eaton (Evanston: Northwestern University Press, 2002), 114–15.

49. Svetlana Boym, *Common Places: Mythologies of Everyday Life in Russia* (Cambridge, MA: Harvard University Press, 1994), 91.

50. Kenez, *Bezhin lug*, 118

51. Kenez, *Bezhin lug*, 118–19.

52. *Pravda*, 19 March 1937.

53. Ian Christie, *The Film Factory: Russian and Soviet Cinema in Documents, 1896–1939* (New York: Routledge, 1994), 378–81.

54. Kelly, *Comrade Pavlik*, 174–75.

55. Rudolf Ramlow, *Herbert Norkus? — Hier! Opfer und Sieg der Hitler-Jugend* (Berlin: Union Deutsches Verlagsgesellschaft, 1933), 91.

56. Richard Stites, *Revolutionary Dreams, Utopian Vision and Experimental Life in the Revolution* (New York and Oxford: Oxford University Press, 1989), Nina Tumarkin, *Lenin Lives! The Lenin Cult in Soviet Russia* (Cambridge: Cambridge University Press, 1983), and Emilio Gentile, *The Sacralisation*, 41.

57. Bill Ellis, "De legendis urbis: Modern legends in ancient Rome," *Journal of American Folklore* 96 (1983): 200–208.

58. *Der Stürmer*, May 1934.

59. Damon T. Berry, "Blood on the Tongue: Reading Abjection in Nationalist Blood Libels From Nazi Germany to Hamas and the British National Party," *Journal of Hate Studies* 10 (2012): 111–12.

60. Elisabeth Bemporad, "Empowerment, Defiance, and Demise: Jews and the Blood Libel Specter under Stalinism," *Jewish History* 26 (2012): 347.

61. Ellis, Bill, "De legendis urbis," 201.

62. Allan Dundes, "The Ritual Murder or Blood Libel Legend: A Study of anti-Semitic Victimization through Projective Inversion," in *The Blood Libel Legend: A Casebook in Anti-Semitic Folklore*, ed. Allan Dundes (Madison: University of Wisconsin Press, 1991), 355.

SIX

Communism's Compelling Grasp

Enduring the Gulag and Enduring Loyalty

Nanci Adler

When the Russian television station, NTV, announced the death of Aleksandr Iakovlev on the evening of October 18, 2005, the broadcaster stated that Iakovlev was the only former high Party leader to apologize for the "sin of Bolshevism."[1] The listeners were implicitly invited to consider the similarities between Bolshevism and religion.[2] Among the ideological currents that converged within this public announcement were individual responsibility, religious confession, and a repudiation of a political ideology, now increasingly viewed with nostalgia.

Iakovlev progressed from committed Communist and ideologue to critic of the repressive practices of the system, eventually to become a chief architect of the Gorbachev-era perestroika policies. After the collapse of the Soviet Union, he chaired the Presidential Commission on the Rehabilitation of Victims of Unlawful Repression which eventually rehabilitated over four million citizens. In the first post-Soviet decade, Iakovlev not only denounced the former political system, but encouraged people to remember and "repent," even calling for the traditional November 7 Revolution Holiday to be renamed "The Day of Agreement and Reconciliation" (which failed because no one understood what conflicts they were supposed to be reconciling). In one perspective, Iakovlev escaped from the gravitational field of one ideology—Communism—only to be drawn into another—religion. Iakovlev's labeling of the moral transgressions committed in the name of Bolshevism as sinful, wittingly or unwittingly, leads us to reflect on Karl Marx's disparagement of religion as an opiate of the people.[3] The CPSU had effectively appropriated the role and function of religion in the lives of some citizens. It was a driving force that may have sustained them through and beyond the Gulag.

Communism and Nazism may share the power of religious conviction to impose authoritarian codes of behavior and to sustain hardships. This thread can be discerned in a number of narratives I gathered from loyalist Gulag prisoners and returnees. They draw from oral histories with survivors, unpublished and published memoirs of Gulag prisoners and returnees, and Party and state archives. For purposes of discussion, these examples will be divided into separate categories, each conveying the power and function of a strongly held belief system. They illustrate how Bolshevism functioned as a secular religion; how Communism assumed the prerogatives of a faith-based belief; how the charismatic appeal of the Party or the movement enthralled its followers; and finally the enduring, post-regime influence of an assimilated ideology. These authoritarian values have come to dominate national memory and a national narrative that marginalizes the Gulag, and by extension, its victims and survivors.

However, even as we call attention to the way these authoritarian regimes violated individual rights and failed to deliver promised material benefits, we also recognize that they provided believers with an immaterial, but essential, ingredient of human life—a vital sense of "meaning." Meaningfulness is not conferred by the material universe, but created by human systems of belief. Recognition of the essential need for *meaning* should inform our understanding of the appeal of authoritarian systems, and their enduring grasp.

THE GULAG PRISONER AND THE BOLSHEVIK SOUL

Oksana Lazarevna taught socioeconomics at Odessa University and was the mother of two. She was also the wife of an "enemy of the people," who had been arrested and taken away. Oksana was a committed Party member, but as she watched the arrest of one after another of her cohorts, she suspected that the enemy had "penetrated the Party, and it was the NKVD."[4] One day, while Oksana was nursing her infant son, they came for her too. The NKVD agents tore the baby from her, and dispatched her sons to her parents. Oksana was taken to an Odessa prison. There, the suspicions she had previously harbored were confirmed by what she witnessed in prison.

By the time Oksana was sent to the Gulag, she had resolved to "clear the names of honest Communists."[5] From her barracks, she began to write letters to Stalin and the Central Committee. She charged that, "lawlessness reigns in the organs of the NKVD . . . it has lead to the destruction of the Odessa Party ranks and many sincere Leninist-Communists."[6] Her camp-mates were terrified. They warned, "you will have to give these letters to the NKVD authorities in the camp. Don't you understand what the consequences will be? You will die, and you will kill your children." In her response, Oksana illustrated how the dedication to a set of values can override even so strong a human devotion as motherhood, let alone personal survival. She declared: "I am a Communist in the first place, and after that a mother."[7] Oksana was transferred, and her story, recorded in the memoirs of a camp-mate, ends there. The author, also a committed Party member, wrote in 1963:

> In these days of the triumph of truth and justice, the complete unmasking of the cult of personality of Stalin, the restoration of the Leninist principles in life and Party leadership, I would love to know what ever happened to Oksana Lazarevna—a sincere Communist with a Capital C.[8]

Given the content of Oksana's letters, however it is unlikely that she even survived transport to the camps. It is likely that she maintained her faith until the very end.

In the aftermath of Khrushchev's Secret Speech, the great wave of return and rehabilitation was followed by thousands of requests for Party reinstatement.[9] The motivation of some of the applicants invites comparison between Bolshevism and religion, among other things, because of the frequent references among some prisoners and returnees to their "Bolshevik soul."[10] Despite the fact that Bolshevism presented itself as a secular political movement, many of its adherents described themselves as possessing a Bolshevik soul. This self-description is consistent with the predisposition of humans to transcend their individual, material being and connect with something greater than their *self*, and it is not unique to religion. It is an innate property of being human—a property used and exploited by both religious and secular "total institutions."

For the Party faithful, their belief in the CPSU incentivized their labor even within the camps, because they considered themselves to be the builders of socialism who were participating in its construction with their bare hands. The sense of identity of a number of prisoners was imbued by their youthful dreams of building a better life and forging a new society, goals that merged their identity with that of the Party. Their faith in the morality of socialism was largely unshaken by the repression, which they interpreted either as a perversion of an inherently good ideology or as an opportunity to "offer up," as it were, tangible physical labor in support of their ideology. Viktor Frankl has called our attention to the defining function of *meaning* by pointing out that "suffering ceases to be suffering in some way at the moment it finds a meaning, such as the meaning of a sacrifice."[11] To the extent that the meaning of life, including its fulfilling sacrifice, depended on being in good standing with the Party, its behavior could be immune from challenge.

Some prisoners went to great lengths to prove their loyalty. Lev Gavrilov was arrested in 1937 and sentenced to ten years of incarceration. He spent the early war years in Kolyma, and wrote about his experiences in his memoirs. He entitled his story, "z/k: *zapasnoi kommunist*" (reserve Communist)—a play on words with the Russian word "*zek*," a colloquial term for "*zakliuchenyi*" (prisoner). His memoirs describe how he extracted his own gold teeth to contribute to the war effort. His interrogators were apparently equally pious devotees; they did not want to accept this offer from an "enemy of the people." Gavrilov refused to accept their assessment that he was someone who had violated his right to be a Communist, hence the title of his narrative.[12]

The ability to find a redeeming value in the endurance of hardships that serve a higher purpose is a widely accepted human virtue, accounting for secular heroism as well as religious martyrdom. In the vacuum left by the destruction of religions, the essential needs for trusted leadership, social coherence, and meaning were appropriated by the secular ideology of Communism, accompanied by a cult of personality akin to what Weber described as "charismatic authority." Under Lenin, Stalin, and their dictatorial heirs, this authority was promoted by crafting a form of "hero worship" through the combination of (real or feigned) devotion and obedience. While charisma is an imprecise, multi-determined descriptor, as are all compelling attractions, such as love, it is a real and powerful motivator. The attraction to a strong leader is no less real or powerful when it is impelled by fear rather than love.

RELIGION AND BOLSHEVISM

While the cognitive frames of secular systems answer *what* and *how* questions, religion answers *why* questions—the purpose and meaning of events. A further distinguishing characteristic of religious systems is that their claims are not falsifiable. As Bolshevism increasingly came to operate as a non-falsifiable system, it merged with the practice of religion. Apparently inconsistent empirical evidence—if admitted at all—could be interpreted as serving a higher purpose.

As the stories presented in this chapter will illustrate, people live for belief systems, die for them, and kill for them. Nor is the allegiance of ardent believers impaired by seemingly contradictory evidence. Some of the narratives suggest that there was no contradictory evidence because the worldview of true believers admitted none.

In addition to the immortality conferred on individuals to belonging to the collective, Bolshevism promised a workers' paradise in this life—a promise that seemed credible because it was consonant with the Russian Orthodox belief that an ultimate paradise was achievable here on earth.[13] However, the secular hero worship promoted by the cult of personality lacked the gravitas of a divinity embedded in Russian Orthodoxy, thus Bolshevism did not have an eternity to create this paradise. So, how does one account for the failure to deliver on their promise in this life? It appears that this conundrum was obfuscated by a combination of denial of official misbehavior or deflection of blame, discrediting dissident voices, propaganda supporting the position that the promised reward was just ahead and within reach, and the fact that there was no precisely stated delivery date.

Many of the powerless victims were encouraged to take comfort in the officially promoted belief that their individual fate was less relevant than the fate of the Soviet project. This redeeming participation in a wholeness that transcended the individual helped some to survive, and others to face death. A number of well-known purge victims such as Bukharin and Iakir made public declarations exonerating the state for their execution. Witness Bukharin's oft-quoted parting words to his wife, " . . . remember the great deed called the Soviet Union lives; only this is really important. Our personal fates are transient and pitiful."[14] Given the absolute power of the state to punish the victim's family, as well as its record of coerced confessions, the sincerity of Bukharin's parting words cannot be assumed. However, given that Bukharin was a founding father, he may have sincerely believed in what he said. Regardless, for true believers, this declaration was a common affirmation of their faith in the Soviet system.

THE GOSPEL ACCORDING TO THE PARTY

Gaining entrance into the ranks of the Party was a sanctifying event in the lives of many, because Party dictates were accorded the authority of gospel. In consequence, previous descriptors such as personal interest, familial loyalty, martyrdom, murder, violence, and "victimization" all came to be reinterpreted and re-oriented toward the goal of serving the Party. Olga Shatunovskaia, an Old Bolshevik who spent seventeen years in the Gulag and emerged to work for the Party, addressed this issue in an exchange with her son later in life. He asked, "Mama, how was it possible that you, communists, could carry out such evil as the murder of the entire family of the czar, including small children and the servants?" From the more informed perspective of the present, she replied, "It now seems like wild nonsense to me, but at the time we thought that this sacrifice was absolutely necessary for the good of the world proletariat. Revolutionary legality was higher than moral legality."[15] In this summary phrase, "revolutionary legality was higher than moral legality," Shatunovskaia succinctly identified a core issue that regularly challenged the "Bolshevik soul." The "revolutionary legality" had become the "higher power," but unlike God, this absolute power did not reside with a remote being, located in a remote place. Rather it resided with Stalin, or Ezhov, or the NKVD, and it was always located nearby.

Mikhail Baital'skii, Party member and Trotsky supporter, had been arrested and interned three times—in 1929, in 1935, and in 1950—for supporting Oppositionist tendencies. In 1958, during Khrushchev's Thaw, he began writing his memoirs, titled *Notebooks to the Grandchildren*. In the 450 pages of these nine notebooks, he records his observations of the Party, the people he knew, the system, and the camps. His wife, Eva, who eventually left him, was such an ardent Party devotee that she fainted at the news of Lenin's death. When their son was born, the couple honored the Soviet founding father by using Lenin's initials to name him.[16] The Party's dictates determined Eva's assessment of everything, including the criteria for good and evil. According to Baital'skii, the question, "what would the Party think of this?" was always on her mind. She assumed that if the Party sanctioned the execution of its former leaders for espionage or murder, "then they absolutely were spies and murderers."[17] The Party's decision was sufficient evidence for Eva.

Party entrance, expulsion, and reinstatement were personal and political landmarks. One memoirist, N. S. Kuznetsov, was arrested in 1938. He claimed that he had been "accused of horrible things without a shred of evidence." After a two-year period of interrogation, which included isolation in the Butyrka, he was sentenced to eight years of labor camp in Arkhangelsk, where he worked as a lumberman. It was not until about 1950 that he was released and subsequently rehabilitated.

Kuznetsov persisted in filing requests for restoration of his Party membership, and his memoir illustrates that these became defining moments in his life. Kuznetsov describes the consequences from his last petition in epic terms. What would turn out to be a life-changing missive arrived one day in the form of an ordinary postcard. It was from the Central Committee requesting him to come to the Party Control Commission to discuss his Party rehabilitation. He immediately set out for Moscow, and as he approached the meeting, he felt himself "gripped with fear" over the possibility that he might not be reinstated.[18] When he was told that he would be reinstated, he felt the ecstatic surge of a numinous experience. This is how he described the vital renewal wrought by his "born-again" Communist experience: "I was born for the third time. The first birth was in the northern Urals, the second in Samara when I was accepted into the Leninist Party, and the third in the building of the CC KPSS in December of 1955."[19]

In the seventeen years that had passed from arrest to reinstatement, his wife had died in camp, his sister was killed in the war, and his estranged children had survived, grew up without parents, completed their education, and had their own children. None of the deficits he endured during the years of his pariah status disconfirmed his faith in the rightness of his Communist-Leninist beliefs. Despite his losses and those of his family, Kuznetsov was steadfast in his claim that he had retained his humanity and his Party allegiance. His faith was redeemed when the long-awaited Leninist truth prevailed. One of Kuznetsov's children became a teacher, the other a geologist. He emphasizes their fortunate education, rather than his misfortunes. In his memoirs he writes:

> their employment confirms the fact that the cult of personality with its anti-Leninist essence, had nothing in common with the nature of our Soviet system. In the Soviet system, even children discarded under the cult of personality to fend for themselves not only did not perish, but got an education without their parents and actively participated in the building of a new Communist society. [20]

For Kuznetsov and many others, membership in the Party was experienced, profoundly, as "belonging," acceptance into the Party was celebrated as a "birth." For true believers, such as L. A. Ol'bert, who spent twenty years in prisons and camps, Party affiliation continued beyond the grave. As his widow recorded, just before Ol'bert's 1972 death, he requested that his Party card, "with which he was connected his whole life," be turned over to the Council of Old Bolsheviks. In the last hours of his life, he reminisced about what the Party card had meant to him. His dying wish was fulfilled. [21] He wrote the following about his Party reinstatement:

> How joyful it was and at the same time painful and unbearably hard to read the lines "rehabilitated for lack of crime" after having been incarcerated for almost twenty years, having lost the best years of [my] youth, and not being guilty of anything against the Party or the motherland. It brought happiness, tears, and excitement, not only to me but to all prisoners who lived with a single-minded interest and hope. Everything revolved for us around the Party and the Soviet government. [22]

An ardent belief in an ideology can imbue experience with a meaning that helps the believer adjust to otherwise intolerable predicaments. Even in the Nazi camps there were still some religious inmates who maintained their belief in God, in spite of their suffering—perhaps because of their suffering. For those in the Nazi concentration camp who continued to believe in God, and those in the Gulag who continued to believe in the Party, there was always the paradox—how could the "higher power" be powerful and good, and yet permit evil? Some prisoners believed that if only Stalin could be informed of their mistaken arrest and incarceration, he would rescue them. Others resolved the issue by assuming that their incarceration was part of a larger purpose which a wise and good Stalin was pursuing. [23]

Ol'bert's salvation, typical of other wrongly incarcerated prisoners, rested with the hope that the Party would discover their "true circumstances" and absolve them. Then, the wrongly accused would be returned to their normal life. He wrote, "this strong belief inspired many and helped them to morally endure the hardships."[24] Later, such hopes were borne out. The Party was officially presented and perceived as the savior rather than the culprit.

Viewed from the perspective of its utopian ideology, it seemed surprising that the practice of Communism, which aspired to be secular and scientific, should have veered toward the same type of reliance on dogma, faith, and infallibility that characterizes religion. However, this turn toward political absolutism seems inevitable when viewed from the perspective of a competition between two total institutions—Communism and religion. In justifying their coercive means by their ideological end, the Communist party was adopting the practice that religion had already demonstrated to be successful for converting and controlling large, often resistant, populations. Prisoners were rendered powerless by an absolute authority, deprived of their previous social support, blamed for their incarceration, and forced to labor in grueling, wretched conditions that were termed "corrective." In an ironic convergence, the Gulag thus recreated the existential conditions for which religions have historically provided a solution.

Devoted communists who were Gulag prisoners had to address the issue of theodicy that also challenges the religious faithful—how could the idealized State abide evil? The justifying response often paralleled the religious explanation that the ways of God are inscrutable. The ways of the Party were equally inscrutable, but must also be trusted. Another ready explanation for the existence of evil was that it is the work of the Devil or Stalin, or Beria, or the local NKVD. Such rationalizations, masquerading as rational explanations, have been successfully employed by religion throughout history to foreclose criticism.

THE REAL WORLD OF THE CAMP

The stories of those whose belief in Communism survived the Gulag ordeal should not be considered as representative. Rather, they illustrate one functional way of processing the experience of enduring a closed system, both in the Big Zone (Soviet society) and the Small Zone (the camps). Solzhenitsyn's prisoner Ivan Denisovich painstakingly laid brick upon brick and enthusiastically continued his task even after roll was called.[25] But there were many others who clearly could not see the greater good; they could only see the persistent evil. This group did not consider their camp experience as having any redemptive meaning. They strove only to survive, not to contribute to the cause. When possible, they faked work output, but this could be a lethal risk. Ekaterina Olitskaia, Socialist Revolutionary and Gulag returnee, recalled the often futile efforts of her Kolyma camp-mates in the sewing factory to meet their output quota in order to keep their indoor jobs. Failure could result in transfer to an outside job in the brutal Arctic climate. When they managed to meet their quotas, the camp administration's cynical response was to create new, unattainable ones.[26]

Olitskaia spent the better part of the twenties, thirties, forties, and fifties in the camps or in exile, from Solovetsky to Magadan.[27] In her memoirs, Olitskaia expressed nothing but horror at the amorality of the camps. She could not fathom the psychology of fellow camp-mates who simultaneously supported the justice of Communism, while claiming that only their own arrests were unjustified.[28] The camp experience motivated Olitskaia to undertake the mission of telling the world her story and the story of those who did not survive to tell their own. When she wrote her memoirs in the sixties, she expressed concern that so few manuscripts were being published,[29] and tried to speak for the silent:

> The survivors have been rehabilitated. Those who perished have been rehabilitated posthumously. . . . "Human progress is built on flesh and bones," say some, "When you cut wood, chips fly," say others, "Revolutions are not made with white gloves on," say still others. . . . And what do the people have to say about this? Ordinary people? They are silent.[30]

Their stifled silence was given voice by some writers. Among them were Shalamov, who described the camps as "only making a person worse."[31] Hundreds of lesser known memoirists added their testimony to the resounding recognition that the suffering of the camps provided no greater good or salvation. These eyewitnesses chronicled the workings of the system, and presented abundant evidence in their damning cases. Their stories contain no ennobling themes, and reflect no religious devotion to a redemptive cause. "Hell" is the word they use to characterize the camp experience. The harshness of living and dying described in these works refutes the claims of a heroic perspective proffered by some. Vasily Grossman scornfully addresses that heroic perspective in his novel, *Forever Flowing*. In a telling exchange, a fictional former Party official-turned-inmate provides his fellow prisoner, Ivan Grigorevich, with a vapidly formulaic explanation of how he accepts his fate:

> When they chop down the forest, the chips fly, but the Party truth remains the truth and it is superior to my misfortune. . . . I myself was one of those chips that flew when the forest was cut down.[32]

The protagonist, Ivan, deftly skewers this argument by challenging the assumption of a "license to cut" uncritically smuggled into the apologia: "That's where the whole misfortune lies—in the fact that they're cutting down the forest. Why cut it down?"[33]

Raising the question of a prior "why" for the ensuing violence was absent from most of the accounts of committed communists. Without this prior authorization of the necessity of violence, the issue of guilt (*Die Schuldfrage*), as Karl Jaspers so aptly termed it, was not protected by the mantle of religion, unless the Communist Party admitted to being a religion. Nevertheless, the Party appropriated to itself the prerogatives of religion. Personal misfortunes were to be accepted with resignation or satisfaction in fulfillment of the Party's definition of a greater purpose.

After their release, some survivors like Olga Shatunovskaia continued to work within the Party organization, first on de-Stalinization, and then on "building socialism" in the Brezhnev years. During this period, the Gulag was designated as a non-issue. Olga, her cohorts, and their children continued to work for and ostensibly believe in the Party under Gorbachev, right up until the end of the Soviet Union. Others later turned away from the cause with the same fervor with which they had embraced it.

LEGACIES: THE CHILDREN OF COMMUNISTS

Gertruda Evgen'evna Chuprun was born to Party devotees who, like many of their peers, gave their daughter a Party name: *geroina truda'* (heroine of labor), or Gertruda for short. Her father, Evgenii Borisovich Ioel'son-Grodzianskii, was a professor at the Baumann (Technical) Institute and a director at the Institute of the Refrigeration Industry. In the late twenties he worked in Hamburg, arranging for refrigerators and their component parts to be sent to the Soviet Union. An acknowledged expert on refrigeration, he was consulted about problems with the cooling system in the Lenin Mausoleum. His privileged life was to suddenly spiral downward in 1937. In December of that year he was arrested as a "German spy," and a month later he was executed; his body was disposed of in the "Kommunarka" mass grave on the outskirts of Moscow.

Gerta's mother, Dina Evdokiia Sidorovna, had been a factory worker, who advanced to become a deputy in the Moscow Soviet from 1931 to 1934, and then went on to study medicine. In 1937 she was excluded from the Party for being married to a "traitor to the motherland." On the day of her husband's execution, she was arrested and sentenced to eight years in Karaganda. Their two children, Aleksandr and Gerta, were placed in the Children's Detention Center on the grounds of the Danilov Monastery in Moscow. Gerta was five at the time.

Dina was released from her camp in Kazakhstan in 1948, and she and Gerta reunited. They harbored the vain hope of reunion with Evgenii until 1956. They harbored other hopes as well. Dina, along with many others, clung to the illusion of Stalin's integrity, which was dispelled by the XX Party Congress in 1956. No longer could Dina's generation maintain the comforting fiction that Stalin did not know about the repressions, and that Ezhov and Beria were the real malefactors. Khrushchev's revelations of Stalin's complicity came as a political and psychological shock. In the aftermath of Khrushchev's Secret Speech, Gerta was also forced to abandon the illusion that her father had somehow survived. She received a death certificate, stating that he had died of pneumonia, during an epidemic in 1939. Later, apparently during perestroika, she was issued a second death certificate. The new document gave the cause of death as "execution," and the year as 1938. Gerta's father was posthumously rehabilitated, and her mother immediately applied for and received rehabilitation, Party reinstatement, and a personal pension with privileges. Gerta received a coveted rehabilitation certificate as well, so her situation was much better than that of many of her cohorts, who, as children of the repressed, struggled with a stigmatized past and fought hard for their status as "victims"—both for the recognition and the privileges this status conferred. Gerta was contemptuous of the compensation: "they paid 20,000 rubles—two months' salary—for the dead body of my father." Her mother bought furniture with the money.

Gerta became an engineer, but never joined the Party. She subscribed to the tenets of Communism, but did not feel the need for Party membership. She explained that it was not that she did not believe in "the bright future" promised by the Party. "It was just," she laughingly added, "that many of the people who joined believed in their own personal bright futures."[34] Gerta's mother was not one of that group; the Party took priority over everything else. Dina's emotional dependence on the Party was so central to her experience of life that she held no opinions contrary to the Party line. She was grateful to Khrushchev for liberating her, never conceded that she was guilty of the crimes for which she was imprisoned, and did not blame those who had imprisoned her. Gerta recalled a vivid illustration of how powerfully her mother was motivated by the Party. Dina was addicted to nicotine, and smoked incessantly, in spite of frequent admonitions from everyone. Dina would respond by saying: "if I am reinstated in the Party, I will stop smoking, but now I need it for my nerves." After reinstatement, Dina became actively re-engaged in Party and community work, and stopped smoking. As Karl Marx presciently observed, a strong religious belief can activate the same reward circuits as those activated by addictive substances.

In the meantime, Gerta got married and had a child, but her mother, now also a grandmother, placed her responsibilities to the Party above those to her family. She would not commit to babysitting because she worried that "there might be a Party meeting" she would have to miss. All during the stagnation of Brezhnev's period, Dina proudly donned her "Party veteran" medal and never uttered one negative comment about the Party.

Then, shortly after perestroika/glasnost was introduced, Dina became ill and was hospitalized in a clinic for Old Bolsheviks. From her sickbed, Dina experienced a more personal glasnost. She confessed to Gerta that she had had some doubts about Brezhnev, and the direction the Party had taken. Gerta came to believe that these doubts had been building for a while, but Dina was afraid to admit them, even to herself, because she did not want to live without the "bright idea" — the ideology and promise of Communism that gave meaning to her life. In addition to Dina's psychological reasons, Gerta believed that her mother also had practical reasons to shield herself from doubting. Dina was afraid of the very same political repression that had intimidated everyone. No matter how exemplary their behavior had been or where they stood in the hierarchy, Gerta claimed, "the entire country was in deep fear of speaking ill of the Party" — perhaps, of thinking ill of the Party. When Dina died in 1987, she was still a devoted Party member. She had occasionally doubted, but never dissented.

Current discussions of the "Soviet self" have raised the pivotal question of whether "faith in the revolutionary utopia and socialist mores" could co-exist with "disbelief, irony, and even resistance to certain aspects of the system."[35] The narratives presented in this study confirm that this is possible because at the macro level faith can override doubt. At the micro level, faith and doubt can co-exist in the same person without colliding because each may be about different issues. On Dina's white marble tombstone, engraved in gold letters, Gerta memorialized so much that was central to her mother's life with the inscription "Veteran of the CPSU."[36]

Another woman interviewed for this study was Mariia Il'ina, whose Party loyalist father was executed, her mother incarcerated, and she was sent to an orphanage. Until Gorbachev lifted the censorship on public discussions of the terror and exposed it to the scrutiny of public discourse, she knew little of the chronology and scope of the repression. Now, she was forced to revisit and critically assess the old, mutually validating interpretations of the repression that she had learned from her mother and her cohorts. Now she came to realize that the use of physical coercion to promote the Communist ideology was also practiced under Lenin. She admitted: "I was the last of everyone I knew to really understand that so much of the system of repression started with Lenin, we always wrote everything off to Stalin."[37] Mariia would have preferred to remain oblivious to this because it undermined so much of the ideology that was foundational to her understanding of her family and her country.

ASSIMILATION OF OR ACCOMMODATION TO IDEOLOGY?

In forging a successful approach to moving past the repressive past, one of the complexities is assessing the meaning of Party membership. For example the question of how far down the chain of command of a repressive regime should culpability be assigned remained open in Iraq after the overthrow of Saddam Hussein. De-Ba'athification policies, introduced by reformers shortly after the fall of the regime, created an "epic struggle" between the regime's opponents and supporters, and with regard to what principles of justice should be applied to the lower level functionaries.[38]

Some saw their wholesale dismissal as a form of "collective punishment," while others resented the fact that hundreds of thousands of lower-level Ba'athists, who may have been guilty of abuses, were permitted to remain in civil service positions.[39] As with the lower levels of Nazi Party membership under Hitler and Communist Party membership in Russia, Ba'ath Party membership may primarily have reflected fear and careerism.[40]

Still, these determinants can lead from the accommodation to repression to the assimilation of and allegiance to a repressive ideology. This psychological transition could account for how it is possible for people to continue to maintain feelings of loyalty to a repressive regime even after they became aware of its inhumane practices.

Regarding prospects for reform, those who had adapted to a repressive regime by acquiescence and accommodation could likewise adapt to a non-repressive regime. But those who had adapted by the assimilation of the repressive ideology would probably be resistant to change in at least two ways: First, any evidence that might conflict with their assimilated ideology could be re-interpreted as irrelevant or even confirmatory of a high-minded principle. For example, evidence of human rights violations could be overshadowed by the demands of patriotism, and false imprisonment, as a necessary personal sacrifice for the greater good. Second, the meaningful experience of feeling connected to a revered leader, a cohesive group, and a visionary ideology can be so emotionally satisfying that it needs no more validating evidence than does religious faith. The endurance of the Communist ideology despite the Party's failure to deliver the "bright future" and despite the Party's betrayal of its self-professed values suggests that it occupies a psychosocial niche similar to that inhabited by religion.

COMMUNISM'S LEGACY AND STALIN'S HEIRS

For many ex-prisoners as well as other citizens, the process of coming to terms with an ambivalently repudiated national past required coming to terms with the way it permeated their personal past. For the older generation who were committed to the Party, who considered themselves to be the "builders of socialism," even while in camp, a disconfirmation of their original ideology could raise unsettling questions about how they (mis)spent their lives.[41] Such unsettling questions can lead to unsettling answers. They direct us to look at how the human need for safety, meaning, structure, and social cohesion can be manipulated by the closed systems of repressive regimes, and can transform the "individual" into a constituent part. The present regime is also suffering from the effects of the repression because it has found no better way to deal with this integral part of its past than historical revisionism, which is buttressed by textbooks that sanitize the Stalinist repression, the re-classification of archives, the arrest and harassment of researchers of Stalin-era archives, and the marginalization of the Gulag.

Over two decades after the collapse of the Soviet Union, Stalin's popularity has risen in nationwide polls, reflecting the longing of many to restore the country's former prestige as well as the security of a more strictly ordered society.[42] A series of measures, including the restoration of an ode to Stalin engraved in a Moscow metro station and the 2009 creation of a state commission to guard against the "falsification of history to the detriment of Russia's interests,"[43] has led Memorial, the chief human rights watchdog organization, to argue that, "de-Stalinization is Russia's acutest problem at the moment."[44]

The problem is newly acute but not new. Decades earlier, in 1962, Yevgeni Yevtushenko's acclaimed poem "The Heirs to Stalin" celebrated the removal of Stalin's body from the Lenin Mausoleum, but presciently asked how Stalin was to be removed from Stalin's heirs. In a 2005 survey, 1,600 Russians were asked their opinion of Stalin and his role in the country's history. Their assessment was quite positive. Most credited him with having led his people to victory in the Great Patriotic War, and 32 percent of the respondents believed this overshadowed whatever defects he might have had and any mistakes he may have made. By 2008, another survey found that respondents viewed Stalin as one of the three "most prominent figures of all times." In 2013, on the sixtieth anniversary of Stalin's death, polls reflected even higher support for Stalin, particularly for his wartime leadership; Stalin now ranked first among the great figures of Russian history.[45] Meanwhile, on the seventieth anniversary of the Battle of Stalingrad in February 2013, buses were covered with the dictator's image, and Volgograd was renamed Stalingrad for a day. Communists had collected 100,000 signatures to permanently reinstate its name to Stalingrad, a name that enshrined the heroic sacrifice and Russian victory in the Great Patriotic War.[46] Chief among the resurrected Soviet symbols today is Stalin himself, whose role in history has been fashioned to fit a mythologized narrative. This refurbished postmortem popularity of Stalin may represent an "invisible Stalinism," unblemished by an invisible Gulag, once more asserting the principle that the order attendant to centralized power justifies the deprivation of individual rights.[47]

But while events can be selected for or deleted from the official narrative, they still exist in the real world of mass graves and archival records, and in the personal narratives, or "counter-histories" of the survivors. An inclusive history could be based on the dynamic reconciliation of a dialogue between the personal narrative and national narrative, between the past and the present. But this dialogue has been stifled. Indeed, the persistence of these competing narratives on the past attests to a post-Communist repression and totalitarian culture even after its formal demise. Perhaps a comparative scrutiny and reappraisal of Stalinism and Nazism could contribute to resolving this and other impasses to creating a good future out of a bad past. Such an angle of inquiry may also shed important light on complex questions regarding optional and obligatory agency, responsibility, culpability of the individual and the collective, and the under-researched grey zone of the victim-perpetrator divide. Along the way, it will contribute to our historical understanding of the personal and political legacy of repressive regimes.

NOTES

Parts of this chapter were excerpted from Nanci Adler, *Keeping Faith with the Party: Communist Believers Return from the Gulag* (Bloomington: Indiana University Press, 2012).

1. "Segodnia," NTV, October 18, 2005.
2. See, for example, Rene Fulop-Miller, *The Mind and Face of Bolshevism* (London and New York: G.P. Putnam's Sons, 1926), Mikhail Vaiskopf, *Pisatel' Stalin* (Moscow: Novoe literaturnoe obozrenie, 2002), Oleg Kharkhordin, *The Collective and the Individual in Russia* (Berkeley: University of California Press, 1999), Isaac Deutscher, *Stalin: A Political Biography* (London: Oxford University Press, 1967); see also notes 24, 31, 33, and 34.
3. Karl Marx, "Introduction," *Marx's Critique of Hegel's Philosophy of Right (1843)* (Cambridge: Cambridge University Press, 1970).
4. "Vospominaniia—ocherki Slavianinoi O.A.," RGASPI, f. 560, op. 1, d. 36, ll. 4–6.
5. Ibid., l. 72.
6. Ibid., l. 5.
7. Ibid., l. 73.
8. Ibid., l. 6.
9. More specifically, a report by Shvernik on the work of the Party Control Commission (KPK) from February 1956 to June 1961 states that 30,954 Communists received Party rehabilitation, many posthumously (RGANI, f. 6, op. 6, d. 1165, l. 2). Elsewhere this report states that 24,038 appeals from former P.O.W.s were sent to the XX and XXI Party Congress, and 12,498 other applicants appealed to the KPK for restoration of Party membership. Approximately 55 percent of the appeals to the XX Party Congress, and 40.6 percent of those to the XXI Party Congress, were honored. *Reabilitatsiia: Kak eto bylo, fevral' 1956—nachalo 80-x godov, t. II*, ed. A. N. Iakovlev et al (Moscow: Mezhdunarodnyi Fond 'Demokratsiia', 2003), 363; see also 252). A 1957 report attributes the high percentage of reinstatements to the fact that "among the applicants were many rehabilitated [persons], who were excluded from the Party for political reasons" (RGANI, f. 6, op. 6, d. 1077, l. 2). Tens of thousands more were to apply only a few decades later. This backlog was handled during Gorbachev's de-Stalinization. According to a memorandum by Boris Pugo, chairman of the Party Control Commission from 1988–1990, 80,000 applications for Party membership were honored. *Reabilitatsiia: Kak eto bylo*, 520.

10. Igal Halfin was one of the first historians to explore this phenomenon in *Terror in My Soul: Communist Autobiographies on Trial* (Cambridge, MA: Harvard University Press, 2003).

11. Viktor Frankl, *Man's Search for Meaning: An Introduction to Logotherapy* (London: Hodder & Stoughton, 1964), 115.

12. Lev Gavrilov, "Zapasnoi kommunist," in *Dodnes Tiagoteet* 2, ed. Semen Vilenskii (Moscow: Vozvrashchenie, 2004), 225–34.

13. My thanks to Leona Toker for drawing my attention to this aspect of Russian Orthodoxy through Nikolai Lossky's 1957 work, *Kharakter Russkogo Naroda* (in *Usloviia absoliutnogo dobra*) (Moscow: Politicheskaia literatura, 1991).

14. Cited in Halfin, *Terror in My Soul*, 282.

15. Dzhana Kut'ina, Andrei Broido, Anton Kut'in, *Ob ushedshem veke, rasskazyvaet Ol'ga Shatunovskaia* (La Jolla, CA: DAA Books, 2001), 333.

16. Mikhail Davidovich Baital'skii, "Tetradi dlia vnukov," Memorial, f. 2, op. 1, d. 8, l. 0698.

17. Ibid.

18. Ibid., l. 102.

19. Ibid.

20. Ibid., l. 103.

21. "Vospominaniia Kuznetsova N.S.," l. 72.

22. "Nezabyvaemoe," Vospominaniia Ol'berta L.A., RGASPI, f. 560, op. 1, d. 29, l. 69.

23. For a discussion of the "blind discipline" of believing in the ultimate wisdom of Stalin, see L. A. Man'kovskii, "K voprosu o psikhologii kul'ta Stalina," *Voprosy Filosofii* (1989) 162–66.

24. Ol'bert, RGASPI, f. 560, op. 1, d. 29, l. 39.

25. Alexander Solzhenitsyn, *One Day in the Life of Ivan Denisovich* (New York: Bantam Dell, 1963), 88–89.

26. Anne Applebaum, *Gulag: A History* (New York: Anchor Books, 2004), 227.

27. Lesia Padun-Luk'ianova, "Ekaterina Olitskaia," in Vilenskii, *Dodnes' Tiagoteet* 2, 44–45.

28. Ekaterina Olitskaia, "Na Kolyme," in *Dodnes' Tiagoteet* 2, 46.

29. From 1990–2004, editor S. Vilenskii writes in a footnote, over 1.5 million books of remembrance were published in the Soviet Union and successor states.

30. Oltiskaia, "Na Kolyme," 65.

31. Varlam Shalamov, "Inzhener Kiselev," *Grani*, No. 76, 1970, 25.

32. Vasily Grossman, *Forever Flowing* (New York: Harper & Row, 1972), 105.

33. Ibid.

34. Ibid.

35. For an interesting comment on the complexities of the Soviet self that possesses "contradictory sensibilities" and exhibits "mixed emotions," see Choi Chatterjee and Karen Petrone, "Models of Selfhood and Subjectivity: The Soviet Case in Historical Perspective," *Slavic Review* 67 (2008): 984–85.

36. Gertruda Evgen'evna Chuprun, interview with author, Moscow, March 20, 2008.

37. Mariia Il'inichna Kuznetsova, interview with author, Moscow, March 15, 2008.

38. Miranda Sissons, "Briefing Paper: Iraq's New 'Accountability and Justice' Law," International Center for Transitional Justice, January 22, 2008, 2.

39. Ibid., 5.

40. See Ella Rolfe, "Addressing the Baathist Legacy in Iraq," *ICTJ in the News*, 26 February 2010.

41. Such questions could be settled by the re-interpretative process of cognitive dissonance. A different psychosocial process might be employed by those whose "conversion" to the regime's form of communism was rewarded; see Herbert M. Adler and Van Buren O. Hammett, "Crisis, Conversion, and Cult Formation: An Examination of a Common Psychosocial Sequence," *American Journal of Psychiatry* 130 (1973): 861–64.

Such rewards included the promise of psychosocial, political, vocational, and material benefits. Survival was enhanced by authentically embracing the ideology.

42. Ellen Barry, "Communism's ghosts haunt Moscow streets," *International Herald Tribune*, 14 October, 2008, "Stalin lidiruet v oprose," *30 oktiabria*, 88, 2008, "Rossiia i istoricheskaia pamiat,'" *30 oktiabria*, 81, 2007, Iaroslav Leont'ev, "Marks perevernul'sia by v grobu," *30 oktiabria*, 57, 2005, Elina Bestaeva, "Ch'ia eta ulitsa," ibid.; "Nostal'giia po tiranu," *30 oktiabria*, 50, 2005, Yevgeny Kiselyov, "Why Russians Put Stalin at the Top of the List," *The Moscow Times*, 1 October, 2008, Dan Bilefsky, "Stalin Still Haunts the Land of His Birth," *International Herald Tribune*, 30 September, 2008, Sophia Kishkovsky, "What's in a street name? Moscow is finding out," *International Herald Tribune*, 19 September, 2008, "Russia Remembers Victims of Stalinism, But Tyrant Still Popular," *Itar-TASS*, 30 October, 2008.

43. One of Medvedev's last acts as president was to dissolve the scientifically suspect commission.

44. "Russia marks day of victims of political repressions," *Itar-TASS*, 30 October, 2009.

45. Maria Lipman, Lev Gudkov, and Lasha Bakradze, "The Stalin Puzzle: Deciphering Post-Soviet Public Opinion," Washington: Carnegie Endowment for International Peace 2013, 3.

46. Samuel Rachlin, "Stalin's Long Shadow," *International Herald Tribune*, 5 March, 2013. See Nanci Adler, "The Future of the Soviet Past Remains Unpredictable: The Resurrection of Stalinist Symbols Amidst the Exhumation of Mass Graves," *Europe-Asia Studies* 57 (2005), 1093–1119.

47. See Jonathan Brent, "Stalin's Russia and Russia's Stalin: A report on the International Conference on the History of Stalinism," in Jonathan Brent, *Inside the Stalin Archives: Discovering the New Russia* (New York: Atlas & Co., 2008), 252–55, 318, "Opposition Leader Slams 'features of Stalinism' in Russian Life," *Interfax*, 5 March 2008. Writing in 1991, one former prisoner concluded: "In the historical perspective of the development of Russia, the history of the GULAG will not be repeated. But if time and again the liberals and thinkers, humanists, and politicians of the world do not draw the lessons from the GULAG and the historic defeat of its contemporaries, it is hard to believe in the triumph of higher reason." A. Sandler and M. Etlis, *Sovremenniki Gulaga: Kniga vospominanii i razmyshlenii* (Magadan: Kn. Izdatel'stvo 1991), 558. Perhaps unexpectedly even to its author, the years in which these lines were written ended up being the peak of anti-Stalinist revelations and public discourse on the Gulag.

SEVEN

The Lontsky Street Prison Memorial Museum

An Example of Post-Communist Holocaust Negationism

John-Paul Himka

A former prison in Lviv, Ukraine, which had been used for decades particularly to hold political prisoners, is now the National Museum-Memorial of Victims of the Occupation Regimes "Prison on Lontsky Street."[1] The building complex started as military barracks in 1889–1890, when Lviv (known also as Lemberg and Lwów) was the capital of the crownland of Galicia in the Habsburg monarchy.[2] The construction of the prison took place after the fall of the Habsburg monarchy, in 1918–1920, when Lviv became part of the restored state of Poland. In the Polish period, 1918–1939, the prison on Lontsky St. held some prominent political offenders, including members of both the radical right Organization of Ukrainian Nationalists (OUN) and the Communist Party of Western Ukraine. The history of the Lontsky St. prison during the Second World War is a brutal, tangled tale that this study will seek to clarify in order to show how the current museum presents a one-sided, politically motivated version of what transpired on its site. In brief, Lviv, and with it the prison, came under Soviet rule from September 1939 until June 1941. In addition to severe maltreatment of prisoners at Lontsky St. and at other prisons in Lviv, a maltreatment that was typical enough of Stalinist incarceration, the Soviets ended their control of the prisons in June 1941 with a horrific crime. Unable to evacuate the prisoners fast enough after the German attack on the Soviet Union on June 22, the NKVD prison administration murdered the political prisoners to prevent their cooperation

137

with the German enemy. As the posters in the museum inform visitors, in the last days of June 1941, the Soviets killed 1,681 prisoners at the Lontsky St. prison, 971 in the prison on Zamarstyniv St., and 739 in the Brygidki prison in Lviv. These killings, known as the NKVD murders, are the primary focus of the memorial museum today.

When the Soviets retook Lviv in July 1944, they once again used the Lontsky St. prison to hold political prisoners for interrogation. At this time OUN and its armed force, the Ukrainian Insurgent Army (UPA), were fighting a desperate struggle against the reimposition of Soviet rule on Western Ukraine, while Soviet forces retaliated with tremendous force.[3] Lontsky St. prison was an important instrument of the counterinsurgency. In 1944–1953 a number of activists of OUN and UPA were held here, including prominent figures in the movement, such as Mykhailo Soroka and Liubomyr Poliuha. In the 1960s, 1970s, and 1980s many well-known Ukrainian dissidents were also detained on Lontsky St., including Viacheslav Chornovil, Ivan Hel, Bohdan and Mykhailo Horyn, and Ihor and Iryna Kalynets.

The most controversial aspect of the way the memorial museum presents history concerns the period between the two Soviet eras, that is, the German occupation that came right after the first Soviet occupation of 1939–1941 and just before the Soviet reconquest in 1944. Those three years in which the Germans held Lontsky St. prison, 1941–1944, witnessed at the outset a bloody interplay of Soviet and German violence. The museum exhibition glides lightly over the Nazi occupation. The little it has to say highlights the suffering of OUN members. The information for visitors has nothing at all to say about the persecution of Jews at Lontsky St. prison during the war, although a small amount of information is available on the museum website. Most important, the museum glorifies OUN without mentioning or admitting that the militia associated with OUN was deeply involved in murders and other atrocities against Jews on the very premises of the Lontsky St. prison and in the other Lviv prisons in July 1941. Thus the museum is a place where Jewish memory is erased as well as the memory of crimes against Jews perpetrated by Ukrainian nationalists. This is part of a broader trend in areas of western Ukraine where the nationalists had once been strong.[4] The memorial museum on Lontsky St., however, is a particularly intense site of this kind of memory and oblivion as well as a place where a local and international public is steeped in a historical narrative woven of falsehoods. It is a site that embodies what Michael Shafir has termed "deflective negationism," that is, it "transfers the guilt for the perpetration of crimes to members of other nations, or it minimizes own-nation participation in their perpetration to insignificant 'aberrations.'"[5] The museum's presentation of history, which is at variance with the results of professional historical research, is able to be sustained not only because of regional support in Ukraine and formerly because of Ukrainian government patronage, but also because of a strong and mutually rein-forcing alliance with OUN in the North American diaspora. The national-ists in the diaspora use their connections with and influence upon ethnic academic outposts, Canadian politicians, and the press to reinforce the message of the Lontsky St. museum and to make deflective Holocaust negationism appear respectable.

Before examining and analyzing the ideational content of the memori-al museum and its situation within broader structures, let us look briefly at how the prison turned into a museum. The idea to make a memorial museum out of the prison on Lontsky St. emerged in 2005, that is, in the aftermath of the Orange Revolution that brought Viktor Yushchenko into power in Ukraine. As president of Ukraine (2005–2010), Yushchenko pro-moted a nationalist-inspired historical policy (*Geschichtspolitik*) that had two main elements: 1) a campaign to have Ukrainians and the world at large recognize the famine of 1932–1933 (the Holodomor) as a genocide against the Ukrainian people and 2) the glorification of Ukrainian nation-alists, namely members of OUN and UPA, as heroes of Ukraine.[6] Both of these elements were primarily anti-communist, and both were outfitted with xenophobic undertones. Yushchenko pursued his memory politics openly and intensely as of spring 2006. In that year he established the Ukrainian Institute of National Memory, awarded the former OUN acti-vist and UPA supreme commander Roman Shukhevych the posthumous title of Hero of Ukraine, and issued a directive to institute a Day of Memory for the Victims of the Holodomors and Political Repressions. The latter directive, dated October 12, 2006, served, according to the mu-seum's explanatory posters, as the impetus to turn the prison into a place of commemoration and public education. The initiative to found the mu-seum received support from the Lviv city council, the Lviv oblast council, and the Security Service of Ukraine. A working group to establish the museum was put together, comprised of the above-mentioned govern-ment organs as well as a nationalist research organization in Lviv, the Center for Research of the Liberation Movement, and "well known civil activists."

The Center for Research of the Liberation Movement prepared a photo exhibition in 2006 devoted to the sixty-fifth anniversary of the mass shooting of political prisoners in Western Ukraine in the summer of 1941. Four stands showed reproductions of photos and documents on this theme. In the years that followed the center "conducted fundamental research on the history of the prison" (Posters) and collected memoirs and testimonies of former prisoners as well as artifacts from this period.

The territory of the prison was first opened to the Lviv public in 2006. A Christian memorial service (*panakhyda*) was conducted, and a cross was erected in the outer courtyard of the museum. As of 2008, the public was for the first time allowed to visit inside the prison, including the cells. In that same year the Security Service of Ukraine gave the prison and its surrounding property for use of the future museum. In June 2009 the museum was opened, with an exposition prepared by the Center for Research of the Liberation Movement and the Security Service of Ukraine (Posters). According to the museum's website, 8,799 persons visited the museum in 2010, 15,733 in 2011, and 16,277 in 2012. But attendance in 2013 has been declining.[7]

The description of the museum that follows describes what I found there and photographed when I visited it on June 3, 2010. I have also been able to obtain some supplemental information.

THE NKVD MURDERS

The NKVD murders are not widely known to the Anglophone public, even to the educated public. The murders are succinctly and correctly described in Timothy Snyder's recent bestseller, *Bloodlands*: "The German invasion prompted the NKVD to shoot some 9,817 imprisoned Polish citizens rather than allow them to fall into German hands. The Germans arrived in the western Soviet Union in summer 1941 to find NKVD prisons full of fresh corpses."[8] Snyder's book, however, describes so many atrocities and murders committed by both Nazis and Soviets that it is unlikely that this particular incident would stick in the mind of readers.

Although they have made little mark on public awareness, the NKVD murders have generated a substantial evidentiary and scholarly literature. In the immediate aftermath of the discovery of the corpses in the prisons, the Germans conducted a detailed war crimes investigation.[9] As part of their propaganda war against "Jewish Bolshevism," the executions in the Lontsky St. prison and other prisons in Western Ukraine were given wide press coverage in the occupied territories, in Germany, and internationally.[10] The corpses of the victims were shown on newsreels, and they also appeared in films and photos taken by German personnel for military or private usage. After World War II Ukrainian émigrés in the West published memoirs of what they had seen when the Germans opened the prisons or of what they themselves had experienced inside them.[11] The memoirs in these volumes were supplemented by the republication of articles that had appeared in the Ukrainian press in the summer of 1941, but with the anti-Semitic phrases of the originals discreetly excised. A collection published in Ukraine two years after independence, though having a wider scope, also included memoirs of witnesses of the 1941 massacres and a substantial compendium of articles that had appeared in the Ukrainian press; the republished articles included the anti-Semitic statements of the originals, without editorial comment.[12] Another volume published later in Ukraine took some materials from earlier collections, but now added substantial documentation emanating from the perpetrators themselves, the NKVD and other Soviet bodies. It also included lists of all the victims of the NKVD massacres, in so far as they could be reconstructed. The first two chapters provided a scholarly overview of the course of the murders.[13] A Polish-language collection with a similar profile, containing lists of victims, Polish testimonies, and NKVD documents, appeared a few years later.[14] Much earlier, in 1988, Jan Gross had already published an account of the prison massacres based on Polish testimonies.[15] His book, *Revolution from Abroad*, differed from those previously mentioned in that it had a larger purpose of analyzing the sociology of the interaction between a totalitarian regime and a newly conquered society. This study of the Soviet state in the eastern borderlands of what had recently been the Second Polish Republic was a companion to an earlier volume he had written about Polish society under Nazi occupation. The NKVD murders were the primary subject of a study by Bogdan Musial, which appeared in both German and Polish.[16] Although Musial's is the most comprehensive monograph on the massacres, it has generated controversy because of the way it portrays the role and fate of Jews on the eve of and immediately following the German invasion.[17]

Given all the evidence, including NKVD internal reports on the progress of the shootings, there can be no doubt that the thousands of prisoners found dead in Lviv prisons in late June and early July 1941 were killed by the NKVD. Nonetheless, for a very long time the Soviets denied their responsibility for the murders, blaming instead the Germans, a move most familiar from the case of Katyn but also employed in the case of the exhumations of NKVD victims in the Ukrainian city of Vinnytsia.[18] Thus, while collecting information on German war crimes on the territory of Western Ukraine, the Soviets made any witnesses who mentioned the NKVD murders ascribe them instead to the Germans. An example of this, extraordinary because of the person of the witness, is the testimony of the pioneer of Holocaust studies, Philip Friedman, before the Commission for the Study of History of the Great Patriotic War on January 30, 1946. He knew perfectly well, as he later wrote in his study of Ukrainian-Jewish relations during the Nazi occupation, that "Ukrainian fighters and leaders were killed in prison by the Bolsheviks before their retreat."[19] However, his recorded testimony told a different story altogether: that right after the Germans took Lviv on June 30, 1941, they herded Jews into the prisons, shot them, and mutilated their bodies beyond recognition; then they claimed that the corpses were those of political prisoners killed by the NKVD in order to arouse hatred against communism and to provide a pretext for further attacks on Jews.[20]

Additional confusion between Nazi and Soviet crimes arose in regard to pictures that were included in the exhibition on the war crimes of the Wehrmacht on the Eastern Front, which toured Germany in one form in 1995–1999 and in a revised form in 2001–2004. One of the issues that led to the revision of the exhibition was that it included photographs that depicted corpses of the NKVD victims, thus crimes not of the Wehrmacht but of the Soviets. Bogdan Musial wrote a powerful indictment of this aspect of the *Wehrmachtausstellung* under the title "Pictures From an Exhibition."[21] But his critique overreached its goal. Other scholars have argued that some of the pictures Musial criticized were not of political prisoners killed by the NKVD at all, but of Jews who had been pressed into duty to exhume the corpses and who were subsequently executed.[22] One of the better known of these disputed photographs was taken in the courtyard of Lontsky St. prison,[23] but neither it nor any other photo of this type is on display in the memorial museum.

The exhibit in the Lontsky St. prison memorial museum of course attributes the murders of late June 1941 to the NKVD. Although these murders are a major focus of the museum, there is very little guiding text relating to the murders. Instead, the museum lets visitors draw their own conclusion based on what they find on display. The exhibition has numerous photographs of relatives and friends moving up and down the rows of corpses, looking for their loved ones. One of these photos, which shows a woman in profound grief and shock after recognizing one of the corpses, has also been made into a life-size poster. The background has been obscured to highlight the woman's face distorted by suffering. The poster also lists the major sites and numbers of victims of the NKVD murders: Horodok 29, Zolochiv (prison no. 3) 749, Drohobych c. 1000, Dobromyl c. 1000, Komarno 200, and so on. The predominant form of information about the murders of June 1941, however, are several walls full of clippings from contemporary Ukrainian newspapers reporting on them in graphic detail, with long lists of victims' names and horrifying descriptions of the tortures the prisoners were imagined to have endured before death. The major problem with these clippings is how they ethnicize the victims and perpetrators of the NKVD murders.[24] (See figure 7.1)

The clippings give the impression that the victims of the NKVD were almost exclusively Ukrainians, and certainly no Jewish victims are mentioned. In this regard the clippings reinforce the whole tone of the museum. Uilleam Blacker, a recent visitor to the museum and a postdoctoral fellow associated with the Memory at War project at Cambridge, has noted: "The museum represents the suffering and struggles of Ukrainians. The exhibition barely mentions the word 'Jew,' while Poles appear, in a historically dubious comparison, only as one side of a triangle of evil 'occupiers' alongside the Nazis and the Soviets."[25] Sofiya Dyak, the director of the Center for Urban History of East Central Europe (located in Lviv), agrees that the Lonskty St. museum "stresses Ukrainian suffering, but does not take cognizance of Polish and Jewish suffering."[26] In actual fact, the NKVD shootings encompassed Jews, particularly Zionists, as well as Poles.

Although the museum exhibition itself provides no information on non-Ukrainian victims, the museum website, which may well be visited

Figure 7.1.

more frequently than the exhibition space, is completely forthcoming on this topic. According to the website, the national composition of the June 1941 victims at the Lontsky St. prison was: 67 percent Ukrainians, 23 percent Poles, 7 percent Jews, 2 percent Russians, and 1 percent others. The website also provides figures demonstrating the very mixed national composition of all those arrested by the NKVD in Western Ukraine from September 1939 through June 1941. At least in recent times, this information has also been conveyed to visitors by the guides. An American professor who visited the museum in August 2013 informed me that his guide "was careful to say several times that the prisoners were not only Ukrainians, but also Poles and Jews."[27]

Thus, the Lontsky St. prison museum has a mixed, but improving record on the matter of ethnicization of the victims: insufficient explanatory material in the exhibits, but exemplary information on the museum website and an effort to inform visitors orally about the situation. The discourse in the commemoration of the NKVD murders elsewhere in the city varies. The monument to victims of communist crimes on Bandera Street is marked by the Ukrainian trident and gives no indication that there were non-Ukrainian victims (see figure 7.2).

But the monument on 20 Zamarstyniv St., which is specifically dedicated to commemorating the NKVD murders, explicitly commemorates Ukrainian, Polish, and Jewish victims and bears images of the Ukrainian trident, the Polish eagle, and the Jewish Star of David. When the photo in Figure 7.3 was taken, May 21, 2009, the word "Jews" and the star of David had been vandalized and rendered barely visible.

The situation is worse with the ethnicization of the perpetrators in the clippings on display at the museum. They identify the murderers as Jews. There is little or no commentary on this either in the museum or on the website.[28] Jeffrey Kopstein, a professor at the University of Toronto, visited the museum in 2011.[29] When he learned that the director of the memorial museum on Lontsky St., Ruslan Zabily, was to be speaking at his university the following year, he sent me his impression of the museum: ". . . The place is literally plastered with OUN anti-Semitic propaganda (OUN-B newspapers line the walls) with virtually no curatorial comment at all. I found this very upsetting when I visited last year."[30] Although the newspapers were not formally affiliated with OUN-B, that is, with the Bandera faction of OUN that dominated Galicia and Volhynia, the Banderite nationalists did help set their tone; it should be kept in mind, however, that a major share of the responsibility for the way Ukrainian

Figure 7.2.

Figure 7.3.

newspapers reported the NKVD murders in July 1941 was borne by the
Nazis who supervised the collaborationist press. The kind of terminology
used for the perpetrators in the numerous clippings is familiar to anyone
who has read Nazi-era propaganda: "Jewish-Bolshevik gang" (49),[31]
"Jewish hirelings" (56), "Bolshevik-Jewish henchmen" (58), and "Jewish-
communist henchmen" (87). A clipping that reviewed the recent Soviet
past leading to the murders stated that when a patriotic Ukrainian was
taken by the NKVD in September 1940, "the Jews of Stryi rubbed their
hands together and were happy about the arrest." The judge who sentenced that Ukrainian patriot was also said to have participated in the
shootings of hundreds of prisoners. He was identified as a Jew, Moisei
Berkovych Hentelman (71–72). Another clipping narrated that in Chork-
tiv the NKVD arrested many Ukrainians immediately after the outbreak
of the German-Soviet war on the basis of denunciations by "local Jewish
communists." "To give the complete picture, it must be pointed out that
after the NKVD fled from Chortkiv Jewish-communist squads spent an
additional three days rampaging in the city, shooting at the innocent
population and sowing terror right and left" (87–88). In Chernivtsi, according to another clipping, "the Jews grew impossibly rich and powerful (*rozpanoshylysia do nemozhlyvosty*) after the Soviet invasion. After a

month or two they constructed an entire network, and the GPU [Soviet security organ] had on its list about three hundred thousand 'suspects,' mainly Ukrainians . . . " (96). These expressions of the Judeo-communist stereotype, which reflected both the hegemonic ideology of the Nazi occupiers as well as the anti-Semitism of Ukrainian nationalists of that era,[32] require contextualization, and distancing from those responsible for installing the exhibition.

THE LVIV POGROM

The emotions unleashed by the discovery of the NKVD victims helped fuel the brutal anti-Jewish pogrom that broke out in Lviv on July 1, 1941. One of the major scenes of pogrom activities was the Lontsky St. prison and its environs, although it was not mentioned anywhere in the museum space until a special exhibition on "the Shoah in Lviv" opened on Holocaust memorial day, January 27, 2013 (website). By that time, the one-sided presentation in the Lontsky St. museum had been the subject of some criticism from both within and outside Ukraine.[33]

Let us look briefly at the historiography of the pogrom. As one of the more spectacular pogroms in a series that broke out from the Baltics to Bessarabia in the wake of the German advance in the summer of 1941, it figured in the very earliest publications on the history of the Holocaust.[34] However, understanding of the events of the Lviv pogrom was thrown off track in 1959–1960, when the Soviets decided to use the pogrom to incriminate the government of Konrad Adenauer. Because Adenauer's minister for refugees, Theodor Oberländer, had been liaison with an OUN-B battalion in German service, Nachtigall, at the start of the German-Soviet war, the KGB manufactured evidence and collected false testimony that blamed the Lviv pogrom on that battalion. Identifying the Lviv pogrom with Nachtigall was also convenient for the Soviets in that the battalion's Ukrainian commander, Roman Shukhevych, was later to become commander of the anti-Soviet insurgency of the late 1940s. That the evidence against Nachtigall had been falsified was evident to many from the start, but in 2008 the paper trail of the KGB's manipulations was made public.[35] It is quite possible that some members of Nachtigall nonetheless participated in the pogrom in Lviv and it is reasonably certain that the battallion committed mass murders of Jews as it marched from Lviv to Vinnytsia,[36] but it was not a prime actor in the pogrom in Lviv.

Although some perceptive scholarship on the Lviv pogrom and other pogroms in Eastern Poland/Western Ukraine in 1941 predates 2000,[37] that year marked a turning point. The publication of Jan Gross's account of the pogrom in Jedwabne, first in Polish and then a year later in English,[38] heralded a new historiographic era in several respects. Not only did it initiate intensive scholarly research on the local violence of the summer of 1941,[39] but it also argued and demonstrated the necessity of incorporating victims' testimony into Holocaust research. It was not that no survivor testimony had been incorporated into scholarship earlier, but the classics of Holocaust literature eschewed such sources, relying rather on documents produced by the German perpetrators. This was true of such outstanding and deservedly influential works as Hannah Arendt's *Eichmann in Jerusalem*, Christopher Browning's *Ordinary Men*, and Raul Hilberg's indispensible and pioneering *The Destruction of the European Jews*. It was also true of the path-breaking study of the Holocaust in Galicia by Dieter Pohl based on newly opened Soviet archives.[40] Moreover, Gross's *Neighbors* was the first major work in which a specialist in East European studies, not in Holocaust studies or the Third Reich or Jewish history, brought to bear specialized knowledge of local history and languages to study aspects of the Holocaust.[41]

What Gross started in 2000 trickled with some delay also into public discourse and scholarship regarding Ukraine. Debate over the Ukrainian role in the pogroms appeared in the Kyiv periodical *Krytyka*, which models itself on the *New York Review of Books*, in 2005.[42] Not long after, Dieter Pohl wrote an article calling for scholars to put the West Ukrainian pogroms on their research agenda.[43] Since 2010 at least, historical research on these pogroms has been carried out in a tense, polarized atmosphere. In his swan song before stepping down from office as president of Ukraine in January 2010, Viktor Yushchenko posthumously named Stepan Bandera, the leader of the largest faction of OUN during wartime, a Hero of Ukraine. Shortly thereafter he called upon Ukrainians to name streets, squares, and schools after OUN and its members. The president who replaced Yushchenko, Viktor Yanukovych, pursued historical policies that were the opposite of Yushchenko's, and a year after taking office, he revoked Bandera's hero status. Ukraine is deeply divided over identity issues, and the place of OUN and Bandera is one of the points of conflict. Yushchenko's glorification of Bandera and OUN had repercussions in Canada, where the Ukrainian Canadian Congress, which is dominated by members and sympathizers of the current Banderite OUN in Canada, called upon the Canadian government in February 2010 to recognize OUN and its armed force, UPA, as resistance organizations whose wartime members deserved veterans' benefits from the Canadian government. Scholars working on OUN's involvement in the pogroms of 1941 and on OUN's responsibility for ethnic cleansing of the Polish population of Volhynia objected to both Yushchenko's and the Ukrainian Canadian Congress's glorification of OUN in light of the historical record.[44]

The new millennium saw the publication of a substantial new scholarly literature on the pogroms in Lviv and Western Ukraine, although a great deal more work remains to be done. The opening of the Soviet archives made a large body of captured OUN documents available to researchers. The new documentation made clear that OUN even before

1941 envisaged a Ukraine purged of national minorities, including Jews.[45] For example, the formulator of OUN's military doctrine, Mykhailo Kolodzinsky, wrote in 1938, in a manual that was studied carefully by the entire OUN leadership: ". . . We will not slaughter three and a half million Jews during the insurrection . . . [but] the more Jews who perish during the insurrection the better for the Ukrainian state."[46] Much more literature concerned the pogroms themselves, in Lviv and elsewhere.[47]

Two large points have emerged unequivocally from this research that have a direct bearing on how the history is presented in the memorial museum on Lontsky St. First, the Lontsky St. prison was a major site of the pogrom. The course of the pogrom in Lviv is now fairly well understood. From June 30, through the first few days of July, Jews were rounded up and made to exhume the corpses, wash them, and lay them out in rows for identification by the populace. The working conditions were horrible—the decomposing bodies had to be handled with bare hands and without the gas masks that some of the Germans wore to keep out the stench. Throughout the process, the Jews were beaten.[48]

Because Jews were assembled there, the pogromist mob also converged on the prisons. Leon Berk, who was brought to Lontsky St. on July 1, the day of the pogrom, remembered:

> When I crawled into the backyard, I saw a colossal wall on the right side, an empty, dark-brick, tall wall, and all the Jews were pushed to that wall by beating, by the onslaught of the Ukrainian crowds. I found myself unable to breathe, there was no air. That hitting and beating and screaming lasted for the whole day. It was a sunny, beautiful day. It was really hot. On the fence were Ukrainians sitting like vultures screaming "Death to the Jews! Death to the capitalists! Death to the communists! You wanted Stalin, you will have him now." Stones, sticks, and clubs were thrown at us. Every time the mob of Ukrainians attacked, we pushed ourselves further to the wall, trying to pierce the wall. Then we would sit down, bleeding and full of pain. That lasted almost the whole day.[49]

An unknown number of the Jews pressed into the exhumation were also executed on the premises of the prison.

In addition to the Lviv pogrom, another significant event in Holocaust history took place on the premises of the Lontsky St. prison, the Petliura days of July 25–26, 1941. Jews were brought to Lontsky St. and beaten savagely for hours before being taken away in trucks for execution on the outskirts of the city. Altogether over a thousand Jews were murdered in this action. Specialists in the history of the Holocaust in Ukraine had been able to reconstruct the general outline of what happened from survivors' memoirs, but a comprehensive study of the incident, based on extensive documentation as well as memoirs and testimonies, has only recently been written.[50] Both the Lviv pogrom and the Petliura days should constitute an integral part of the remembered history of the Lontsky St. prison memorial museum. The current exhibition on "the Shoah in Lviv" does present some information on the pogrom (though not on the Petliura days), as does the museum website. But the accuracy and objectivity of this information is problematic in light of the second point that arises from the research that has been completed on the pogrom.

The second point is that the OUN militia was responsible for arresting the Jews who were brought to the prisons.[51] This is borne out by many and diverse survivors' and witnesses' accounts as well as by photographic evidence. There are no surviving militia records from the first days of the German occupation, so we do not have the same kind of perpetrators' documentation that exists for the NKVD murders. It is also known that this same militia rounded up Jews for execution by an Einsatzgruppe unit a few days after the pogrom[52] and that it rounded up and tortured Jews during the Petliura days three weeks later. It is further known that many militiamen then entered German service in the Ukrainian Auxiliary Police, that OUN encouraged infiltration of the police by its members, and that this police force was a major instrument for the extermination of the Jewish population of Lviv and Galicia.[53]

All this is known and documented, yet not acknowledged by the memorial museum on Lontsky St., neither in its exhibition space nor on its website. One of the four posters that make up the special exhibition on the Shoah states that the German administration and propaganda office provoked the pogroms.[54] A lecture by Meylakh Sheykhet at the opening of the special exhibition was even more emphatic: "The pogroms in Lviv were planned by the Einsatzgruppen, the result of German propaganda."[55] The museum website, however, does not hold the Germans directly responsible: "The German authorities, which were just being established, shut its eyes with regard to the anti-Jewish pogroms. Nonetheless, the pogroms of the Jews were convenient for them." Ascertaining the exact role of the Germans in the many pogroms that swept the western territories of the invaded Soviet Union in summer 1941 is not just difficult for the museum, but it has been a difficult problem for research on the summer 1941 violence in general.

The museum identifies the main perpetrators of the pogrom to have been the urban crowd or riff raff or criminal elements, which is a common response of those who wish to deny any Ukrainian nationalist complicity in the Lviv pogrom.[56] The Canadian writer Larry Warwaruk described his visit to the museum in May 2011. He and his wife were given a personal tour of the museum by its director, Ruslan Zabily. "I questioned him about the killing of Jews immediately following the NKVD's flight from the German invasion in the summer of 1941 when the NKVD, as they were leaving killed off the Ukrainian Nationalist prisoners. Ruslan gave me an interesting answer. He said that the NKVD, before they left the prison, released common criminals, giving them instructions to kill Jews, and that Lviv's Ukrainian Nationalists had nothing to do with the slaughter of Lviv's Jews."[57] A very similar message is conveyed by the text on one of the special exhibition posters: "The criminal element of the city, which was freed from the prisons in the last days of the existence of Soviet power, took part in the pogroms." With such an explanation, a Nazi and Ukrainian nationalist crime becomes transformed into yet another Soviet crime.

A more neutral explanation of the pogrom can be found on the museum website: "The mass pogroms, which are written about quite a bit in the press, took place in the city spontaneously. They had no organizers, not Ukrainians or Poles, or any national orientation. It was, in our opinion, the chaos and anarchy of a city on the front." In his lecture at the exhibition opening, Sheykhet stated that the German presence and German propaganda "mobilized some marginal elements. But even with regard to these elements, they [the Germans] bear the responsibility." Sheykhet was adamant that OUN had nothing to do with the Lviv pogrom and those statements to the contrary were anti-Ukrainian Soviet and German propaganda, hoping to displace responsibility for the crimes onto the Ukrainians. Some of it seemed to be "commissioned with the goal of whitewashing Nazism and blaming only the Ukrainians, who themselves also suffered terribly from Nazism."

The following assertion appears on one of the posters for the special exhibition: "The Nazi administration approached the leader of the Home Executive of OUN Ivan Klymiv—'Lehenda' with the proposition to take part in pogroms, but Klymiv ordered all structures of OUN to ignore similar propositions and categorically forbade participating in pogroms." This information is taken from the so-called "Book of Facts" (*Knyha faktiv*). The Book of Facts, which is composed in the form of a chronicle, states, under the dates July 4–7, that the Gestapo approached "Ukrainian circles" in Lviv to organize a three-day pogrom as a reprisal against the Jews. They assured the Ukrainians that the German authorities, neither police nor military, would not interfere.

> The leading personnel of OUN, when they learned of this, informed all members that this was a German provocation in order to compromise the Ukrainians by pogroms, in order to provide a pretext for the German police to intervene and "restore order," and—most important—to divert the attention and energy of the Ukrainians in general from political problems and the struggle for independent statehood toward the slippery road of anarchy, crimes, and plunder. . . . Only thanks to the decisive attitude of the OUN cadres there did not result in the first days after the retreat of the Bolsheviks a massive slaughter of Jews in Lviv and in other Ukrainian cities, in spite of the tremendous wave of indignation called forth by the Bolsheviks' murder of eighty thousand Ukrainian political prisoners and in spite of the numerous provocations of the German Gestapo to incite Ukrainians to slaughter Jews.

Ivan Klymiv is not specifically mentioned in this passage, but he appears just a bit further down the page of the same document as leading the supposed resistance to the Germans in the first half of July 1941.[58]

This account would seem to clear OUN-B of any responsibility for the pogrom. But the Book of Facts is a deception. In February 2008 the Security Service of Ukraine mounted a major campaign to deny that OUN or UPA had anything to do with the murder of Jews, but instead rescued them. Among the documents unearthed at that time to promote this viewpoint was this Book of Facts. It was presented as "essentially a chronicle of the activities of OUN during March-September 1941."[59] In fact, however, it was prepared shortly after World War II. This is clear from the text itself, which states that OUN leaders were arrested by the Gestapo and detained *"throughout the war* in prisons and concentration camps."[60] Thus it was not a contemporary chronicle at all, but a post-war codification of history emanating from OUN itself, in fact a revision of the actual history. It had revised history to such an extent that it denied that any pogroms had occurred at all in Ukrainian territories under Nazi occupation. Moreover, this revisionist text can be linked to OUN's conscious decision, once it understood that Germany would lose the war, to prepare alternative evidence with regard to how it had behaved toward Jews under the Nazi occupation. An OUN document from October 27, 1943 labelled "strictly confidential" ordered the preparation of "lists (*spysy*) that would confirm that the Germans carried out anti-Jewish pogroms and liquidations by themselves, without the participation or help of the Ukrainian police. . . ."[61] Thus, the Book of Facts represents a double deception, first by OUN propagandists, then some six decades later by the Security Service of Ukraine as it pursued President Yushchenko's historical politics. The deception was exposed not long after the Security Service revealed the Book of Facts to the public.[62] Nonetheless, this would-be chronicle continues to be employed by deflective negationists in the Ukrainian diaspora in North America[63] and, obviously, by the deflective negationists who run the memorial museum of Lontsky St. prison.

Uilleam Blacker, whose critique of the Lontsky St. museum has already been cited earlier, seems to interpret what is going on at the museum as something less than deflective negationism: "It is not Holocaust obfuscation as such that is the primary motivation behind Lonts'kyi's narrative, as some have suggested; it is rather a paranoid determination not to undermine the purity of Ukrainian victimhood that precludes openness about the role of Ukrainian nationalists in the Holocaust. Of course, this is a subtle distinction, which many observers will not recognize."[64] Two points must be made in regard to this interpretation. First, deflective negationism is almost never motivated by the desire for Holocaust obfuscation *as such.* Austrians, for example, who engaged or engage in deflective negationism have done so because of their concern for Austria's reputation, for its self-image as the first victim of Nazism, and for the memory of their fathers and grandfathers who fought in German forces during World War II.[65] Similar reasons feed Holocaust obfuscation and denial in all its forms, particularly in Europe. Moreover, following Blacker's line of argument, one could say that former Iranian president Mahmoud Ahmadinejad was not a Holocaust obfuscator as such either, but rather an opponent of Israel and the West. No abstract classification, including deflective negationism of the Holocaust, can exist in pure form, but only in concrete forms. Second, while Blacker recognizes that the museum is not open about "the role of Ukrainian nationalists in the Holocaust," he seems not to have recognized the museum's glorification of these very Ukrainian nationalists.

GLORIFICATION OF OUN

The long-standing omission of the history of the Lviv pogrom in the museum, its recent appearance in distorted form, the adamant denial of OUN involvement in it in spite of the consensus among Holocaust researchers internationally, and the resort to deceptive documentation in an attempt to buttress that denial is linked to the museum's intention to glorify and exalt the martyrology of OUN.

As the museum's posters inform us, during the prison's Polish period, in 1936, inmates included the top leadership of OUN in Galicia—Stepan Bandera (later head of the eponymous faction of OUN), Yaroslav Stetsko (head of the short-lived Ukrainian government proclaimed in Lviv on June 30, 1941 and an ardent anti-semite),[66] Mykola Lebed (head of security in Stetsko's government and later in the war acting head of OUN-B), and Kateryna Zarytska (courier for UPA commander Shukhevych and head of the Ukrainian Red Cross during the war). The portraits of these OUN leaders are reproduced on the poster.

The poster on the history of the prison during the first Soviet period features the portrait and biogram of Dmytro Kliachkivsky who was arrested by the Soviets in 1940 and held in Lontsky awaiting deportation. Kliachkivsky managed to escape during transport. The biogram tells us: "In 1943 he was the Supreme Commander of UPA. He died in battle with NKVD units in 1945." It does not mention that he directed a vicious ethnic cleansing campaign against the Polish population of Volhynia.

Another poster explains the history of the Lontsky St. prison during the Nazi occupation as follows: "During the Nazi occupation (1941–1944) an investigative prison of the Gestapo was set up on Lontsky St. In the first days of the occupation of Lviv the Einsatsgruppen of the SD (security service) were located in the prison. In this period prisoners suffered not only from hunger and maltreatment but also from typhus epidemics. The main target of the Gestapo was members of OUN, mass arrests of whom started at the end of 1941." Although it is more than doubtful that OUN members were the Gestapo's "main target," it is certainly true that relations between the Germans and OUN-B deteriorated in the fall of 1941 and that the Germans were persecuting OUN leaders they caught with some severity. And in spring 1943 UPA revolted against the Germans, only reaching a new accommodation in 1944, as the Red Army approached Western Ukraine. The history of German-OUN relations is much more complicated than this, but the point here is that the museum is correct that OUN members were incarcerated and tortured on the premises of the Lontsky St. prison. The most famous OUN victim of this period of the prison's history was Ivan Klymiv, mentioned previously in connection with the Book of Facts. The biogram accompanying Klymiv's portrait reads: "Ivan Klymiv (1909–1942). Member of OUN. Home Leader of OUN on Western Ukrainian lands in 1940–1941. Minister of the state administration of Ya. Stetsko. Died in the prison on Lontsky St. during interrogation on 4 December 1942." What the biogram omits is that on the day of the Lviv pogrom he issued proclamations calling for the implementation of collective responsibility and urging the destruction of Poles, Russians, Hungarians, and Jews.[67]

Although the approach to history exemplified by the Lontsky St. prison museum is at variance with the mainstream intellectual, political, and moral values of present-day North America, Australasia, and Western Europe, very similar treatments of the past can be found elsewhere in post-Communist Europe. In Romania, for example, there are still those who lionize Marshall Ion Antonescu, head of the wartime Romanian state, denying his thoroughly documented role in the murder of hundreds of thousands of Jews. Analogous is the case of Slovakia and Monsignor Jozef Tiso. In both cases, those who honor the memory of these leaders claim that they rescued rather than murdered Jews. In these two countries and in Croatia, one finds similar revisionist accounts of the OUN's equivalents—the legionnaires of the Archangel Michael, the Hlinka Guard, and the Ustaša.[68] The Lontsky St. museum is only one symptom of a larger problem.

ENTR'ACTE: THE DETENTION OF THE MUSEUM'S DIRECTOR, RUSLAN ZABILY

After Viktor Yushchenko was replaced by Viktor Yanukovych as president of Ukraine early in 2010, historical politics made a U-turn, which deprived the Lontsky St. museum of its formerly powerful patronage. Moreover, Yanukovych introduced a much more authoritarian form of government than any of his predecessors, even to the point of jailing the most important opposition figures in 2011. On September 8, 2010 the reoriented Security Service of Ukraine detained the director of the museum on Lontsky St., Ruslan Zabily. They held him for fourteen hours and confiscated two external hard drives with historical documents, claiming that he was about to pass on state secrets.

Scholars around the world immediately reacted in protest. Among those who spoke out publicly against the arrest or signed a petition of protest were a number of scholars who disagreed fundamentally with the kind of historical politics Zabily represented, but who insisted on the need to protect freedom of speech.[69] Nationalist activists in the Ukrainian diaspora, however, recognized that the Zabily case—with its violation of human rights and its confirmation of a familiar, frequently reiterated narrative of Ukrainian victimization—could be effectively utilized to legitimize the kind of historical presentation found in Zabily's museum. This legitimization campaign was successfully conducted in, among other venues, the Canadian political sphere.

THE MUSEUM AND CANADIAN POLITICS

Some background is necessary. There was a time when the Ukrainian diaspora in North America was less dominated by the direct political descendants of the Bandera faction of OUN, but at present it is this political tendency which dominates the organized Ukrainian community. The president of the Ukrainian Canadian Congress (UCC) is Paul Grod, who is in the leadership of the Canadian branch of the OUN-B youth organization SUM. The treasurer of the UCC, Wolodymyr Dlugosh, has also been involved in SUM. Among the other six members of the UCC executive committee two, Serhiy Kasyanchuk and Oleh Romanyshyn, have served as president of the primary Banderite organization, the League of Ukrainian Canadians.[70] As has been mentioned above, after Yushchenko proclaimed Bandera and OUN as a whole to be heroes, the UCC asked the Canadian government to extend recognition to OUN and UPA as resistance fighters entitled to veterans' benefits. Although the UCC claims to represent 1.25 million Ukrainians in Canada, the majority of persons of Ukrainian heritage that are being included in this claim have little or no contact with the organized Ukrainian community. In fact, precisely the dwindling numbers in the organized community have allowed the Banderites, a minority with an activist agenda, to consolidate power in the diaspora.[71] Although not as numerous as the claim of 1.25 million indicates, the organized Ukrainian community can still effectively deliver campaign donations, campaign workers, and votes, particularly in the major Canadian cities of Toronto, Edmonton, and Winnipeg.

The organized Ukrainian diaspora has cultivated political connections and influence with all Canadian parties, but especially with the Conservatives (and their variously named predecessors). Canada's official policy of multiculturalism, which was introduced in 1971 and confirmed by the Canadian Multiculturalism Act of 1988, has invited ethnic politics into the national arena. The present Conservative government of Canada headed by Prime Minister Stephen Harper has relied partly on ethnic alliances to stay in power. His Department of Foreign Affairs, according to a well-informed analyst, is also employed "to capture the ethnic-minority vote." "For some time now, the department has toyed with the idea of a 'global citizens' agenda, a nascent policy that would see Ottawa tapping into expatriate and diaspora expertise to advance Canadian trade and cultural and development interests overseas."[72] Indeed, UCC president Paul Grod has been named among the top eighty persons influencing Canadian foreign policy; he was listed among "diaspora group and NGO reps" immediately after Shimon Fogel, CEO of The Centre for Israel and Jewish Affairs.[73] This situation has allowed the Banderite OUN to have a disproportionate influence on Canadian politics.

Not long after the detention of Ruslan Zabily, Prime Minister Harper himself visited Ukraine. In Lviv on October 26, 2010, he went to the memorial museum on Lontsky St. and met with Zabily. This was intended to send a strong signal of disapproval to President Yanukovych for clamping down on free speech. The reporter from Toronto's *Globe and Mail* noted: "Whether Mr. Yanukovych cares about any messages Mr. Harper might send is problematic. But Ukrainian Canadians will care, and they represent an important voting bloc in the Prairies."[74] The delegation included a number of persons who served in executive positions in Banderite organizations, not only UCC president Grod, but also Ivanna Baran, Taras Podilsky, Borys Potapenko, and Lisa Shymko.[75] Marco Levytsky, the editor of *Ukrainian News* and a defender of OUN's innocence in the Holocaust, also accompanied the delegation and received more access to the Prime Minister and to the events of his tour than did the mainstream media. In a bizarrely ironic episode, Prime Minister Harper wrote in the Lontsky St. musuem's guest book: "It is important that the terrible things here not be forgotten or repeated."[76]

Scholars of the Holocaust and of Holocaust memory in Ukraine were taken aback by the Prime Minister's visit to the museum, which, as Omer Bartov later reflected, ended up "legitimizing skewed representations of a past cleansed of complicity in genocide and ethnic cleansing."[77] Several scholars, including me, contacted PostMedia news reporter Peter O'Neil, who was covering the Prime Minister's tour for that news service's 4.1 million readers, and explained the museum's context. O'Neil ended up writing a piece that was subsequently published in *The National Post*, *Edmonton Journal*, *Montreal Gazette*, and other newspapers. Scholars, he wrote, had alerted him "to the beating, humiliation and murder of Jews in Lviv by Ukrainians—with Nazi encouragement—in the days after the Soviets were routed by Hitler's forces in the early summer of 1941. The Jews were also forced to exhume and to clean the mutilated, decomposing bodies in the prison." He quoted, among others, a leading specialist on the Lviv pogrom: "German scholar Kai Struve, who visited the museum last year, said the Soviet massacre of prisoners was a 'horrible crime' that must be acknowledged and remembered. 'But if it is done in such a one-sided, selective way, it does not do a good service even to the Ukrainian victims of this crime.'"[78]

O'Neil's article was roundly criticized by a leading Banderite from America, a former president of the World Congress of Ukrainians, Askold S. Lozynskyj. O'Neil had in fact consulted Lozynskyj before publishing his article, since the UCC had encouraged him to speak to Lozynskyj about the historical issues.[79] In his critique of O'Neil, which was published in the expatriate newspaper *Kyiv Post*, Lozynskyj claimed that "Canada's mainstream media" did not carry the article, just PostMedia newspapers. "PostMedia is a restructuring of CanWest Global," and "CanWest Global was founded and controlled by a Canadian-Jewish family, the Aspers." He considered the article by O'Neil that we are discussing, as well as another one by O'Neil about the Prime Minister's inflation of the number of victims of the Ukrainian famine of 1932–1933, to be an "excessive reaction by Jewish media as a self-preserving defense tactic since, statistically, a disproportionate component of the Holodomor's executioners were Jews and an equally overwhelming amount of Soviet accomplices during the Soviet's [*sic*] two years in western Ukraine from 1939–1941 were Jews." He ended by asserting that "those who control the Jewish Canadian press" are "bigoted and insensitive."[80]

The meeting between Prime Minister Harper and Lontsky St. museum director Ruslan Zabily on October 26, 2010 was not their last. At the end of a cross-Canada lecture tour sponsored by Canadian Banderites,[81] Zabily was received by Prime Minister Harper once again on October 19, 2012. In his speech to a Canadian delegation about to monitor the parliamentary elections of Ukraine, Harper praised Zabily's courage and his museum's preservation of memory. Harper ended his brief speech with the slogan associated with the Bandera movement: *Slava Ukraini*, that is, "Glory to Ukraine."[82]

During this visit to Canada, Zabily met with a number of other prominent Canadian politicians. For example, Ihor Broda, a leading Banderite activist in Edmonton, took Zabily to visit Linda Duncan, a parliamentary deputy from the left-wing New Democratic Party, at her constituency office. Duncan had already met Zabily in spring of 2012 when she participated in a Canadian parliamentary human rights commission that visited Ukraine. Duncan brought to the meeting a student from Kyiv who is serving as a parliamentary intern for her. The intern told Zabily that her grandfather had fought in UPA. Duncan and Zabily spoke for an hour and a half, with Broda translating. Duncan said she would try to visit Zabily when she goes to Ukraine as an election observer.[83]

The Canadian ambassador to Ukraine, Troy Lulashnyk, also visited the museum on December 8, 2011. He penned into the guest book: "So that we remember the tragedy and heroism of Ukraine."[84]

Jason Kenney, Minister of Citizenship, Immigration, and Multiculturalism in the Harper government, visited the Lontsky St. prison museum on March 1, 2013. He seems to have been completely unaware that the museum not just revealed history, but also concealed it.[85] While he was on his visit to Ukraine, the Ukrainian Canadian Civil Liberties Association[86] tweeted on March 3: "@kenneyjason on impressive 3day Ukraine trip. Hope u pay tribute 2 Ukrn freedomfighters in OUN, massacred by Nazis, Soviets & their enablers." Kenney tweeted them back that same day: "@UCCLA I did, eg at the Lonski Prison Museum, where hundreds of Ukrainian nationalists were tortured & killed." At the same time, in one of the many ironies that arise when a commitment to human rights is unwittingly wedded to a narrative of denial about perpetration, Kenney wanted to use this same trip in Ukraine to move the country forward on coming to terms with its Holocaust past. In two tweets of March 2, Kenney wrote: "Sadly, local authorities erected large crosses at Sambir's mass grave, with no recognition of the ~2,000 jews buried there. Canada is encouraging Sambir to right this wrong, just as we are encouraging Ukraine to pursue serious holocaust commemoration, education & research."

BACK TO THE FUTURE?

Perhaps every nation has a difficult past to integrate into its historical consciousness. And it is a measure of its intellectual, political, and moral maturity to what extent it is able to think and carry on discourse openly and honestly about the dark elements of its historical heriditament, whether it be the conquest of neighboring countries, the extermination and dispossession of aboriginals, the elimination of ethnic minorities, the bombing of civilian populations, the destruction of Jews, the creation of famines, or mass political terror. This kind of maturation has been particularly difficult in post-communist Europe, even more so in post-Soviet Europe, and still more so in the territories that experienced both Nazi and Soviet occupation, "the Bloodlands," as Timothy Snyder has dubbed them. Ukraine is in the heart of these Bloodlands. The territories of Ukraine that formed part of the Soviet Union prior to 1939 have barely begun a serious reckoning with their complicated history under Communism. And Western Ukraine, particularly the former Galicia, is in the same situation with regard to its history in the period when the nationalism of OUN was hegemonic, particularly during the period of the Nazi occupation.

At present Western Ukraine faces a choice. It can proceed through the painful process of learning its difficult history and slowly accommodating itself to living with the conflicting emotions and thoughts arising from it. This is a way forward, into the future. Or, it can postpone the self-reckoning, deny its necessity, and surrender to the past. This is the way to remain stunted in development, to be imprisoned in the *Gedanken* and *Geisteswelt* of the 1930s and 1940s, perforce in the grip of nationalist intolerance, xenophobia, anti-Semitism, and censorship. The museum on Lontsky St. has chosen the latter alternative, as has the leadership of the organized Ukrainian community in North America. They reinforce each other's position, with the ignorant complicity of the most prominent figures in Canadian political life and government. The memorial museum of the Lontsky St. prison misinforms an international public about what happened in Lviv in the summer of 1941, presenting a one-sided picture of communist crimes, while suppressing knowledge of the involvement in pogroms and mass executions of Jews at Lontsky St. prison itself and elsewhere. These crimes were committed by a nationalist movement that the museum glorifies and whose direct political heirs in the overseas diaspora have a vested interest in their concealment. It is hoped that the present article contributes to a reassessment of this situation on the part of those in Canadian politics and government, who have tolerated and often facilitated it. The prominent Canadians who have visited and praised the museum should look for ways to help the museum reconsider how it presents the history of the Holocaust. The way forward leads through admitting all of what happened at Lontsky St. prison in July 1941 and desisting from glorifying the perpetrators.

NOTES

1. As in so much of my work, I am grateful for the help of other scholars in the field who have shared materials with me. In this regard, I would particularly like to thank Per Anders Rudling. I am also indebted to Chrystia Chomiak and Eva Himka who read the first draft and whose insightful comments have improved it. I wish too to thank Johan Dietsch, who commented on this paper at the Harriman Institute Workshop "Russian and Ukrainian Nationalism: Entangled Histories" (22–23 April 2013); others at the workshop also offered me valuable comments. I alone, however, am responsible for the interpretations advanced in this text.

2. General information on the history of the prison and of the museum has been taken from the text of the posters on display when I visited and photographed the museum on 3 June 2010 as well as from the website of the museum, http://www.lonckoho.lviv.ua/, accessed 1 April 2010. I will cite these sources further simply as Posters and Website.

3. Grzegorz Motyka, *Ukraińska partyzantka 1942–1960: działalność Organizacji Ukraińskich Nacjonalistów i Ukraińskiej Powstańczej Armii* (Warsaw: Instytut Studiów Politycznych PAN, RYTM, 2006), Alexander Statiev, *The Soviet Counterinsurgency in the Western Borderlands* (Cambridge: Cambridge University Press, 2010).

4. See Omer Bartov, *Erased: Vanishing Traces of Jewish Galicia in Present-Day Ukraine* (Princeton and Oxford: Princeton University Press, 2007).

5. Michael Shafir, *Between Denial and "Comparative Trivialization": Holocaust Nega-tionism in Post-Communist East Central Europe* (Analysis of Current Trends in Anti-semitism, 19, Jerusalem: The Hebrew University of Jerusalem, The Vidal Sassoon International Center for the Study of Antisemitism, 2002), 10.

6. Wilfrid Jilge, "Competing Victimhoods—Post-Soviet Ukrainian Narratives on World War II," in *Shared History—Divided Memory: Jews and Others in Soviet-Occupied Poland, 1939–1941*, in ed. Elizabeth A. Cole et al. (Leipzig: Leipziger Universitätsverlag, 2007): 103–31, Stefan Rohdewald, "Post-Soviet Remembrance of the Holocaust and National Memories of the Second World War in Russia, Ukraine and Lithuania," *Forum for Modern Language Studies* 44 (2008): 173–84, Irena Cantoro-vich, "Honoring the Collaborators—The Ukrainian Case," *Kantor Program* Papers, June 2012, http://www.kantorcenter.tau.ac.il/sites/default/files/ukraine-collaborators_4.pdf (accessed 29 April 2013); Georgiy Kasianov, "Revisiting the Great Famine of 1932–1933: Politics of Memory and Public Consciousness (Ukraine after 1991)," in *Past in the Making: Historical Revisionism in Central Europe after 1989*, ed. Michal Kopeček, (Budapest: Central European University Press, 2008): 197–219. Heorhii Kas′ianov, *Danse macabre: holod 1932–1933 rokiv u politytsi, masovii svidomosti ta istoriohrafii (1980-ti–pochatok 2000-kh)* (Kyiv: Nash chas, 2010).

7. Mariana Pietsukh, "Muzei strakhu v 'nichnomu' formati. Reportazh z Nochi Muzeiv," *Istorychna pravda*, 27 May 2013, http://www.istpravda.com.ua/articles/2013/05/27/124888/ (accessed 23 October 2013).

8. Timothy Snyder, *Bloodlands: Europe between Hitler and Stalin* (New York: Basic Books 2010), 194–95.

9. Alfred M. De Zayas, with the collaboration of Walter Rabus, *The Wehrmacht War Crimes Bureau, 1939–1945* (Lincoln and London: University of Nebraska Press, 1980), 214–27.

10. John-Paul Himka, "Ethnicity and the Reporting of Mass Murder: *Krakivs′ki visti*, the NKVD Murders of 1941, and the Vinnytsia Exhumation," in *Shatterzone of Empires: Coexistence and Violence in the German, Habsburg, Russian, and Ottoman Borderlands*, Omer Bartov and Eric D. Weitz eds., (Bloomington: Indiana University Press, 2013), 382–83.

11. Milena Rudnyts'ka, ed., *Zakhidnia Ukraina pid bol'shevykamy, IX.1939–VI.1941*, (New York, 1958), 399–492. *Zlochyny komunistychnoi Moskvy v Ukraini v liti 1941 roku* (New York: Proloh, 1960). The abbess of the Studite nuns, Sister Olena Viter, re-counted her interrogation by the NKVD at Lontsky St. prison in May 1941; Rud-nyts'ka, *Zakhidnia Ukraina*, 403.

12. Iu. Slyvka et al., *Litopys neskorenoi Ukrainy. Dokumenty, materialy, spohady*, book 1 (Lviv: Prosvita, 1993). The collection lists the following organizations as involved in the project: the Institute of Ukrainian Studies of the Academy of Sciences of Ukraine, the Lviv branch of the Institute of Archeography of the Academy of Sciences of Ukraine, the All-Ukrainian Brotherhood of Soldiers of UPA, and the All-Ukrainian Association of Political Prisoners and Victims of Repression. The State Administration of Lviv Oblast was the "sponsor of the book."

13. Oleh Romaniv and Inna Fedushchak, *Zakhidnoukrains′ka trahediia 1941* (Lviv and New York: Naukove tovarystvo im. Shevchenka, 2002).

14. Krzysztof Popiński, Aleksandr Kokurin, and Aleksandr Gurjanow, *Drogi śmierci. Ewakuacja więzeń sowieckich z Kresów Wschodnich II Rzeczypospolitej w czerwcu i lipcu 1941* (Warsaw: Karta, 1995).

15. Jan T. Gross, *Revolution from Abroad: The Soviet Conquest of Poland's Western Ukraine and Western Belorussia* (Princeton and Oxford: Princeton University Press, 1988), 144–86.

16. Bogdan Musial, *"Konterrevolutionäre Elemente sind zu erschießen": Die Brutalisie-rung des deutsch-sowjetischen Krieges im Sommer 1941* (Berlin: Propyläen, 2000), Bogdan Musial, *"Rozstrzelac elementy kontrrewolucyjne!" Brutalizacja wojny niemiecko-sowieckiej latem 1941 roku* (Warsaw: Fronda, 2002).

17. Review by Dieter Pohl in H-Soz-u-Kult (internet), 30 April 2001. Per Anders Rudling, "Bogdan Musial and the Question of Jewish Responsibility for the Pogroms in Lviv in the Summer of 1941," *East European Jewish Affairs* 35 (2005): 69–89.

18. Irina Paperno, "Exhuming the Bodies of Soviet Terror," *Representations* 75 (2001): 89–118. See also Meir Korzen, "The Extermination of Two Ukrainian Jewish Communities: Testimony of a German Army Officer," *Yad Vashem Studies* 1959: 303–20; here the officer says that the bodies exhumed in Vinnytsia by the Germans in 1943 were Jews killed by the SS and the Ukrainian militia. The truth, however, is that these were political prisoners killed by the Soviet security organs in the late 1930s. The editors of *Yad Vashem Studies* seem not to have understood what they were publishing.

19. Philip Friedman, "Ukrainian-Jewish Relations during the Nazi Occupation," in Philip Friedman, *Roads to Extinction: Essays on the Holocaust*, ed. Ada June Friedman (New York: Conference on Jewish Social Studies, Jewish Publication Society of America, 1980), 183; see also 198, note 24.

20. Tsentral'nyi derzhavnyi arkhiv hromads'kykh ob"iednan' Ukrainy, f. 166, op. 2, spr. 295, ark. 2. I am grateful to Oleksandr Melnyk for making this document available to me.

21. Bogdan Musial, "Bilder einer Ausstellung: Kritische Anmerkungen zur Wanderausstellung 'Vernichtungskrieg. Verbrechen der Wehrmacht 1941 bis 1944,'" *Vierteljahrshefte für Zeitgeschichte* 47 (1999): 563–91.

22. Bernd Boll, "Złoczów. July 1941: The Wehrmacht and the Beginning of the Holocaust in Galicia: From a Criticism of Photographs to a Revision of the Past," in *Crimes of War: Guilt and Denial in the Twentieth Century*, ed. Omer Bartov et al. (New York: The New Press, 2002), 61–99, 275–83.

23. John-Paul Himka, "The Lviv Pogrom of 1941: The Germans, Ukrainian Nationalists, and the Carnival Crowd," *Canadian Slavonic Papers* 53 (2011): 216–17. In this text I erroneously identified the photo as from Brygidki not Lontsky St. prison. The photo is from the collection of David Lee Preston.

24. Inappropriate ethnicization of these murders and the murders at Vinnytsia is the theme of John-Paul Himka, "Ethnicity and the Reporting of Mass Murder," 378–98. I took the photo of the clippings at the museum.

25. Uilleam Blacker, "The Prison on Lonts'kyi Street: Memory Dialogue or Memory Monologue?" *Current Politics in Ukraine*, 4 January 2013, http://ukraineanalysis. wordpress.com/2013/01/04/the-prison-on-lontskyi-street-memory-dialogue-or-memory-monologue/ (accessed 23 March 2013). At the opening of the museum, the head of the Security Service of Ukraine at the time, Valentyn Nalyvaichenko, made a speech that seemed to equate the interwar Polish regime with the Nazis and Soviets. This provoked indignation in Poland's mass media. See Tarik Cyril [Syril] Amar, "Lonts'koho: pam"iat' pro tiurmu chy uv"iaznena pam"iat'?," *Zaxid.net*, 3 August 2009, http://zaxid.net/home/showSingleNews.do?lontskogo_pamyat_pro_tyurmu_chi_uvyaznena_pamyat&objectId=1083037 (accessed 15 April 2013). I am grateful to Per Anders Rudling for calling my attention to this article.

26. Shimon Briman, "L'vov: evreiskii uzel," *Den'* (Kyiv), 21 May 2013, http://www. day.kiev.ua/ru/article/mirovye-diskussii/lvov-evreyskiy-uzel (accessed 23 October, 2013).

27. Email from Arthur Greene to the author, 8 August 2013.

28. When an earlier version of this paper was delivered at the Harriman Institute, the historian Volodymyr Viatrovych stated that there is some kind of statement contextualizing the clippings on exhibit. I asked him to send me the text of the statement and preferably a photo, but he has not done so.

29. Kopstein, a political scientist, has been researching the pogroms of 1941. Jeffrey S. Kopstein and Jason Wittenberg, "Deadly Communities: Local Political Milieus and the Persecution of Jews in Occupied Poland," *Comparative Political Studies* 20 (2010): 1–25. Kopstein presented a paper on the pogroms in Western Ukraine in 1941 at the conference Jewish Life and Death in the Soviet Union during World War II, held 24–25 March 2012 at the University of Toronto.

30. Email of 2 October 2012.

31. These numbers refer to the pages in Slyvka, *Litopys neskorenoi Ukrainy*, where the text of the clipping is reprinted. My account here does not exhaust the anti-Semitic statements in the clippings displayed at the museum.

32. See Taras Kurylo, "The 'Jewish Question' in the Ukrainian Nationalist Discourse of the Inter-War Period," *Polin* 26. On the Judeo-communist stereotype, see particularly Joanna B. Michlic, "Żydokomuna—Anti-Jewish Images and Political Tropes in Modern Poland," *Simon Dubnow Institute Yearbook* 4 (2005): 303–29.

33. The absence of information on the pogrom and many other problems of the way the museum presented history were raised already in August 2009 by the then director of the Center for Urban History of East Central Europe in Lviv, Amar, "Lonts'koho."

34. Notably in Philip Friedman, *Zaglada Zydów lwowskich w okresie okupacji niemieckiej* (Munich: Monachium, 1947), 7–8.

35. "U Sluzhbi bezpeky Ukrainy vidbulys' Hromads'ki istorychni slukhannia 'Zvynuvachennia proty "Nakhtihaliu"—istorychna pravda chy politychni tekhnolohii,'" press release of the Security Service of Ukraine, 6 February 2008, http://www.ssu.gov.ua/sbu/control/uk/publish/article?art_id=74369&cat_id=74549 (accessed 6 April 2013). "Iak tvorylasia lehenda pro Nachtigall," *Dzerkalo tyzhnia*, 16 February 2008, available on the website of the Security Service of Ukraine: http://www.ssu.gov.ua/sbu/control/uk/publish/article?art_id=74855&cat_id=74589 (accessed 6 April 2013).

36. Per A. Rudling, *The OUN, the UPA and the Holocaust: A Study in the Manufacturing of Historical Myths* (Carl Beck Papers in Russian & East European Studies, Pittsburgh: Center for Russian & East European Studies, University Center for International Studies, University of Pittsburgh, 2011), 8–9.

37. Günter Plum, [Report on OUN involvement in 1941 pogroms,] Munich: Institut für Zeitgeschichte, 1965, in archives of Institut für Zetigeschichte, Gutachten 3547 (copy provided to the author by Marco Carynnyk); a copy of this typescript can also be found in the Mykola Lebed archives at Harvard Ukrainian Research Institute, box 1, file 3. (Plum's report is particularly important because it already identified the OUN militia as a major perpetrator in the Lviv pogrom.) Andrzej Zbikowski, "Local Anti-Jewish Pogroms in the Occupied Territories of Eastern Poland, June-July 1941," in *The Holocaust in the Soviet Union: Studies and Sources on the Destruction of the Jews in the Nazi-Occupied Territories of the USSR, 1941–1945*, Lucjan Dobroszycki and Jeffrey S. Gurock eds. (Armonk, New York and London: M. E. Sharpe, 1993), 173–79.

38. Jan T. Gross, *Neighbors: The Destruction of the Jewish Community in Jedwabne, Poland* (Princeton: Princeton University Press, 2001).

39. Andrzej Żbikowski, "Pogromy i mordy ludności żydowskiej w Łomżyńskiem i na Białostocczyźnie latem 1941 roku w świetle relacji ocalałych Żydów i dokumentów sądowych," in *Wokół Jedwabnego*, Vol. 1: *Studia*, Paweł Machcewicz and Krzysztof Persak ed. (Warsaw: Instytut Pamięci Narodowej, Komisja Ścigania Zbrodni przeciwko Narodowi Polskiemu, 2002), 159–271. This is a detailed account of pogroms in the general vicinity of Jedwabne commissioned by Poland's Institute of National Remembrance; it was a direct response to Gross's book.

40. Dieter Pohl, *Nationalsozialistische Judenverfolgung in Ostgalizien 1941–1944: Organisation und Durchführung eines staatlichen Massenverbrechens* (Munich: R. Oldenbourg Verlag, 1997).

41. For a more detailed exposition, see John-Paul Himka, "Introduction: A Reconfigured Terrain," in *The Holocaust in the East: Local Perpetrators and Soviet Responses*, ed. Michael David-Fox et al. (Pittsburgh: University of Pittsburgh Press, 2014), 1–3, and Marci Shore, "Conversing with Ghosts: Jedwabne, Żydokomuna, and Totalitarianism," *Kritika: Explorations in Russian and Eurasian History* 6 (2005): 345–74.

42. The debates are summarized and contextualized in John-Paul Himka, "Debates in Ukraine over Nationalist Involvement in the Holocaust, 2004–2008," *Nationalities Papers* 39 (2011): 353–70.

43. Dieter Pohl, "Anti-Jewish Pogroms in Western Ukraine—A Research Agenda," in *Shared History—Divided Memory: Jews and Others in Soviet-Occupied Poland,*

1939–1941, ed. Eleazar Barkan, et al. (Leipzig: Leipziger Universitätsverlag, 2007), 305–13.

44. Tarik Cyril [Syril] Amar, Ihor Balyns'kyi, and Iaroslav Hrytsak, eds., *Strasti za Banderoiu* (Kyiv: Hrani-T, 2010). The Ukraine List (UKL) compiled by Dominique Arel, Nos. 441 and 442. Timothy Snyder, "A Fascist Hero in Democratic Kiev," *The New York Review of Books* Blog, 24 February, 2010, http://www.nybooks.com/blogs/nyrblog/2010/feb/24/a-fascist-hero-in-democratic-kiev/ (accessed 30 October 2013). John-Paul Himka, "The Organization of Ukrainian Nationalists and the Ukrainian Insurgent Army: Unwelcome Elements of an Identity Project," *Ab Imperio* 4 (2010): 83–101.

45. Marco Carynnyk, "Foes of Our Rebirth: Ukrainian Nationalist Discussions about Jews, 1929–1947," *Nationalities Papers* 39 (2011): 315–52.

46. Oleksandr Zaitsev, "'Voienna doktryna ukrains'kykh natsionalistiv' Mykhaila Kolodzins'koho," *Ukraina Moderna*, 6 October, 2012, http://www.uamoderna.com/event/186 (accessed 10 April, 2013).

47. Hannes Heer, "Einübung in den Holocaust: Lemberg Juni/Juli 1941," *Zeitschrift für Geschichtswissenschaft* 49 (2001): 409–27; Hannes Heer, "Lemberg 1941: Die Instrumentalisierung der NKVD-Verbrechen für Judenmord," in *Kriegsverbrechen im 20. Jahrhundert*, ed. Wolfram Wette and Gerd R. Ueberschär (Darmstadt: Primus Verlag, 2001), 165–77; Bogdan Musial, *"Konterrevolutionäre Elemente sind zu erschießen,"* Ivan Fostii, *Pivnichna Bukovyna i Khotynshchyna u Druhii svitovii viini 1939–1945 rr.* (Chernivtsi: Oblasne viddilennia Poshukovo-vydavnychoho ahenstva "Knyha pam"iati Ukrainy, 2005), 130–32, Delphine Bechtel, "De Jedwabne à Zolotchiv: Pogromes locaux en Galicie, juin-juillet 1941," *Cultures d'Europe Centrale*, 5 (2005); *La destruction des confins*, 69–92, Vladimir Solonari, "Patterns of Violence: The Local Population and the Mass Murder of Jews in Bessarabia and Northern Bukovina, July–August 1941," *Kritika: Explorations in Russian and Eurasian History* 8 (2007): 749–87; John-Paul Himka [Ivan Khymka], "Dostovirnist' svidchennia: reliatsiia Ruzi Vagner pro l'vivs'kyi pohrom vlitku 1941 r.," *Holokost i suchasnist'* 4 (2008): 43–79; Christoph Mick, *Kriegserfahrungen in einer multiethnischen Stadt: Lemberg 1914–1947* (Wiesbaden: Harrassowitz Verlag, 2010), 471–76; Aleksandr Kruglov, "Pogromy v Vostochnoi Galitsii letom 1941 g.: organizatory, uchastniki, masshtaby i posledstviia," in *Voina na unichtozhenie. Natsistskaia politika genotsida na territorii Vostochnoi Evropy. Materialy mezhdunarodnoi nauchnoi konferentsii (Moskva, 26–28 aprelia 2010 goda)*, ed. A. R. Diukov and O. E. Orlenko (Moscow: Fond "Istoricheskaia pamiat,'" 2010), 324–41; Grzegorz Rossoliński-Liebe, "The 'Ukrainian National Revolution' of 1941: Discourse and Practice of a Fascist Movement," *Kritika: Explorations in Russian and Eurasian History* 12 (2011): 83–114 (about the context for the pogroms), Christoph Mick, "Incompatible Experiences: Poles, Ukrainians and Jews in Lviv under Soviet and German Occupation, 1939–1944," *Journal of Contemporary History* 46 (2011): 336–63, Wendy Lower, "Pogroms, Mob Violence and Genocide in Western Ukraine, Summer 1941: Varied Histories, Explanations and Comparisons," *Journal of Genocide Research* 13 (2011): 217–46; John-Paul Himka, "The Lviv Pogrom of 1941," 209–43, Kai Struve, "Rites of Violence? The Pogroms of Summer 1941," *Polin* 24 (2012): 257–74, Witold Mędykowski, *W cieniu gigantów. Pogromy 1941 r. w byłej sowieckiej strefie okupacyjnej. Kontekst historyczny, społeczny i kulturowy* (Warsaw: Instytut Studiów Politycznych Polskiej Akademii Nauk, 2012), Alexander V. Prusin, "A 'Zone of Violence': The Anti-Jewish Pogroms in Eastern Galicia in 1914–1915 and 1941," in *Shatterzone of Empires: Coexistence and Violence in the German, Habsburg, Russian, and Ottoman Borderlands*, ed. Omer Bartov and Eric D. Weitz (Bloomington: Indiana University Press, 2013), 362–77; Kai Struve, "Tremors in the Shatterzone of Empires: Eastern Galicia in Summer 1941," in *Shatterzone of Empires: Coexistence and Violence in the German, Habsburg, Russian, and Ottoman Borderlands*, ed. Omer Bartov and Eric D. Weitz (Bloomington: Indiana University Press, 2013), 463–84. The best and most detailed treatment is Kai Struve, "'Vergeltung' und Exzess. Gewalt gegen Juden während des Sommers 1941 in Ostgalizien," Habilitationsschrift, der Martin-Luther-Universität Halle-Wittenberg, 2013.

48. The photo is from the collection of David Lee Preston. For a Jewish woman's personal account of her experience in the Lontsky St. prison yard on 1 July 1941, see Vladimir Melamed, "Organized and Unsolicited Collaboration in the Holocaust: The Multifaceted Ukrainian Context," *East European Jewish Affairs* 37 (2007): 233.

49. USC Shoah Foundation Institute for Visual History and Education, interview with Leon Berk, 1339.

50. Kai Struve, "'Vergeltung' und Exzess," 411–20, Kai Struve,"Komanda osobogo naznacheniia 'L'vov,' ukrainskaia militsiia i 'Dni Petliury' 25 i 26 iuliia 1941 g," *Problemy istorii Holokostu* 6 (2013): 102–24.

51. On the OUN militia, see I. K. Patryliak, *Viis'kova diial'nist' OUN (B) u 1940–1942 rokakh* (Kyiv: Kyivs'kyi natsional'nyi universytet imeni Tarasa Shevchenka Instytut istorii Ukrainy NAN Ukrainy, 2004). David Alan Rich, "Armed Ukrainians in L'viv: Ukrainian Militia, Ukrainian Police, 1941 to 1942," *Canadian-American Slavic Studies* 48 (2014): 271–87.

52. John-Paul Himka, "The Lviv Pogrom of 1941," 219–21; Kai Struve, "'Vergeltung' und Exzess," 389–98.

53. Gabriel N. Finder and Alexander V. Prusin, "Collaboration in Eastern Galicia: The Ukrainian Police and the Holocaust," *East European Jewish Affairs* 34 (2004): 95–118.

54. I am grateful to Sergiy Kudelia, who sent me photos and an account of the exhibition on 7 February 2013. His father had visited it a few days earlier.

55. Meilakh Sheikhat, "Holokost: Den' pam"iati chy borot'by iz revizionizmom? (chastyna 1)," *iPress.ua*, 30 January 2013, http://ipress.ua/articles/yevrei_14851.html, and "Holokost: Den' pam"iati chy borot'by iz revizionizmom? (chastyna 2)," *iPress.ua*, 31 January 2013, http://ipress.ua/articles/golokost_den_pamyati_chy_borotby_iz_revizionizmom_chastyna_2_14909.html (accessed 25 March 2013).

56. See John-Paul Himka, "The Lviv Pogrom of 1941," 235.

57. Email of Larry Warwaruk to me, 14 November 2012.

58. The Embassy of Ukraine in Canada sent me scans of the first three pages of the Book of Facts.

59. "U Sluzhbi bezpeky Ukrainy vidbulys' Hromads'ki istorychni slukhannia." "Iak tvorylasia lehenda pro Nachtigall" (source of quotation). "Dokumenty SBU sprostovuiut' zvynuvachennia proty batal'iony 'Nakhtihal,'" press release of the Embassy of Ukraine in Canada, 22 March 2008.

60. Emphasis added.

61. Carynnyk, "Foes of Our Rebirth," 345 (discussion and translation of passage) and 346 (photoreproduction of the original document). The document is held in Tsentral'nyi derzhavnyi arkhiv vyshchykh orhaniv vlady ta upravlinnia Ukrainy, f. 3833, op. 1, spr. 43, 9.

62. John-Paul Himka, "Be Wary of Faulty Nachtigall Lessons," *Kyiv Post*, 27 March 2008, Dmitrii Rybakov, "Marko Tsarynnyk: Istorychna napivpravda hirsha za odvertu brekhniu," *LB.ua*, 5 November 2009, http://lb.ua/news/2009/11/05/13147_marko_tsarinnik_istorichna.html (accessed 6 April 2013). "Falsifying World War II History in Ukraine," *Kyiv Post*, 9 May 2011, http://www.kyivpost.com/news/opinion/op_ed/detail/103895/ (accessed 6 April 2013).

63. Marco Levytsky, "Ukrainian Nationalists Played No Part in Massacre of 4,000 Jews," *The Ukraine List (UKL)*, no. 441 (16 February 2010), item 3. Marco Levytsky, "Open Letter Villifies Freedom Fighters, Minimizes Holodomor", *Kyiv Post*, 6 May, 2011, http://www.kyivpost.com/opinion/op-ed/open-letter-villifies-freedom-fighters-minimizes-h-103827.html (accessed 6 April 2013). In the first of these pieces, Levytsky wrote: "Prior to the German invasion, the Soviet NKVD, in which Jews had disproportionate membership, was involved in the killing of 4,000 to 8,000 civilian prisoners. . . ." At the time of the NKVD murders, however, Jews were not particularly overrepresented in the NKVD.

64. Uilleam Blacker, "The Prison on Lonts'kyi Street."

65. Heidemarie Uhl, "Of Heroes and Victims: World War II and Austrian Memory," *Austrian History Yearbook* 42 (2011): 185–200.

66. Karel C. Berkhoff and Marco Carynnyk, "The Organization of Ukrainian Nationalists and Its Attitude toward Germans and Jews: Iaroslav Stets'ko's 1941 *Zhyttiepys*," *Harvard Ukrainian Studies* 23 (1999): 149–84.

67. Marco Carynnyk, "Foes of Our Rebirth," 332–35. Marco Carynnyk has written an evocative portrait of Klymiv as a nationalist fanatic and xenophobe. He even suggests that Klymiv may have been the link between the Germans and OUN in organizing the Lviv pogrom and other anti-Jewish violence in early July 1941. Marco Carynnyk, "'Jews, Poles, and Other Scum': Ruda Różaniecka, Monday, 30 June 1941," paper presented at the Fourth Annual Danyliw Research Seminar on Contemporary Ukrainian Studies, University of Ottawa, 23–25 October 2008, http://www.ukrainianstudies.uottawa.ca/pdf/P_Danyliw08_Carynnyk.pdf (accessed 6 April 2013).

68. For a country by country survey and two synthesizing and interpretive essays on these issues, see John-Paul Himka and Joanna Michlic, ed. *Bringing the Dark Past to Light: The Reception of the Holocaust in Post-Communist Europe* (Lincoln: University of Nebraska Press, 2013).

69. These included, among others, Tarik Cyril Amar, Omer Bartov, Karel Berkhoff, Jeffey Burds, Marco Carynnyk, Sofia Grachova, David Marples, Jared McBride, Joanna B. Michlic, Per Anders Rudling, and Timothy Snyder. Natalia A. Feduschak, "Harassment of Historian Raises Censorship Fears", *Kyiv Post*, 17 September 2010, http://www.kyivpost.com/content/ukraine/harassment-of-historian-raises-censorship-fears-82719.html (accessed 23 March 2013). Timothy Snyder, "Who's Afraid of Ukrainian History?," *NYR Blog*, 21 September 2010, http://www.nybooks.com/blogs/nyrblog/2010/sep/21/whos-afraid-ukrainian-history/ (accessed 8 April 2013). "Petition by Historians in Response to Detention of Their Colleague Ruslan Zabilyi"0, *Kyiv Post*, 15 September 2010, http://www.kyivpost.com/opinion/op-ed/petition-by-historians-in-response-to-detention-of-82471.html (accessed 23 March 2013).

70. Ukrainian Canadian Congress website, http://www.ucc.ca/about-ucc/leadership-1/executive-committee/ (accessed 8 April 2013).

71. The contemporary Ukrainian diaspora requires more study. Starting points for an orientation are: Vic Satzewich, *The Ukrainian Diaspora* (London and New York: Routledge, 2002) (now outdated). John-Paul Himka, "A Central European Diaspora under the Shadow of World War II: The Galician Ukrainians in North America," *Austrian History Yearbook* 37 (2006): 17–31. Per Anders Rudling, "Multiculturalism, Memory, and Ritualization: Ukrainian Nationalist Monuments in Edmonton, Alberta," *Nationalities Papers* 39 (2011): 733–68, and "Erratum," *Nationalities Papers* 39 (2011): 1031. A difference in interpretation between Rudling and this author is that Rudling sees more continuity in the present Banderite domination of the diaspora.

72. David Carment, "It's about Ethnic Votes, Not Church and State," *Globe and Mail*, 21 February 2013. Carment is Canadian Defence and Foreign Affairs fellow and editor of the *Canadian Foreign Policy Journal* at Carleton university. On the Harper government's subordination of foreign policy to ethnic voting blocs, see also Jeffrey Simpson, "This Commonwealth 'Principle' Is Naked Self-Interest," *Globe and Mail*, 9 October 2013.

73. Kristen Shane and Ally Foster, "The Top 80 Influencing Canadian Foreign Policy," *Embassy*, 6 March 2013 (updated 13 March 2013), http://www.embassynews.ca/top-80-influencers/2013/03/05/the-top-80-influencing-canadian-foreign-policy/43401 (accessed 25 March 2013).

74. John Ibbitson, "Stephen Harper Stresses Freedom in Ukraine", *Globe and Mail*, 25 October 2010, http://www.theglobeandmail.com/news/politics/stephen-harper-stresses-freedom-in-ukraine/article1381111/ (accessed 8 April 2010).

75. Andrew MacDougall (Press Secretary, Prime Minister's Office), email to author, 24 November 2010.

76. Taras Podilsky, "Honour to Visit Ukraine with PM", *Edmonton Journal*, 31 October 2010, http://www2.canada.com/edmontonjournal/news/letters/story.html?id= cfdc8ea9-7519-4708-aa79-9bbd42829f56 (accessed 8 April 2013).

77. Omer Bartov, "Conclusion," in *Bringing the Dark Past to Light: The Reception of the Holocaust in Post-Communist Europe*, ed. John-Paul Himka and Joanna Michlic (Lincoln: University of Nebraska Press, 2013), 690.

78. I had originally consulted O'Neil's article on the *Edmonton Journal* site on 5 November 2010: http://www.edmontonjournal.com/news/Ukrainian+museum+toured +Harper+show+sided+history+atrocities+critics/3785861/story.html. But the article has been removed from public access (it is standard practice for PostMedia to move most articles behind a paywall after three months). A copy is preserved on the Internet, however, on the website of Holocaust denier Will Zuzak, who presents it as an exhibit item of "Ukrainophobia" in the media. Peter O'Neil, "Ukrainian Museum Toured by Harper Shows 'One-Sided' History of Atrocities, Critics Say," http://www.telusplanet. net/public/mozuz/ukrainophobia/oneil20101105CanadaCom.html (accessed 26 March 2013); Zuzak took the article originally from *canada.com*, 5 November 2010, http:// www.canada.com/news/world/story.html?id=3785861.

79. Peter O'Neil, "My Role in a Dark Conspiracy," *ocanada.com*, 10 November 2010, http://o.canada.com/2010/11/10/my-role-in-a-dark-conspiracy/ (accessed 27 March 2013).

80. Askold S. Lozynskyj, "How Insensitive Bigots Continue to Play Ukrainians and Jews against Each Other," *Kyiv Post*, 8 November 2010, http://www.kyivpost.com/ opinion/op-ed/how-insensitive-bigots-continue-to-play-ukrainians-89252.html (accessed 26 March 2013).

81. Zabily was brought to North America by a consortium calling itself the Canadian Conference in Support of Ukraine. The group is completely Banderite, composed of the League of Ukrainian Canadians, its sister organization the League of Ukrainian Canadian Women, the youth association SUM, the Society of Veterans of UPA, and the Banderite newspaper *Homin Ukrainy/Ukrainian Echo*. orys Potapenko, "Ruslan Zabily Tours N. American Universities, Visits Ukrainian Communities, Meets with Government Leaders," *Ukrainian Vancouver*, 30 October 2012, http://ukrainianvancouver.com/ eng/?p=1255 (accessed 8 April 2010).

82. "PM Delivers Remarks to Election Ukraine Mission Canada," *Prime Minister of Canada Stephen Harper*, 19 October 2013, http://www.pm.gc.ca/eng/media.asp?id=5319 (accessed 8 April 2013). Potapenko, "Ruslan Zabily." On the slogan *Slava Ukraini*: "Following its second conference [April 1941], the OUN-B also employed the fascist salute of raising the right arm "slightly to the right, slightly above the peak of the head" while calling "Glory to Ukraine!" (*Slava Ukraini!*) and responding "Glory to the Heroes!"(*Heroiam Slava!*). Rossoliński-Liebe, "The 'Ukrainian National Revolution' of 1941," 89. The photo of the meeting originally appeared on the website of the Prime Minister's Office, but it is not there any longer.

83. "Poizdka Ruslana Zabiloho do Edmontonu ta Kalgar," *Homin Ukrainy*, 13 January 2013.

84. Website, http://www.lonckoho.lviv.ua/fotohalereya/imprezy-hosti/troj-lulash nyk-v-tyurmi-na-lontskoho-8-12-2011 (accessed 14 April 2013).

85. "Ministr bahatokul'turnosti Kanady vidviduie ukrains'ki mistsia pam'iati zlochyniv totalitaryzmu," website of the Center for Research of the Liberation Movement, 4 Maqrch 2013, http://www.cdvr.org.ua/content/міністр-багатокультурності-канади-відвідує-українські-місця-пам'яті-злочинів-тоталітаризму (accessed 25 March 2013).

86. This Association, which originated as an organization to defend Ukrainian Canadians accused of war crimes, celebrates OUN and has been spearheading a campaign against a permanent Holocaust exhibition in the as yet unopened Canadian Museum of Human Rights in Winnipeg. A. Dirk Moses, "The Canadian Museum for Human Rights: The "Uniqueness of the Holocaust' and the Question of Genocide," *Journal of Genocide Research* 14 (2012): 215–38. Karyn Ball and Per Anders Rudling "The

Underbelly of Canadian Multiculturalism: Holocaust Obfuscation and Envy in the Debate about Canadian Museum for Human Rights," *Holocaust Studies* 20 (2014): 33-80. See also Rhonda Spivak, "Does This Postcard Suggest Jews are Pigs?" *Winnipeg Jewish Review*, 13 April 2011, http://www.winnipegjewishreview.com/article_detail. cfm?id=987&sec=6&title=DOES_THIS_POSTCARD_SUGGEST_JEWS_ARE_PIGS_ HEAR_SOME_FEEDBACK,_AND_QUESTIONS_POSED_TO_THOSE_WHO_SENT_ IT_OUT (accessed 8 April 2013).

EIGHT

Writing History, Denying the Past

On Revisionism, the Holocaust, and Soviet Terror

Maria Karlsson

If the twentieth century has presented us with one still largely unchallenged lesson, it is this: Adolf Hitler was not a good man. In him, posterity has rather concentrated all the main evils of modernity: anti-semitism and racism, virulent nationalism, ruthless bureaucratic zeal, and senseless mass communication combined with rigorous censorship. And then, on top of it all, stands the Holocaust, as the utmost symbol of the barbarity that is said to have saturated both Hitler and his time. Naturally, this demonized image of Hitler has not been all-prevailing. In some scholarly works, such as Joachim Fest's or Ian Kershaw's well-known and read biographies, Adolf Hitler has been allowed to emerge as something other than the devil in disguise. However, the popular image or cultural representation of Hitler has remained rather one-dimensional.[1] Of further importance, the direct link between Hitler and the Holocaust has remained firmly in place. Not even the well-researched and convincingly argued functionalist interpretations of the Holocaust, arguing that Hitler's intentions alone could not have built the death camps nor executed the victims, completely remove Hitler from the equation.[2] His intentions, motives, and worldviews are downplayed, but they are never gone—and both Hitler and the consequences of his ideology still represent a hell on earth to many people.

Joseph Stalin, Hitler's once comrade in arms and subsequently mortal enemy, was not necessarily a much better man. Leading the Soviet Union through decades of terror and purges, Stalin's reign did—as much as the reign of his next door neighbor—help usher in and perpetuate the age of social, and humanitarian, catastrophe.[3] Regardless, Stalin's legacy has never been one of evil reincarnated. To a younger generation, lacking individual memories and experiences of both the Second World War and the Cold War crises, these two very different legacies are still viable. While we, for example, would name our children Joseph we would be much more hesitant to name them Adolf. And, in a less personal context, even a young cultural genre such as computer and video games replicate the difference. Hitler has, for example, assumed the role of the main antagonist in several more or less successful titles.[4] Stalin has, on the other hand, been used quite differently—or not at all—in accordance with the overall pattern.[5]

This differing cultural representation is mirrored in much of the professional historiography surrounding Hitler, the Holocaust, Stalin, and the Soviet terror as well. Historian Robert Thurston, for instance, referred to Stalin as a man "initializing and reacting to developments, not the cold mastermind of a plot to subdue the party and the nation" in his book *Life and Terror in Stalin's Russia* (1996).[6] This depiction of Stalin's intentions (there were none) and his relationship with the Soviet terror (coincidental) was completely in line with an influential revisionist, or functionalist, school of interpretation. On the other hand, when the today discredited Holocaust denier David Irving wrote a similar passage about Hitler in his 1977 book *Hitler's War*, he has been judged to be crossing over to denial, whitewashing, falsification, or obfuscation. What Irving had written was that "in wartime, dictatorships are fundamentally weak—the dictator himself, however alert, is unable to oversee all the functions of his executives acting within the confines of his far-flung empire."[7] In addition to this extremely functionalist interpretation, Irving argued that Hitler had never willed the Holocaust. That he was, in fact, actively attempting to stop any physical outbursts of anti-semitism whenever he was able to do so.[8] In a similar sense, and in line with the quote above, Thurston claimed that Stalin had been very cautious about the terror and the purges of the 1930s. If anything, he had acted as a voice of moderation during the years of the "great terror," and he had even declared, seemingly without effect, that "there was to be no witch hunt."[9]

Taken out of their respective historiographic contexts, both interpretations and quotes say essentially the same thing. Both tell of a dictator placed at the top of the state hierarchy but lacking in intention, power, influence, or control. To Thurston, Stalin was a weak leader, reacting to events simply out of convenience and chance, never possessing any grand plan of terror or societal transformation. To Irving, Hitler could be described along the same lines; Hitler had been a pragmatic politician, unfairly judged by both his Allied enemies and post-war historians. Yet, though Hitler and Stalin are described along the same lines, the reception of Thurston's and Irving's interpretations has been widely different. As already mentioned, Thurston's account of Stalin's lack of control, lack of intentions, and cautious and moderate approach has been more or less in line with a legitimate Western revisionist account of Soviet history. Though controversial in its origin phase, this revisionist school has become an integral part of Soviet historiography, responsible for what historian Sheila Fitzpatrick has characterized as a paradigm shift in Soviet historiography.[10] Thurston's work has, in turn, come to add to this corpus of revisionist work.[11] Describing Hitler along the same lines has, however, resulted in (often well-grounded) accusations of denial. While an "early" David Irving—Irving the empirical historian, Irving the archival enthusiast—received praise for his work, Irving post-*Hitler's War* quickly became "the most dangerous spokespersons for Holocaust denial," in the words of American historian Deborah Lipstadt.[12] Hence, the pattern repeats itself. Hitler was bad but Stalin less so, and what can be said about the latter can rarely be implied about the former. Why is this the case? What do we talk about when we talk about revisionism, and what are the fundamental differences and similarities between revising the past and denying it? In this chapter, both the similarities and the differences between a legitimate school of Soviet revisionism and an illegitimate school of Holocaust revisionists, or deniers, will be the central topic of discussion. Patterns of denial and revisionism will be presented and discussed, and it will eventually be argued that although we would like the professional writing of history to be completely separated from the less than scholarly activity that is denial, this is seldom the case. History and denial are rather separated by blurry gray zones, and revisionism are often caught somewhere in-between the two extremes.

"AN EXPLOSIVE BUT SIMPLE-MINDED COMPARISON"

We rarely discuss this dual nature of revisionism—being simultaneously the highest and the lowest form of historical research. Whether the topic is avoided out of established custom, ideological barriers, or out of fear of legitimizing denial, it has been equally potent whenever suggested. In particular, attempts to co-discuss Soviet style revisionism and Holocaust denialism have led to heated debate. To historian Michael David Fox, for instance, fellow historian Martin Malia's (repeated) attempts to compare Soviet revisionists and Holocaust deniers amounted to nothing more than an "explosive but simple-minded comparison."[13] To Fox, Malia's comparison is little more than an attack on revisionism in general, and an accusation toward Soviet revisionists in particular. Comparing Soviet revisionists to the already discredited Holocaust deniers is, he argued, nothing more than Malia's, and others' attempt to "demonize his intellectual opponents."[14] Other proponents of Soviet revisionism, such as Sheila Fitzpatrick, have likewise described attempts to compare (or equate) Soviet and Holocaust revisionisms as unfounded and ridiculous accusations meant only to downplay either the questions posed, or the results reached, by the revisionists of Soviet historiography.[15] Comparing and contrasting legitimate revisionism with illegitimate denial has, therefore, certainly been explosive—but not necessarily simple-minded. Comparisons have rarely brought about constructive discussion, and as a result we barely discuss the dual nature of revisionism, the boundaries of historical scholarship, and the two very different historiographic traditions born out of two of the twentieth century's major crimes against humanity. This chapter will argue that the discussions and the comparisons between differently valued revisionisms *are* important, if given the chance.

The relevance of a topic can, in any case, not be rejected on terms of it being controversial. Most divisive topics are, in fact, especially rewarding and relevant from a scholarly point of view. That being said, Fox raises a good point. Simply asserting that the revisionists are to Sovietology what Holocaust deniers are to the study of Nazi Germany is both trivializing and simple-minded. Equating the two is, however, not the point of this chapter. It will therefore not be argued that Soviet revisionism is the same thing as the Holocaust ditto. The purpose of Soviet revisionists seems never to have been the wish to completely exonerate Stalin in the same sense as the motive behind much Holocaust denial has been the wish to reinstate Hitler. Nonetheless, this seems precisely to have become an unintended consequence in instances where legitimate revisionism and denial has maintained the same things, and advocated very similar interpretations of the Soviet Union and Nazi Germany.

Furthermore, as has been suggested by Fox and many others, both kinds of revisionism need to be put in context. Fox suggests the Cold War and its ensuing fear, competition, and ideological divides as a relevant context to explain Soviet revisionism through.[16] To be fair, however, another relevant context of Soviet historiography is its comparison with the simultaneous historiography of the Holocaust and Nazi Germany—two historiographies that, so far, have been kept incomprehensively separate. How historians have approached the two major dictatorships of Europe's twentieth century warrants comparison. If nothing else, placing one next to the other might help us see the different logics, rules, and conventions of both historiographic traditions.

WRITING HISTORY? DENYING THE PAST?

Revisionism has, in the context of the Holocaust, come to mean an illegitimate revising of the past, signaling a number of different activities often subsumed under the general heading of "denial." Hence, while revisionism and functionalism has referred to more or less the similar interpretations within Soviet historiography they have been completely separate enterprises within Holocaust historiography. Questioning Stalin's role in the terror and repression of the Soviet 1930s and onwards has, hence, been a matter of legitimate scholarship. As a consequence, any critique of Thurston's approach has mainly concerned whether his interpretation makes for good or bad historical research. That being said, even bad historical research is historical research. Few would contemplate critiquing Thurston, or others advocating his views, for outright falsification or abuse of history, and, consequently, criticism of Soviet revisionism has been a matter of quality (historical research done well or badly)—not essence (legitimate historical research or pseudohistorical denial). Questioning Hitler's role in the history of the Holocaust has, on the other hand, resulted in (and warranted) a far-reaching consensus that what Irving had written about Hitler was not simply bad historical research—it was in essence not historical research at all. What Irving had done, it was concluded, was to engage in denial, non-history, pseudo-history, and outright falsification of both history and the "truth."[17] The result has been a Holocaust historiography where "revisionist" has become an invective, a word of abuse, and not even those actually revising past interpretations of the Nazi genocide are entirely comfortable calling themselves revisionists. In this sense, revisionism has come to mean very different things to scholars of Soviet terror and scholars of the Holocaust. While it represents run-of-the-mill historical research to most of the former, it represents the absolute opposite—namely falsification and denial—to the latter.

In light of the similar content, but dissimilar reception and status, of Thurston's and Irving's respective views on Stalin and Hitler, and both dictators' relationship to genocide and terror, it is necessary to talk about the different definitions of revisionism and about the boundaries of historical scholarship. It is often advocated that denial (or whichever term is used to describe the phenomenon of silencing or rewriting the past solely according to concerns of the present, and in complete opposition to both source material and the scholarly community at large) is everything that the professional writing of history is not. As a general rule (and often as a result of moral or political considerations), denial is treated as heresy and as the complete antithesis to history proper. Described as a "rape of history," "an assault on truth and memory," or as a case of pseudo-history, genocide denial is often understood and explained as an epistemological "other," and when approaching it most scholars tend to resort back to the secure grounds of objectivity and truth.[18] Historians are right, it has been concluded, and deniers are wrong. Yet, the picture is often far more dim and nuanced in practice, and denial rarely fits our preconceived notion of being something completely separated from, and something essentially "other" to professional historiography. Michael David Fox has, for instance, noted that one basic difference between revisionism and denial lies in the difference between omission and falsification, that is, between history done badly and pseudo-history. Revisionists can, he concludes, at most be accused of omitting certain parts of the past in ways that are not always excusable, but deniers on the other hand fabricate, falsify, and manipulate on a daily basis.[19] In practice, however, modern Holocaust denial could be accused as much for omission as for falsification as most refined and "soft" Holocaust denial simply willfully and consciously omits what does not fit, and whitewashes whatever is too spectacular. In this sense, the divide is solely theoretical.

Overall, the blurry lines between omission and falsification seem to repeat themselves in many other cases where revisionism faces denialism. Further examples will be presented below, but it should be noted already that denial seems to be separated from professional historiography not by a steep and final divide, but by a scholarly no-man's-land and by gray areas seldom explored or studied. Comparing and contrasting the historiographies of the Holocaust and Soviet terror in particular, highlights many possible gray zones, and the innately ambiguous notion of revisionism is continuously in the spotlight.

WHAT DO WE TALK ABOUT WHEN WE TALK ABOUT REVISIONISM?

Comparing the historiography—its traditions and conventions—of the Soviet Union and Nazi Germany means having to acknowledge "revisionism" as a central focal point. Not simply the term and what it means, but also how it is used and signified as either neutral or invective. There is, however, no escaping "revisionism" and its inherently dual nature.[20]

It can be exemplified further through the very description and self-image of both Soviet revisionists and Holocaust "revisionists." During the fall of 2008, *Slavic Review* sported a number where the self-entitled revisionists of Soviet historiography recounted for their experiences and results over the past few decades. Sheila Fitzpatrick, being one of the most prominent historians and revisionists of Soviet history, wrote a personal account of her role in, and experiences of, the development of Soviet revisionism. Her article deals primarily with the hardships of being a revisionist historian, of the divides within the revisionist group, how she accused others of having ideological blinkers, and how her version of revisionism had included a "commitment both to iconoclasm and 'so-called objective scholarship,'" meaning "not skewing [the] data for political or ideological reasons."[21] Her article does, however, end on a high note as she accounts for the successes of her and her colleagues in what she entitles the "great age of revisionism in Soviet history."[22]

In a deceptively similar case, French Holocaust denier Robert Faurisson has written about his "revisionist method" in the *Journal of Historical*

Review, a California-based journal solely dedicated to publishing Holocaust denial under the guise of legitimate scholarship. Faurisson states, among a number of other things, that "[r]evisionism is not an ideology [. . .], [it] is a method of working."[23] Completely removed from their contexts, Fitzpatrick's and Faurisson's statements about revisionism read as misleadingly similar. They both claim revisionism to be a matter of standing up against an ideologically drenched orthodox historiographical tradition, in Fitzpatrick's case referring to the ideological divides of the Cold War, and in Faurisson's to those originating from the Second World War. Both furthermore emphasize how their revisionism is all but ideologically grounded. In fact, they both in some sense claim to stand above (and beyond) such petty concerns as ideology. In an interesting twist, both explain how their alleged omissions of the larger context and their interest in specific details can be explained by the very nature of revisionism. Fitzpatrick writes, for example, that revisionism always seems to deal with parts rather than the whole because "this is basically a subversive, iconoclastic genre rather than a monumental one."[24] Nonetheless, we react completely different to the two descriptions and assessments of revisionism. While we instinctively place Fitzpatrick's embrace of revisionism within a scholarly context, we simultaneously reject Faurisson's ditto as pseudo-history.

PATTERNS OF DENIAL AND REVISIONISM

What are, then, the main similarities and differences between legitimate revisionism of Soviet history and its illegitimate Holocaust-centered lookalike? This chapter will present a few of these as "patterns" of denial, or revisionism, but it is in no way an exhaustive account. Firstly, it should be noted and highlighted that the foremost difference between revisionism and denial seems to lie in Holocaust and genocide deniers' use of absolute, or hard, denial. Many (or most) Holocaust "revisionists" tend to claim that there simply was no genocide whatsoever. No gas chambers, no concentration camps, no victims, and certainly no perpetrators—in every aspect effectively negating the reality of the genocide. Among legitimate revisionists, within any field of study, there is no equivalent of this. Hence, while deniers question, or assert, that there was a genocide, terror, or mass murder, revisionists rather tend to focus on revising what happened—but not whether or not it did happen—how it happened, as well as who (or what) can be held responsible for the atrocities.

Nonetheless, there are still several similarities to be highlighted. Returning to Thurston and Irving, and to their respective interpretations of Stalin and Hitler, it ought to be clear that one of these important patterns concerns issues of intentionality and control. To both Thurston and Irving, Stalin and Hitler were weak leaders, reacting rather than acting, possessing no preconceived plans of terror and genocide. Both argue, in this sense, in favor of an extreme functionalist point of view, where structure holds sway over agency. However, both also argue effectively against an intentionalist perspective. Not only are Nazi and Soviet terror societal phenomena built on and maintained by different structures, but they also lack any intentional roots. The question of intention, being one of the cornerstones of the United Nations' definition of genocide, has been a fundamental issue within both Holocaust and Soviet studies over the years, and both legitimate revisionists and deniers have devoted much attention to either questioning or denying it. Both Thurston and Irving, furthermore, exemplify different strategies of questioning the issue of intent. The first of these strategies attempts to disqualify the notion of an intent to mass murder by salvaging individual agents and their historical reputation. Irving performed, for instance, a valiant effort directed at convincing his readers that Hitler, for quite some time, was simply unaware of the Holocaust. According to Irving, the true mastermind behind the Holocaust policies was rather Himmler. In a similar sense, Thurston argued in his *Life and Terror in Stalin's Russia* that Stalin had entertained no intentions at all, that his political decisions simply came about as random reactions to different and uncontrollable events and situations. He argued, as mentioned, that Stalin was a voice of moderation concerning the purges. The man responsible and in charge of the terror was, rather, Ezhov. As a second strategy of questioning intentionality, Holocaust deniers usually maintain that Hitler opted for expulsion rather than extermination, in essence arguing that there was an intention of some sort, but that it was far more benevolent than is shown by its unfortunate consequences. In a similar, albeit slightly softer version, Thurston argues in his book that Stalin, in fact, really was afraid of real or imagined "enemies of the people," and had aimed only to protect himself and his people. The end result was, therefore, disproportionate when considering Stalin's original intention.

Beside the issues of intentionality, arguments aiming toward or unintentionally touching upon rationalization and legitimization—claiming, for example, terror and genocide to be inevitable or necessary—have been voiced by revisionists and deniers alike. Common among Holocaust deniers is the notion that the Jews of Germany and Eastern Europe were, contrary to all known facts, conspiring and organizing underground resistance against the Nazi regime. The conclusion being that these revolutionary actions had required the Nazi leaders to react forcefully against a Jewish fifth column.[25] In a rare but similar case, historian Eric Hobsbawm has noted that "any policy of rapid modernization in the USSR, under the circumstances of the time, was bound to be ruthless,"[26] in effect arguing that the Soviet terror and mass atrocities were an inevitable result of societal change, rationalized as a means of attaining a greater good.

Although it does not seem to have been the revisionist intention, some scholars of the Soviet state have additionally steered close to trivializing the Soviet terror in a manner that closely resembles that of deniers of the Holocaust. Questioning numbers and death tolls is, for example, common among deniers. Presenting long and intricate discussions on the number of victims, Holocaust deniers often aim at either downplaying the scope and severity of the Holocaust, or simply claim that the Nazi extermination of the Jews as a whole was a statistical and logistical impossibility. The effect is similar when some Soviet revisionists have presented severely lowered numbers of victims. Historian John Arch Getty noted, for instance, in his book on the purges that the total death toll of the terror amounted to "thousands," and the number of people imprisoned to "several thousand."[27] Here too, the intentions of revisionists and deniers may differ, but the structure and consequences of many of the arguments are similar, effectively highlighting this elusive gray area separating the writing of history from the denial of the past.

On the hunt for the gray areas separating legitimate from illegitimate, proper from pseudo, the 1970s further presents itself as a central crossing point and watershed. At that moment, both revisionists of Soviet history and a new, increasingly refined, generation of Holocaust deniers emerge. During the 1970s, Soviet revisionism truly appeared as an alternative to the, in many ways Cold War-influenced, totalitarian interpretation of Soviet history. Soviet historiography changed as a result of this development, and came from here and onward to present two largely separate histories of the Soviet Union in general, and the road to terror in particular. Almost simultaneously, the genre of Holocaust and genocide denial seems to have changed as well. Previous denial, especially of the Holocaust, had been almost exclusively polemic and unrefined, concentrated only on content and never on form. The result had been crudely written pamphlet-like texts, reminiscent of anti-semitic propaganda rather than scholarly essays. From the 1970s and onward, however, many Holocaust deniers seem to have become aware of the fact that looks matter. Deniers began to publish their writings in a form that would attempt to make it indistinguishable from proper scholarly literature, including hard covers, tables of content, a scholarly looking disposition, criticism of previous denialist literature, and massive amounts of footnotes.[28] Holocaust and genocide denial was, hence, "professionalized" as Soviet history was revised.

These developments, whether seen as completely separate processes or as part of a larger political, societal, or scholarly shift, dovetailed with broader historical and historiographical changes during a tumultuous decade. Interest in the Holocaust continually increased, especially following the end of the decade and the influential broadcasting of the television mini-series *Holocaust*, in part forcing Holocausts deniers to change their tactics. Meanwhile, issues of human rights rose to the top of the political agenda and the principles of social history were placed at the forefront of Western historiography. Therefore, whatever the causal link between the emergence of Soviet revisionism and the new type of Holocaust denial, there are not only similarities in argumentative patterns and structures between revisionist historical writing and denial—but a chronological affinity as well.

CONCLUSIONS

What does, in the end, these sometimes superficial and sometimes fundamental similarities—and the different ways in which they have been received by academia—suggest about the relationships between denial, revisionism, history, and the historiographic traditions of the Holocaust and Soviet terror? Before attempting to answer that question, a few words need to be devoted to what has been emphasized so far. This chapter has, namely, attempted to show that comparing and contrasting Holocaust denial and Soviet revisionism is more than what Michael David Fox referred to as an "explosive but simple-minded comparison." Without attempting to claim that legitimate revisionists equal deniers, or vice versa, it seems clear that there are similarities that cannot be adequately explained by the common idea that denial and historical research are two completely separate activities. In fact, both denial and revisionism are activities that are much more complex than they appear at first glance. History is not simply "the truth about the past," and denial is not always as easy as "lying about the past."[29] Rather, both denialism and revisionism have areas, methods, and objectives in common, perhaps an uncomfortable truth about history as a scholarly discipline but nonetheless an important one. A much more appealing notion describing the relationship between history and denial is that of gray zones, separating denial from history. In addition, it ought to be stressed that these zones appear to be anything but absolute and fixed. Just as time changes how we may interpret past events, it seems clear that what can be said within one field of historical research clearly cannot be said within another. As a result, the truly central question of this chapter is naturally: Why can we pose questions and draw conclusions about Soviet history, when the same questions and conclusions are viewed as either irrelevant, borderline denial or as outright dangerous when uttered within Holocaust historiography?

A first concluding remark has to deal with the often mentioned but seldom studied phenomenon of historical and genocide denial. As much as the professional writing of history has conventions, practices, rules, and regulations, historical and genocide denial seems to have specific demands and practices of its own. Denial, therefore, is more than the historian's equivalent of malpractice, a phenomenon that goes deeper than questions of translations, sources, and footnotes.[30] To some scholars, genocide denial has been characterized as a specific genre, in some cases similar to and in other cases different from the genre of professional historiography.[31] It seems clear that regardless of which genocide or mass murder is being denied, most instances of denial seem to share many common characteristics, strategies, and objectives. Though an intriguing notion, the basic epistemological question still remains: why would one genre's story about the past be more valid or truthful than the other? That is, naturally, *the* million-dollar-question of modern historiography, but it would be tempting to suggest that how we react to and judge Soviet revisionism and Holocaust denial has less to do with what or how revisionists and deniers write, and more to do with what they write about.

Therefore, the reason why we tend to regard David Irving's interpretations of Hitler as disconnected from the Holocaust and as a man who did good in Nazi Germany as both an absurd notion and a matter of pseudo-history has less to do with the past than with the present. And in the present, there is a fundamental difference between Holocaust and Soviet historiography. As the opposite of denial can be, and has been, interpreted as "telling the truth," there has to be a number of agreed-upon truths within a field of study in order for them to be denied. Holocaust historiography has, on one hand, been full of these agreed-upon truths. For example, and this is where this chapter comes full circle, the notion that Hitler has no redeeming qualities, or that he was a bad man, has (with good reason) come to be a basic "truth" advocated by any Holocaust scholar. Similarly, scholars of the Holocaust—whether intentionalist or functionalist in their approach—all argue that whether or not it was Hitler's will and intention that kept the genocidal wheels spinning during the 1940s, Hitler still had an intention to eradicate the Jews one way or another—and that intention was morally wrong. The scholars that have dealt with Soviet history and terror, on the other hand, have as it would seem settled upon much fewer basic "truths" about their object of study. Hence, it is still possible to question not just what Stalin's intention was and what role it played, but whether or not he had an intention at all. The basis for these different historiographical traditions lies, and this is the second point, at least partly in the fact that the moral implications of Nazism, and later the Holocaust as a separate entity, were settled more or less directly after the Second World War. The moral implications of Communism, both in its Soviet incarnation and in others, have been much less clear-cut and readily agreed upon, far more debated among legitimate scholars, and remain ideologically relevant.

NOTES

1. See, for example, the preface to *Unmasking Hitler: Cultural Representations of Hitler from the Weimar. Republic to the Present*, ed. Klaus L. Berghahn and Jost Hermand (Bern: Peter Lang, 2005).

2. In Raul Hilberg's groundbreaking study on the destruction of the European Jews, Hitler is for example placed in a larger context, but rarely removed from the equation entirely. See Raul Hilberg, *The Destruction of the European Jews* (Quadrangle Books: Chicago, 1961). For a more comprehensive discussion on the historiography of the ties between Hitler and the Holocaust see, for instance, Jeremy Noakes, "Hitler and the Third Reich," in *The Historiography of the Holocaust*, ed. Dan Stone (Palgrave Macmillan: Houndmills, 2004).

3. Paraphrasing Robert Gellately's *Lenin, Stalin and Hitler: The Age of Social Catastrophe* (New York: Alfred A. Knopf, 2007).

4. Besides a number of games centered on the history of the Second World War Hitler has appeared, for example, as the "final boss" in an armored body suit in *Wolfenstein 3D* (1992), and was resurrected in the original Japanese version of the game *Bionic Commando* (1988).

5. In comparison, Stalin has seldom appeared as the main antagonist. In some early computer games, such as *Sid Meier's Civilization*, Stalin has even been granted the status of playable character.

6. Robert W. Thurston, *Life and Terror in Stalin's Russia, 1934–1941* (New Haven: Cambridge University Press, 1996), 17.

7. David Irving, *Hitler's War* (London and Sydney: Hodder & Stoughton, 1977), xiii.

8. Irving, *Hitler's War*, 718.

9. Thurston, *Life and Terror*, 44.

10. Sheila Fitzpatrick, "Revisionism in Soviet History," *History and Theory* 36 (2007).

11. Though at times extreme in stressing the terror's lack of planning and central control, Thurston has rarely been argued to be especially radical in his interpretations. See, for example, J. Arch Getty, "'Excesses are not permitted': Mass Terror and Stalinist Governance in the Late 1930s," *The Russian Review* 61 (2002): 114, who, together with his own, Roberta T. Manning's and Robert Weinberg's work, presents Thurston's book as a representative example of Soviet school revisionism.

12. Deborah Lipstadt, *Denying the Holocaust: The Growing Assault on Truth and Memory* (New York and Toronto: The Free Press, 1993), 181.

13. For Martin Malia's comparative article, see "Judging Nazism and Communism," *The National Interest*, 2002. For the debate in *Kritika*—to which editorial staff Michael David-Fox belongs—see, primarily, "From the Editors: Really-Existing Revisionism?" *Kritika: Explorations in Russian and Eurasian History* 2 (2001): 229–32, Martin Malia, "To the Editors," *Kritika: Explorations in Russian and Eurasian History* 3 (2002): 569–71, Michael David-Fox, "On the Primacy of Ideology: Soviet Revisionists and Holocaust Deniers (In Response to Martin Malia)," *Kritika: Explorations in Russian and Eurasian History* 5 (2004): 85–105.

14. David-Fox, "On the Primacy of Ideology," 85.

15. Sheila Fitzpatrick, "Revisionism in Retrospect: A Personal View," *Slavic Review* 67 (2008): 693–94.

16. David-Fox, "On the Primacy of Ideology."

17. A common view voiced in, for example Richard J. Evans's *Telling Lies About Hitler: The Holocaust, History and the David Irving Trial* (London and New York: Verso, 2002), Lipstadt, *Denying the Holocaust*; Michael Shermer and Alex Grobman, *Denying History: Who Says the Holocaust Never Happened and Why Do They Say It?* (Berkeley and Los Angeles: University of California Press, 2000), Kenneth Stern, *Holocaust Denial* (New York: The American Jewish Committee, 1993).

18. Note, as one example among many, the subtitle of Deborah Lipstadt's book: "An Assault on *Truth* and Memory" (my italics).

19. David-Fox 2004, "On the Primacy of Ideology," 89–90.

20. A duality that has, seemingly, spread to fields of study further away as well. See historian Evi Gkotzaridis' interesting article "Revisionism in the Twentieth Century: A Bankrupt Concept or Permanent Practice?" *The European Legacy: Toward New Paradigms* 13 (2008): 725–41. Gkotzaridis wrote the article as her conference entry had been refused by a professor at the European University Institute in Florence. The entry was refused with the motivation that her mere mention of the term "revisionism" aided the Holocaust deniers' cause, and the professor in question maintained that the term should be avoided altogether. Gkotzaridis' text had been about Irish historiography, both literally and figuratively miles from Nazi Germany or the Holocaust.

21. Fitzpatrick, "Revisionism in Retrospect," 690.

22. Fitzpatrick, "Revisionism in Retrospect," 704.

23. Robert Faurisson, "My Revisionist Method," *The Journal of Historical Review* 21 (2002): 7–34.

24. Fitzpatrick, "Revisionism in Retrospect," 703.

25. Richard Harwood, pseudonym for Richard Verall, wrote, for example, in the pamphlet *Did Six Million Really Die? The Truth at Last* (Historical Review Press, 1974) that "[i]t is widely known that world Jewry declared itself to be a belligerent part in the Second World War, and there was therefore ample basis under international law for the Germans to intern the Jewish population as a hostile force." The Nazi actions against the Jews were, therefore, validated and necessary—according to much denialist literature.

26. Eric Hobsbawm, *The Age of Extremes: The Short Twentieth Century 1914–1991* (London: Michael Joseph, 1994): 380–81.

27. J. Arch Getty, *Origins of the Purges: The Soviet Communist Party Reconsidered, 1933–1938* (Cambridge and London: Cambridge University Press, 1985), 8.

28. For further discussion see Lipstadt, *Denying the Holocaust*, chapter 7, 8. The change in both style and form is clearly exemplified in the comparison of different denialist writings from the mid-1970s: Richard Harwood's aforementioned *Did Six Million Really Die?* from 1974 remains crude, badly written, and propagandistic, but Arthur Butz's *The Hoax of the Twentieth Century* from 1976 features, on the other hand, all the stylistic elements we expect to find in an academic text—despite the still unsophisticated title of his book.

29. As suggested by, for example, the main title of Evans' *Telling Lies about Hitler* (2002), and echoed in several other works on Holocaust, and genocide, denial.

30. Insightfully discussed in D. D. Guttenplan's *The Holocaust on Trial: History, Justice and the David Irving Libel Case* (London: Granta, 2002), 15.

31. As suggested in, for example, Robert Eaglestone's brief *Postmodernism and Holocaust Denial* (Cambridge: Icon Books, 2001).

Bibliography

Adler, Herbert M., and Van Buren O. Hammett. "Crisis, Conversion, and Cult Forma-tion: An Examination of a Common Psychosocial Sequence," *American Journal of Psychiatry* 130 (1973): 861–64.

Adler, Nanci. "The Future of the Soviet Past Remains Unpredictable: The Resurrection of Stalinist Symbols Amidst the Exhumation of Mass Graves." *Europe-Asia Studies* 57 (2005): 1093–119.

Adler, Nanci. *The Gulag Survivor: Beyond the Soviet System.* New Brunswick and Lon-don: Transaction Publishers, 2002.

Adler, Nanci. *Keeping Faith with the Party: Communist Believers Return from the Gulag.* Bloomington: Indiana University Press, 2012.

Adler, Nanci, Selma Leydesdorff, Mary Chamberlain, and Leyla Neyzi, eds. *Memories of Mass Repression: Narrating Life Stories in the Aftermath of Atrocity.* New Brunswick and London: Transaction Publishers, 2009.

Albrecht, Gerd. *Nationalsozialistische Filmpolitik.* Stuttgart: Enke, 1969.

Aly, Götz. *Hitler's Beneficiaries: Plunder, Racial War, and the Nazi Welfare State.* New York: Metropolitan Books, 2006.

Applebaum, Anne. *Gulag: A History.* New York: Anchor Books, 2003.

Arendt, Hannah. *The Origins of Totalitarianism.* New York: Harvest, 1979.

Assmann, Aleida. *Erinnerungsräume. Formen und Wandlungen des kulturellen Gedächtnisses.* Munich: C. H. Beck, 1999.

Assmann, Aleida, and Friese Heidrun, eds. *Identitäten, Erinnerung, Geschichte.* Frank-furt am Main: Suhrkamp Verlag, 1998.

Assmann, Aleida, and Ute Frevert. *Geschichtsvergessenheit—Geschichtsversessenheit. Vom Umgang mit deutschen Vergangenheiten nach 1945.* Stuttgart: Deutsche Verlagsanstalt, 1999.

Assmann, Jan. "Collective Memory and Cultural Identity." *New German Critique* 65 (1995): 125–33.

Assmann, Jan. *Das kulturelle Gedächtnis. Schrift, Erinnerung und politische Identität in frühen Hochkulturen.* Munich: C. H. Beck, 1992.

Augstein, Rudolf, ed. *"Historikerstreit": Die Dokumentation der Kontroverse um die Einzi-gartigkeit der nationalsozialistischen Judenvernichtung.* Munich: Piper, 1987.

Baberowski, Jörg, and Anselm Doering-Manteuffel. "The Quest for Order and the Pursuit of Terror: National Socialist Germany and the Stalinist Soviet Union as Multiethnic Empires." In *Beyond Totalitarianism: Stalinism and Nazism Compared,* ed-ited by Michael Geyer and Sheila Fitzpatrick, 180–230. Cambridge: Cambridge Uni-versity Press, 2009.

Baird, Jay W. *To Die for Germany. Heroes in the Nazi Pantheon.* London: Routledge, 1990.

Barner-Barry, Carol, and Cynthia Hody. "Soviet Marxism-Leninism as Mythology." *Political Psychology* 15 (1994): 609–30.

Bartov, Omer. "Conclusion." In *Bringing the Dark Past to Light: The Reception of the Holocaust in Post-Communist Europe,* edited by John-Paul Himka and Joanna Michlic, 663–93. Lincoln: University of Nebraska Press, 2013.

Bartov, Omer. *Erased: Vanishing Traces of Jewish Galicia in Present-Day Ukraine.* Prince-ton and Oxford: Princeton University Press, 2007.

Bartov, Omer. Review of *Europe between Hitler and Stalin,* by Timothy Snyder. *Slavic Review* 70 (2011): 424–28.

Bauer, Yehuda. *Rethinking the Holocaust.* New Haven: Yale University Press, 2001.

Bechtel, Delphine. "De Jedwabne à Zolotchiv: Pogromes locaux en Galicie, juin-juillet 1941." *Cultures d'Europe Centrale* 5 (2005): 69–92.

Behrenbeck, Sabine. *Der Kult um die toten Helden. Nationalsozialistische Mythen, Riten, und Symbole 1923 bis 1945.* Vierow bei Greifswald: SH-Verlag, 1996.

Bemporad, Elisabeth. "Empowerment, Defiance, and Demise: Jews and the Blood Libel Specter under Stalinism." *Jewish History* 26 (2012): 343–61.

de Benoist, Alain. "Nazism and Communism: Evil Twins?" *Telos* 112 (1998): 178–92.

Bensaid, Daniel, and Håkan Blomqvist. *Lenin: Massmördare?* Stockholm: Moteld, 1999.

Berghahn, Klaus L., and Jost Hermand. "Preface." In *Unmasking Hitler: Cultural Representations of Hitler from the Weimar. Republic to the Present,* edited by Klaus L. Berghahn and Jost Hermand. Bern: Peter Lang, 2005.

Berkelaar, Wim. Review of *Stalinism and Nazism. Dictatorships in Comparison,* by Ian Kershaw and Moshe Lewin. *International Review of Social History* 44 (1999): 301–24.

Berkhoff, Karel C., and Marco Carynnyk. "The Organization of Ukrainian Nationalists and Its Attitude toward Germans and Jews: Iaroslav Stets'ko's 1941 *Zhyttiepys.*" *Harvard Ukrainian Studies* 23 (1999): 149–84.

Berlin, Isaiah. *Two Concepts of Liberty: An Inaugural Lecture, Delivered Before the University of Oxford on 31 October 1958.* Oxford: Clarendon Press, 1958.

Berry, Damon T. "Blood on the Tongue: Reading Abjection in Nationalist Blood Libels From Nazi Germany to Hamas and the British National Party." *Journal of Hate Studies* 10 (2012): 99–122.

Besançon, Alain. *A Century of Horrors: Communism, Nazism, and the Uniqueness of the Shoah.* Wilmington: ISI Books, 2007.

Blackbourn, David, and Geoff Eley. *The Pecularities of German History: Bourgeois Society and Politics in Nineteenth-Century Germany.* Oxford: Oxford University Press, 1984.

Blacker, Uilleam. "The Prison on Lonts'kyi Street: Memory Dialogue or Memory Monologue?" *Current Politics in Ukraine,* 4 January 2013, http://ukraineanalysis. wordpress.com/2013/01/04/the-prison-on-lontskyi-street-memory-dialogue-or-memory-monologue. Accessed 23 March 2013.

Blaive, Muriel. "The Memory of the Holocaust and of Communist Repression in a Comparative Perspective: The Cases of Hungary, Poland and Czechoslovakia/the Czech Republic." In *Clashes in European Memory: The Case of Communist Repression and the Holocaust,* edited by Muriel Blaive, Christian Gerbel, and Thomas Lindenberger, 154–72. Innsbruck, Wien and Bozen: Studien Verlag, 2011.

Blaive, Muriel, Christian Gerbel and Thomas Lindenberger, eds. *Clashes in European Memory: The Case of Communist Repression and the Holocaust.* Innsbruck: Studien Verlag, 2011.

Blomqvist, Håkan. "Forum för statlig propaganda" *Aftonbladet,* April 2, 2008.

Bobrenev, Vladimir. *Za otsutstviem sostava prestuplenia.* Moscow: Olimp, 1998.

Bock, Gisela. "Ein Historikerinnenstreit." *Geschichte und Gesellschaft* 18 (1992): 400–404.

Boll, Bernd. "Złoczów. July 1941: The Wehrmacht and the Beginning of the Holocaust in Galicia: From a Criticism of Photographs to a Revision of the Past." In *Crimes of War: Guilt and Denial in the Twentieth Century,* edited by Omer Bartov, Atina Grossmann, and Mary Nolan, 61–99. New York: The New Press, 2002.

von Borries, Bodo. *Geschichtsbewußtsein im interkulturellen Vergleich. Zwei empirische Pilotstudien.* Pfaffenweiler: Centaurus, 1994.

von Borries, Bodo, Hans-Jürgen Pandel, and Jörn Rüsen, eds. *Geschichtsbewußtsein empirisch.* Pfaffenweiler: Centaurus, 1991.

Boym, Svetlana. *Common Places: Mythologies of Everyday Life in Russia.* Cambridge, MA: Harvard University Press, 1994.

Bracher, Karl Dietrich. *The Age of Ideologies: A History of Political Thought in the Twentieth Century.* London: Weidenfeld and Nicolson, 1984.

Brandenberger, David. *National Bolshevism: Stalinist Mass Culture and the Formation of National Identity, 1931–1956.* Cambridge, MA: Harvard University Press, 2002.

Brent, Jonathan. *Inside the Stalin Archives: Discovering the New Russia.* New York: Atlas & Co., 2008.

Brown, Archie. *The Rise and Fall of Communism*. London: The Bodley Head, 2009.

Brown, Kate. *A Biography of No Place: From Ethnic Borderland to Soviet Heartland*. Cambridge, MA and London: Harvard University Press, 2003.

Browning, Christopher, and Lewis Siegelbaum. "Frameworks for Social Engineering: Stalinist Schema of Identification and the Nazi *Volksgemeinschaft*." In *Beyond Totalitarianism: Stalinism and Nazism Compared*, edited by Michael Geyer and Sheila Fitzpatrick, 231–65. Cambridge: Cambridge University Press, 2009.

Brzezinski, Zbigniew. *The Permanent Purge: Politics in Soviet Totalitarianism*. Cambridge, MA: Harvard University Press, 1956.

Buber-Neumann, Margarete. *Under Two Dictators: Prisoner of Stalin and Hitler*. London: Victor Gollancz, 1949.

Bullock, Alan. *Hitler and Stalin: Parallel Lives*. London: Fontana, 1993.

Burleigh, Michael. "National Socialism as a Political Religion." *Totalitarian Movements and Political Religions* 1 (2000): 1–26.

Burleigh, Michael. *Sacred Causes: The Clash of Religion and Politics, from the Great War to the War on Terror*. New York: HarperCollins, 2007.

Cantorovich, Irena. "Honoring the Collaborators—The Ukrainian Case," *Kantor Program* Papers, June 2012. http://www.kantorcenter.tau.ac.il/sites/default/files/ukraine-collaborators_4.pdf. Accessed 29 April 2013.

Caplan, Jane. "The Historiography of National Socialism." In *Companion to Historiography*, edited by Michael Bentley, 545–90. London and New York: Routledge, 2006.

Carynnyk, Marco. "Foes of Our Rebirth: Ukrainian Nationalist Discussions about Jews, 1929–1947." *Nationalities Papers* 39 (2011): 315–52.

Casquete, Jesús. "Martyr Construction and the Politics of Death in National Socialism." *Totalitarian Movements and Political Religions* 10 (2009): 265–83.

Chase, William J. *Enemies within the Gates? The Comintern and the Stalinist Repression, 1934–1939*. New Haven, CT: Yale University Press, 2001.

Chatterjee, Choi, and Karen Petrone. "Models of Selfhood and Subjectivity: The Soviet Case in Historical Perspective." *Slavic Review* 67 (2008): 967–86.

Christie, Ian. *The Film Factory: Russian and Soviet Cinema in Documents, 1896–1939*. New York: Routledge, 1994.

Clark, Katerina, and Karl Schlögel. "Mutual Perceptions and Projections: Stalin`s Russia in the Soviet Union—Nazi Germany in the Soviet Union." In *Beyond Totalitarianism: Stalinism and Nazism Compared*, edited by Michael Geyer and Sheila Fitzpatrick, 396–441. Cambridge: Cambridge University Press, 2009.

Cohen, Stephen. "The Gulag Archipelago." *New York Times*, June 16, 1974.

Connelly, John. Review of *The Dictators: Hitler's Germany, Stalin's Russia*, by Richard Overy. *Kritika: Explorations in Russian and Eurasian History* 7 (2006): 925.

Connelly, John. "The Uses of Volksgemeinschaft: Letters to the NSDAP Kreisleitung Eisenach, 1939–1940." In *Accusatory Practices: Denunciation in Modern European History, 1789–1989*, edited by Sheila Fitzpatrick and Robert Gellately, 153–84. Chicago: University of Chicago Press, 1997.

Conquest, Robert. *The Great Terror: A Reassessment*. New York: Oxford University Press, 1990.

Conquest, Robert. *The Harvest of Sorrow: Soviet Collectivization and the Terror-Famine*. London: Arrow Books, 1988.

Courtois, Stéphane, and Jean-Louis Panné. "The Comintern in Action." In *The Black Book of Communism: Crimes, Terror, Repression*, edited by Stéphane Courtois et al. Cambridge, MA: Harvard University Press, 1999.

Courtois, Stéphane, Nicolas Werth, Jean-Louis Panné, Andrzej Paczkowski, Karel Bartosek, and Jean-Louis Margolin. *The Black Book of Communism: Crimes, Terror, Repression*. Cambridge, MA: Harvard University Press, 1999.

Courtois, Stéphane, Nicolas Werth, Jean-Louis Panné, Andrzej Paczkowski, Karel Bartosek, and Jean-Louis Margolin. *Le livre noir du communisme: crimes, terreur, repression*. Paris: Robert Laffont, 1997.

Dahlmann, Dittmar, and Gerhard Hirschfeld, eds. *Lager, Zwangsarbeit, Deportation und Verfolgung: Dimensionen der Massenverbrechen in der Sowjetunion und in Deutschland 1933 bis 1945.* Essen: Klartext, 1999.

Dal', Oleg. *Ot illiuzii k tragedii: Hnemetskie emigranty v SSSR v 30-e gody.* Moscow: Neues Leben, 1997.

Dallin, David J., and Boris Nikolaevsky. *Forced Labor in Soviet Russia.* New Haven: Yale University Press, 1947.

Danzer, Doris. *Zwischen Vertrauen und Verrat: Deutschsprachige kommunistische Intellektuelle und ihre sozialen Beziehungen (1918–1960).* Göttingen: V & R Unipress, 2012.

David-Fox, Michael. "On the Primacy of Ideology: Soviet Revisionists and Holocaust Deniers (In Response to Martin Malia)." *Kritika: Explorations in Russian and Eurasian History* 5 (2004): 85–105.

David-Fox, Michael. "Introduction: Entangled Histories in the Age of Extremes." In *Fascination and Enmity: Russia and Germany as Entangled Histories, 1914–1945*, edited by Michael David-Fox, Peter Holquist, and Alexander Martin, 1–12. Pittsburgh: University of Pittsburgh Press, 2012.

David-Fox, Michael, Peter Holquist, and Alexander Martin, eds. *Fascination and Enmity: Russia and Germany as Entangled Histories, 1914–1945.* Pittsburgh: University of Pittsburgh Press, 2012.

Deak, Istvan. "The Charnel Continent." *The New Republic*, December 2, 2010.

Deutscher, Isaac. *Stalin: A Political Biography.* London: Oxford University Press, 1967.

Domarus, Max. *Hitler: Speeches and Proclamations 1932–1945. Vol. I.* London: Tauris, 1990.

Druzhnikov, Yuri. "Katriona Kelli, Pavlik Morozov i Lyubianka." *Voprosy literatury* 3 (2006). Accessed February 3, 2015. http://magazines.russ.ru/voplit/2006/3/dru12.html.

Druzhnikov, Yuri. *Informer 001: The Myth of Pavlik Morozov.* New Brunswick: Transaction Publishers, 1996.

Dundes, Allan. "The Ritual Murder or Blood Libel Legend: A Study of anti-Semitic Victimization through Projective Inversion." In *The Blood Libel Legend: A Casebook in Anti-Semitic Folklore*, edited by Allan Dundes, 336–78. Madison: University of Wisconsin Press, 1991.

Eaglestone, Robert. *Postmodernism and Holocaust Denial.* Cambridge: Icon Books, 2001.

Edelman, Murray. *Political Language: Words that Succeed and Politics that Fail.* New York: New York Academic Press, 1977.

Ellis, Bill. "De legendis urbis: Modern legends in ancient Rome." *Journal of American Folklore* 96 (1983): 200–208.

Evans, Richard J. *Telling Lies About Hitler: The Holocaust, History and the David Irving Trial.* London and New York: Verso, 2002.

Fainsod, Merle. *How Russia is Ruled.* Cambridge, MA: Harvard University Press, 1953.

Farmer, Sarah. "Symbols That Face Two Ways: Commemorating the Victims of Nazism and Stalinism at Buchenwald and Sachsenhausen." *Representations* 49 (1995): 97–119.

Faurisson, Robert. "My Revisionist Method." *The Journal of Historical Review* 21 (2002): 7–34.

Ferro, Marc, ed. *Le livre noir du colonialisme.* Paris: Éditions Robert Laffont, 2003.

Figes, Orlando. *The Whisperers: Private Life in Stalin's Russia.* London: Allen Lane, 2007.

Finder, Gabriel N., and Alexander V. Prusin. "Collaboration in Eastern Galicia: The Ukrainian Police and the Holocaust." *East European Jewish Affairs* 34 (2004): 95–118.

Firsow, Friedrich. "Die Komintern und die 'Grosse Säuberung.'" In *Biographisches Handbuch zur Geschichte der Kommunistischen Internationale. Ein deutsch-russisches Forschungsprojekt*, edited by Michael Buckmiller and Klaus Meschkat. Berlin: Akademie Verlag, 2007.

Fitzpatrick, Sheila. *The Cultural Front. Power and Culture in Revolutionary Russia.* Ithaca and London: Cornell University Press, 1992.

Fitzpatrick, Sheila. *Everyday Stalinism: Ordinary Life in Extraordinary Times: Soviet Russia in the 1930s*. Oxford and New York: Oxford University Press, 1999.

Fitzpatrick, Sheila. "Revisionism in Retrospect: A Personal View." *Slavic Review* 67 (2008): 693–94.

Fitzpatrick, Sheila. "Revisionism in Soviet History." *History and Theory* 36 (2007): 77–91.

Fitzpatrick, Sheila. "Signals from Below: Soviet Letters of Denunciation of the 1930s." In *Accusatory Practices: Denunciation in Modern European History, 1789–1989*, edited by Sheila Fitzpatrick and Robert Gellately, 85–120. Chicago: University of Chicago Press, 1997.

Fitzpatrick, Sheila, and Robert Gellately, eds. *Accusatory Practices: Denunciation in Modern European History, 1789–1989*. Chicago and London: The University of Chicago Press, 1997.

Flessau, Kurt-Ingo. *Schule der Diktatur: Lehrpläne und Schulbücher des Nationalsozialismus*. München: Fischer-TB, 1984.

Fostii, Ivan. *Pivnichna Bukovyna i Khotynshchyna u Druhii svitovii viini 1939–1945 rr.* Chernivtsi: Oblasne viddilennia Poshukovo-vydavnychoho ahenstva "Knyha pam"iati Ukrainy, 2005.

Frankl, Viktor. *Man's Search for Meaning: An Introduction to Logotherapy*. London: Hodder & Stoughton, 1964.

Friedman, Philip. "Ukrainian-Jewish Relations during the Nazi Occupation." In *Roads to Extinction: Essays on the Holocaust*, edited by Philip Friedman and Ada June Friedman. New York: Conference on Jewish Social Studies, Jewish Publication Society of America, 1980.

Friedman, Philip. *Zagłada Żydów lwowskich w okresie okupacji niemieckiej*. Munich: Monachium, 1947.

Friedrich, Carl, ed. *Totalitarianism*. Cambridge, MA: Harvard University Press, 1954.

Friedrich, Carl, and Zbigniew Brzezinski. *Totalitarian Dictatorship and Autocracy*. Cambridge, MA: Harvard University Press, 1965.

Fukuyama, Francis. "The End of History?" *The National Interest* (Summer 1989): 3–18.

Fulop-Miller, Rene. *The Mind and Face of Bolshevism*. London and New York: G.P. Putnam's Sons, 1926.

Furet, François. "On Ernst Nolte's Interpretation of Fascism." In *Fascism and Communism*, edited by François Furet and Ernst Nolte, 1–6. Lincoln and London: University of Nebraska Press, 2001.

Furet, François. *Le passé d'une illusion. Essai sur l'idée communiste au XXe siècle*. Paris: Robert Laffont/Calmann-Lévy, 1995.

Furet, François. *The Passing of an Illusion: The Idea of Communism in the Twentieth Century*. Chicago and London: The University of Chicago Press, 1999.

Furet, François, and Ernst Nolte. *Feindliche Nähe. Kommunismus und Faschismus im 20. Jahrhundert*. Munich: F.A. Herbig, 1998.

Gadamer, Hans-Georg. *Truth and Method*. New York: Continuum, 1988.

Gavrilov, Levo. "Zapasnol kommunisto." In *Dodnes Tiagoteet 2*, edited by Semen Vilenskii. Moscow: Vozvrashchenie, 2004.

Gellately, Robert. "Denunciations in Twentieth-Century Germany: Aspects of Self-Policing in the Third Reich and the German Democratic Republic." In *Accusatory Practices: Denunciation in Modern European History, 1789–1989*, edited by Sheila Fitzpatrick and Robert Gellately, 185–221. Chicago: University of Chicago Press, 1997.

Gellately, Robert. *Lenin, Stalin and Hitler: The Age of Social Catastrophe*. New York: Alfred A. Knopf, 2007.

Gentile, Emilio. "Fascism, Totalitarianism, and Political Religion: Definitions and Critical Reflections on Criticism of an Interpretation." In *Fascism, Totalitarianism and Political Religion*, edited by Roger Griffin, 32–81. London and New York: Routledge, 2005.

Gentile, Emilio. "Political Religion: A Concept and its Critics—A Critical Survey." *Totalitarian Movements and Political Religions* 6 (2005): 19–32.

Gentile, Emilio. "The Sacralisation of Politics: Definitions, Interpretations, and Reflections on the Question of Secular Religion and Totalitarianism." *Totalitarian Movements and Political Religions* 1 (2000): 18–55.

Gerlach, Christian, and Nicolas Werth. "State Violence." In *Beyond Totalitarianism: Stalinism and Nazism Compared*, edited by Michael Geyer and Sheila Fitzpatrick, 133–179. Cambridge: Cambridge University Press, 2009.

Getty, J. Arch. "'Excesses are not permitted': Mass Terror and Stalinist Governance in the Late 1930s." *The Russian Review* 61 (2002): 113–38.

Getty, J. Arch. *Origins of the Purges: The Soviet Communist Party Reconsidered, 1933–1938.* Cambridge and London: Cambridge University Press, 1985.

Getty, J. Arch, and Oleg Naumov, eds. *The Road to Terror: Stalin and the Self-Destruction of the Bolsheviks, 1932–1939.* New Haven: Yale University Press, 1999.

Geyer, Michael and Sheila Fitzpatrick, eds. *Beyond Totalitarianism: Stalinism and Nazism Compared.* Cambridge: Cambridge University Press, 2009.

Geyer, Michael, and Sheila Fitzpatrick. "Introduction: After Totalitarianism—Stalinism and Nazism Compared." In *Beyond Totalitarianism: Stalinism and Nazism Compared*, edited by Michael Geyer and Sheila Fitzpatrick, 1–40. Cambridge: Cambridge University Press, 2009.

Gkotzaridis, Evi. "Revisionism in the Twentieth Century: A Bankrupt Concept or Permanent Practice?" *The European Legacy: Toward New Paradigms* 13 (2008): 725–41.

Gleason, Abbot. *Totalitarianism: The Inner History of the Cold War.* New York and Oxford: Oxford University Press, 1995.

Glucksmann, André. *La cuisinière et le mangeur d'hommes. Essai sur les rapports entre l'État, le marxisme et les camps de concentration.* Paris: Seuil, 1976.

Golden, Nathaniel. *Socialization, Survival and Witness: An Investigation of Gulag and Holocaust Literature.* Stoke-on-Trent: Keele University, 2007.

Goldhagen, Daniel Jonah. *Hitler's Willing Executioners: Ordinary Germans and the Holocaust.* New York: Vintage Books, 1997.

Goldman, Wendy Z. *Inventing the Enemy: Denunciation and Terror in Stalin's Russia.* Cambridge: Cambridge University Press, 2011.

Gorlitzki, Yoram, and Hans Mommsen, "The Political (Dis)Orders of Stalinism and National Socialism." In *Beyond Totalitarianism: Stalinism and Nazism Compared*, edited by Michael Geyer and Sheila Fitzpatrick, 41–86. Cambridge: Cambridge University Press, 2009.

Gorsuch, Anne. "Soviet Youth and the Politics of Popular Culture during NEP." *Social History* 17 (1992): 189–201.

Gregory, Paul, and Valery Lazarev. *The Economics of Forced Labor: The Soviet Gulag.* Stanford: Hoover Institution Press, 2003.

Gross, Jan T. *Neighbors: The Destruction of the Jewish Community in Jedwabne, Poland.* Princeton: Princeton University Press, 2001.

Gross, Jan T. *Revolution from Abroad: The Soviet Conquest of Poland's Western Ukraine and Western Belorussia.* Princeton and Oxford: Princeton University Press, 1988.

Grossman, Vasily. *Forever Flowing.* New York: Harper & Row, 1972.

Guttenplan, D. D. *The Holocaust on Trial: History, Justice and the David Irving Libel Case.* London: Granta, 2002.

Halbwachs, Maurice. *The Collective Memory.* New York: Harper & Row Colophon Books, 1980.

Halfin, Igal. *Terror in My Soul: Communist Autobiographies on Trial.* Cambridge, MA: Harvard University Press, 2003.

Halfin, Igal, ed. *Language and Revolution: Making Modern Political Identities.* London and Portland: Frank Cass, 2002.

Harwood, Richard (Richard Verall). *Did Six Million Really Die? The Truth at Last.* Historical Review Press, 1974.

Heer, Hannes. "Einübung in den Holocaust: Lemberg Juni/Juli 1941." *Zeitschrift für Geschichtswissenschaft* 49 (2001): 409–27.

Heer, Hannes. "Lemberg 1941: Die Instrumentalisierung der NKVD-Verbrechen für Judenmord." In *Kriegsverbrechen im 20. Jahrhundert*, edited by Wolfram Wette and Gerd R. Ueberschär, 165–77. Darmstadt: Primus Verlag, 2001.

Hellman, Ben. *Fairy Tales and True Stories: The History of Russian Literature for Children and Young People (1574–2010)*. Boston: Brill, 2013.

Herkommer, Christina. "Women under National Socialism: Women's Scope for Action and the Issue of Gender." In *Ordinary People as Mass Murderers: Perpetrators in Comparative Perspective*, edited by Olaf Jensen and Claus-Christian Szejnmann, 99–119. London: Palgrave Macmillan, 2008.

Hilberg, Raul. *The Destruction of the European Jews*. Chicago: Quadrangle Books, 1961.

Himka, John-Paul, and Joanna Michlic, eds. *Bringing the Dark Past to Light: The Reception of the Holocaust in Post-Communist Europe*. Lincoln: University of Nebraska Press, 2013.

Himka, John-Paul. "A Central European Diaspora under the Shadow of World War II: The Galician Ukrainians in North America." *Austrian History Yearbook* 37 (2006): 17–31.

Himka, John-Paul. "Debates in Ukraine over Nationalist Involvement in the Holocaust, 2004–2008." *Nationalities Papers* 39 (2011): 353–70.

Himka, John-Paul [Ivan Khymka]. "Dostovirnist' svidchennia: reliatsiia Ruzi Vagner pro l'vivs'kyi pohrom vlitku 1941 r." *Holokost i suchasnist'* 4 (2008): 43–79.

Himka, John-Paul. "Ethnicity and the Reporting of Mass Murder: *Krakivs'ki visti*, the NKVD Murders of 1941, and the Vinnytsia Exhumation." In *Shatterzone of Empires: Coexistence and Violence in the German, Habsburg, Russian, and Ottoman Borderlands*, edited by Omer Bartov and Eric D. Weitz, 378–98. Bloomington: Indiana University Press, 2013.

Himka, John-Paul. "Introduction: A Reconfigured Terrain." In *The Holocaust in the East: Local Perpetrators and Soviet Responses*, edited by Michael David-Fox, Peter Holquist, and Alexander M. Martin, 1–4. Pittsburgh: University of Pittsburgh Press, 2014.

Himka, John-Paul. "The Lviv Pogrom of 1941: The Germans, Ukrainian Nationalists, and the Carnival Crowd." *Canadian Slavonic Papers* 53 (2011): 209–43.

Himka, John-Paul. "The Organization of Ukrainian Nationalists and the Ukrainian Insurgent Army: Unwelcome Elements of an Identity Project." *Ab Imperio* 4 (2010): 83–101.

Hitler, Adolf. *Mein Kampf*. New York: Reynal and Hitchcock, 1941.

Hobsbawm, Eric. *The Age of Extremes: The Short Twentieth Century 1914–1991*. London: Michael Joseph, 1994.

Iakovlev, A. N., et al., eds., *Reabilitatsiia: Kak eto bylo, fevral'1956—nachalo 80-x godov, t. II*. Moscow: Mezhdunarodnyi Fond "Demokratsiia," 2003.

Inkeles, Alex, and Raymond Bauer. *The Soviet Citizen: Daily Life in a Totalitarian Society*. Cambridge, MA: Harvard University Press, 1959.

Irving, David. *Hitler's War*. London and Sydney: Hodder and Stoughton, 1977.

Jeismann, Karl-Ernst. *Geschichte als Horizont der Gegenwart. Über den Zusammenhang von Vergangenheitsdeutung Gegenwartsverständnis und Zukunftsperspektive*. Paderborn: Schöningh, 1985.

Jilge, Wilfrid. "Competing Victimhoods—Post-Soviet Ukrainian Narratives on World War II." In *Shared History—Divided Memory: Jews and Others in Soviet-Occupied Poland, 1939–1941*, edited by Eleazar Barkan, Elizabeth A. Cole, and Kai Struve, 3–31. Leipzig: Leipziger Universitätsverlag, 2007.

Jones, Max. "What Should Historians Do With Heroes? Reflections on Nineteenth- and Twentieth-Century Britain." *History Compass* 5 (2007): 439—54.

Judt, Tony. "The Past Is Another Country: Myth and Memory in Post-War Europe." In *Memory & Power in Post-War Europe. Studies in the Presence of the Past*, edited by Jan-Werner Müller, 157–83. Cambridge: Cambridge University Press, 2002.

Kandel, Isaac. "Education in Nazi Germany." *Annals of the American Academy of Political and Social Science* 182 (1935): 153–63.

Kandel, Isaac. *The Making of Nazis*. Connecticut: Greenwood Press, 1970.

Karlsson, Klas-Göran. "Historical Consciousness—The Fundament of Historical Thinking and History Teaching." In *The Process of History Teaching. An International Symposion Held at Malmö University, Sweden, March 5–7 2009*, edited by Per Eliasson, Kenneth Nordgren, and Carina Rönnqvist, 13–34. Karlstad: Karlstad University Press, 2011.

Karlsson, Klas-Göran. "The Holocaust as a Problem of Historical Culture. Theoretical and Analytical Challenges." In *Echoes of the Holocaust. Historical Cultures in Contemporary Europe*, edited by Klas-Göran Karlsson and Ulf Zander, 9–58. Lund: Nordic Academic Press, 2003.

Karlsson, Klas-Göran. "The Holocaust, Communist Terror and the Activation of Swedish Historical Culture." In *Geschichtspolitik im erweiteren Ostseeraum und ihre aktuellen Symptome—Historical Memory Culture in the Enlarged Baltic Sea Region and its Symptoms Today*, edited by Oliver Rathkolb and Imbi Sooman, 195–212. Vienna: Vienna University Press, 2011.

Karlsson, Klas-Göran. "Processing Time—On the Manifestation and Activation of Historical Consciousness." In *Historicizing the Uses of the Past. Scandinavian Perspectives on History Culture, Historical Consciousness and Didactics of History Related to World War II*, edited by Helle Bjerg, Claudia Lenz, and Erik Thorstensen, 129–44. Bielefeld: Transcript Verlag, 2011.

Karlsson, Klas-Göran. "Public Uses of History in Contemporary Europe." In *Contemporary History on Trial. Europe since 1989 and the Role of the Expert Historian*, edited by Harriet Jones, Kjell Östberg and Nico Randeraad, 27–45. Manchester: Manchester University Press, 2007.

Karlsson, Klas-Göran. "The Reception of the Holocaust in Russia: Silence, Conspiracy, and Glimpses of Light." In *Bringing to Light the Dark Past: The Reception of the Holocaust in Postcommunist Europe*, edited by John-Paul Himka and Joanna Michlic, 487–515. Lincoln: Nebraska University Press, 2013.

Karlsson Klas-Göran. "The Uses of History and the Third Wave of Europeanisation." In *A European Memory? Contested Histories and Politics of Remembrance*, edited by Malgorzata Pakier and Bo Stråth, 38–55. New York and Oxford: Berghahn Books, 2010.

Karsen, Fritz. "Some Remarks on the Nazi Philosophy of Education." *The German Quarterly* 14 (1941): 135–42.

Kasianov, Georgiy. "Revisiting the Great Famine of 1932–1933: Politics of Memory and Public Consciousness (Ukraine after 1991)." In *Past in the Making: Historical Revisionism in Central Europe after 1989*, edited by Michal Kopeček, 197–219. Budapest: Central European University Press, 2008.

Kas'ianov, Heorhii. *Danse macabre: holod 1932–1933 rokiv u politytsi, masovii svidomosti ta istoriohrafii (1980-ti—pochatok 2000-kh)*. Kyiv: Nash chas, 2010.

Kelly, Catriona. *Comrade Pavlik. The Rise and Fall of a Soviet Boy Hero*. London: Granta Books, 2005.

Kenez, Peter. "Bezhin lug (Bezhin Meadow)." In *Enemies of the People: The Destruction of Soviet Literary, Theater and Film Arts in the 1930s*, edited by Katherine Bliss Eaton, 113–26. Evanston: Northwestern University Press, 2002.

Kershaw, Ian, and Moshe Lewin, eds. *Stalinism and Nazism: Dictatorships in Comparison*. Cambridge: Cambridge University Press, 1997.

Kershaw, Ian, and Moshe Lewin. "Introduction. The Regimes and Their Dictators: Perspectives of Comparison." In *Stalinism and Nazism: Dictatorships in Comparison*, edited by Ian Kershaw and Moshe Lewin, 1–25. Cambridge: Cambridge University Press, 1997.

Keys, Barbara. "The Body as a Political Space: Comparing Physical Education under Nazism and Stalinism." *German History* 27 (2009): 395–413.

Kharkhordin, Oleg. *The Collective and the Individual in Russia*. Berkeley: University of California Press, 1999.

Klemperer, Victor. *LTI. Notizbuch eines Philologen*. Leipzig: Reclam Verlag, 1975.

Kocka, Jürgen. "Asymmetrical Historical Comparison: The Case of the German *Sonderweg*." *History & Theory* 38 (1999): 40–50.

Kocka, Jürgen. "Comparison and Beyond." *History & Theory* 42 (2003): 39–44.

Kopstein, Jeffrey S., and Jason Wittenberg. "Deadly Communities: Local Political Milieus and the Persecution of Jews in Occupied Poland." *Comparative Political Studies* 20 (2010): 1–25.

Kort, Michael. *The Soviet Colossus: History and Aftermath*. Armonk and London: M.E. Sharpe, 1996.

Korzen, Meir. "The Extermination of Two Ukrainian Jewish Communities: Testimony of a German Army Officer." *Yad Vashem Studies* (1959): 303–20.

Koselleck, Reinhart. *Futures Past: On the Semantics of Historical Time*. New York: Columbia University Press, 2004.

Kössler, Reinhart. "Entangled history and politics: Negotiating the past between Namibia and Germany." *Journal of Contemporary African Studies* 26 (2008): 313–39.

Kotkin, Steven. *Magnetic Mountain: Stalinism as a Civilization*. Berkeley, Los Angeles and London: University of California Press, 1995.

Kozlov, Vladimir. "Denunciation and Its Functions in Soviet Governance: A Study of Denunciations and Their Bureaucratic Handling from Soviet Police Archives, 1944–1953." In *Accusatory Practices: Denunciation in Modern European History, 1789–1989*, edited by Sheila Fitzpatrick and Robert Gellately, 121–52. Chicago: University of Chicago Press, 1997.

Kramer, Alan. *Dynamic of Destruction: Culture and Mass Killing in the First World War*. Oxford: Oxford University Press, 2007.

Kruglov, Aleksandr. "Pogromy v Vostochnoi Galitsii letom 1941 g.: organizatory, uchastniki, masshtaby i posledstviia." In *Voina na unichtozhenie. Natsistskaia politika genotsida na territorii Vostochnoi Evropy. Materialy mezhdunarodnoi nauchnoi konferentsii (Moskva, 26–28 aprelia 2010 goda)*, edited by A. R. Diukov and O. E. Orlenko, 324–41. Moscow: Fond "Istoricheskaia pamiat,'" 2010.

Kurylo, Taras. "The 'Jewish Question' in the Ukrainian Nationalist Discourse of the Inter-War Period." *Polin* 26.

Kut'ina, Dzhana, Andrei Broido, and Anton Kut'in. *Ob ushedshem veke, rasskazyvaet Ol'ga Shatunovskaia*. La Jolla, CA: DAA Books, 2001.

Lambert, Peter. "Heroisation and Demonisation in the Third Reich: The Consensus-building Value of a Nazi Pantheon of Heroes." *Totalitarian Movements and Political Religions* 8 (2007): 523–46.

Lammers, Karl Christian. "Nazism." In *Nationalencyklopedin*, Vol. 14. Höganäs: Bra Böcker, 1994.

Lane, Christel. *The Rites of Rulers: Ritual and Industrial Society—the Soviet Case*. Cambridge: Cambridge University Press, 1981.

Laqueur, Walter. *Russia & Germany: A Century of Conflict*. New Brunswick: Transaction Publishers, 1990.

Lefort, Claude. *Complications: Communism and the Dilemmas of Democracy*. New York: Columbia University Press, 2007.

Lenin, Vladimir. *Imperialism, the Highest State of Capitalism: A Popular Outline*. Beijing: Foreign Languages Press, 1969.

Lévy, Bernard-Henri. *La barbarie à visage humain*. Paris: Grasset, 1977.

Liedman, Sven Eric. "Kommunism." In *Nationalencyklopedin*, Vol. 11. Höganäs: Bra Böcker, 1993.

Lindgren, Stefan. "*Kommunismens svarta bok*—slutet på 'body-count.'" In *Utan heder. En bok om ohederliga debattörer och högerns rädsla för förändring*, edited by Aron Etzler, 25–52. Stockholm: Röd Press Förlag, 1999.

Lipstadt, Deborah. *Denying the Holocaust: The Growing Assault on Truth and Memory*. New York and Toronto: The Free Press, 1993.

Littmann, Arnold. *Herbert Norkus und die Hitlerjungen vom Beusselkietz*. Berlin: Steuben Verlag, 1934.

Lorentz, Chris. "Drawing the Line: 'Scientific History' Between Myth-Making and Myth Breaking." In *Narrating the Nation: Representations in History, Media and the Arts*, edited by Stefan Berger, Linas Eriksonas, and Andrew Mycock, 35–55. Oxford: Oxford University Press, 2008.

Lossky, Nikolai. *Kharakter Russkogo Naroda* (in *Usloviia absoliutnogo dobra*). Moscow: Politicheskaia literatura, 1991.

Lower, Wendy. "Pogroms, Mob Violence and Genocide in Western Ukraine, Summer 1941: Varied Histories, Explanations and Comparisons." *Journal of Genocide Research* 13 (2011): 217–46.

Lukacs, John. *June 1941: Hitler and Stalin*. New Haven: Yale University Press, 2006.

Maier, Charles S. "Consigning the Twentieth Century to History: Alternative Narratives for the Modern Era." *The American Historical Review* 105 (2000): 807–31.

Maier, Charles S. *The Unmasterable Past: History, Holocaust, and German National Identity*. Cambridge, MA and London: Harvard University Press, 1997.

Maier, Hans, ed. *Totalitarianism and Political Religions: Concepts for the Comparison of Dictatorships*. London and New York: Routledge, 2004.

Malia, Martin. "Judging Nazism and Communism." *The National Interest* 64 (2002): 63–78.

Malia, Martin. "The Lesser Evil?" *Times Literary Supplement*, March 27, 1998.

Malia, Martin. *The Soviet Tragedy: A History of Socialism in Russia, 1917–1991*. New York: The Free Press, 1994.

Malia, Martin. "To the Editors," *Kritika: Explorations in Russian and Eurasian History* 3 (2002): 569–71.

Man'kovskii, L. A. "K voprosu o psikhologii kul'ta Stalina." *Voprosy Filosofii*, No. 1, 1989.

Mann, Michael. "The Contradictions of Continuous Revolution." In *Stalinism and Nazism: Dictatorships in Comparison*, edited by Ian Kershaw and Moshe Lewin, 135–57. Cambridge: Cambridge University Press, 1997.

Marjanen, Jani. "Histoire croisée of concepts as transnational history: Undermining methodological nationalism." In *Transnational Political Spaces: Agents—Structures—Encounters*, edited by Mathias Albert, Gesa Bluhm, Jan Helmig, Andreas Leutxsch, and Jochen Walter, 239–63. Frankfurt and New York: Campus, 2009.

Martin, Terry. *The Affirmative Action Empire: Nations and Nationalism in the Soviet Union, 1923–1939*. Ithaca and London: Cornell University Press, 2001.

Martin, Terry. "The Origins of Soviet Ethnic Cleansing." *The Journal of Modern History* 70 (1998): 813–61.

Marx, Karl. "Introduction." *Marx's Critique of Hegel's Philosophy of Right (1843)*. Cambridge: Cambridge University Press, 1970.

Marx, Karl, and Friedrich Engels. *The Communist Manifesto*. Rendlesham: The Merlin Press, 1998.

von Mayenburg, Ruth. *Hotel Lux*. Bielefeld: W. Bertelsmann Verlag, 1978.

Mazower, Mark. *Dark Continent: Europe's Twentieth Century*. London: Penguin Books, 1998.

McDermott, Kevin. "Stalinist Terror in the Comintern: New Perspectives," *Journal of Contemporary History* 30, No. 1 (1995): 111–30.

Mead, Margaret, and Rhoda Métraux. "An Analysis of the Nazi Film Hitlerjunge Quex: Gregory Bateson." In *The Study of Culture at a Distance*, edited by Margaret Mead and Rhoda Métraux, 302–11. Chicago: Chicago University Press, 1953.

Mędykowski, Witold. *W cieniu gigantów. Pogromy 1941 r. w byłej sowieckiej strefie okupacyjnej. Kontekst historyczny, społeczny i kulturowy*. Warsaw: Instytut Studiów Politycznych Polskiej Akademii Nauk, 2012.

Melamed, Vladimir. "Organized and Unsolicited Collaboration in the Holocaust: The Multifaceted Ukrainian Context." *East European Jewish Affairs* 37 (2007): 217–48.

Mensing, Wilhelm. "Einem deutschen Sowjetbürger wird bei Stalin das Schreiben abgewöhnt: Aus dem Leben des Dresdner jüdischen Schriftstellers Helmut Weiss," *Exil: Forschung, Erkenntnisse, Ergebnisse* 23 (2003).

Mensing, Wilhelm. *Von der Ruhr in den GULag: Opfer des Stalinschen Massenterrors aus dem Ruhrgebiet*. Essen: Klartext, 2001.

Michlic, Joanna B. "*Żydokomuna*—Anti-Jewish Images and Political Tropes in Modern Poland." *Simon Dubnow Institute Yearbook* 4 (2005): 303–29.

Mick, Christoph. "Incompatible Experiences: Poles, Ukrainians and Jews in Lviv under Soviet and German Occupation, 1939–1944." *Journal of Contemporary History* 46 (2011): 336–63.

Mick, Christoph. *Kriegserfahrungen in einer multiethnischen Stadt: Lemberg 1914–1947*. Wiesbaden: Harrassowitz Verlag, 2010.

Möller, Horst, ed. *Der rote Holocaust und die Deutschen. Die Debatte um das "Schwarzbuch des Kommunismus."* Munich and Zürich: Piper, 1999.

Montefiore, Simon. *Stalin: The Court of the Red Tsar*. New York: Vintage Books, 2005.

Moses, Dirk A. "The Canadian Museum for Human Rights: The 'Uniqueness of the Holocaust' and the Question of Genocide." *Journal of Genocide Research* 14 (2012): 215–38.

Mosse, George L. *Toward the Final Solution: A History of European Racism*. New York: Howard Fertig, 1978.

Mosse, George L. *The Image of Man: The Creation of Modern Masculinity*. New York and Oxford: Oxford University Press, 1996.

Mosse, George L. *Nazi Culture. Intellectual, Cultural and Social Life in the Third Reich*. Madison: The University of Wisconsin Press, 1966.

Motyka, Grzegorz. *Ukraińska partyzantka 1942–1960: działalność Organizacji Ukraińskich Nacjonalistów i Ukraińskiej Powstańczej Armii*. Warsaw: Instytut Studiów Politycznych PAN, RYTM, 2006.

Musial, Bogdan. "Bilder einer Ausstellung: Kritische Anmerkungen zur Wanderausstellung 'Vernichtungskrieg. Verbrechen der Wehrmacht 1941 bis 1944.'" *Vierteljahrshefte für Zeitgeschichte* 47 (1999): 563–91.

Musial, Bogdan. *"Konterrevolutionäre Elemente sind zu erschießen": Die Brutalisierung des deutsch-sowjetischen Krieges im Sommer 1941*. Berlin: Propyläen, 2000.

Musial, Bogdan. *"Rozstrzelac elementy kontrrewolucyjne!" Brutalizacja wojny niemiecko-sowieckiej latem 1941 roku*. Warsaw: Fronda, 2002.

Müller, Reinhard. *Die Akte Wehner: Moskau 1937 bis 1941*. Berlin: Rowohlt, 1993.

Müller, Reinhard. *Herbert Wehner: Moskau 1937*. Hamburg: Hamburger Edition, 2004.

Müller, Reinhard. "'Wir kommen alle dran': Säuberungen unter den deutschen Politemigranten in der Sowjetunion (1934–1938)." In *Terror: Stalinistische Parteisäuberungen 1936–1953*, edited by Hermann Weber and Ulrich Mählert. Paderborn: Ferdinand Schöningh, 1998.

Naimark, Norman. *Fires of Hatred: Ethnic Cleansing in Twentieth-Century Europe*. Cambridge, MA and London: Harvard University Press, 2001.

Naimark, Norman. *Stalin's Genocides*. Princeton and Oxford: Princeton University Press, 2010.

Nimmo, Dan, and James E. Combs. *Subliminal Politics: Myths and Mythmakers in America*. Englewood Cliffs: Prentice-Hall, 1980.

Noakes, Jeremy. "Hitler and the Third Reich." In *The Historiography of the Holocaust*, edited by Dan Stone, 24–51. Houndmills: Palgrave Macmillan, 2004.

Nolte, Ernst. "Between Historical Legend and Revisionism? The Third Reich in the Perspective of 1980." In *Forever in the Shadow of Hitler? Original Documents of the Historikerstreit, the Controversy Concerning the Singualarity of the Holocaust*, 1–15. New Jersey: Humanities Press, 1994.

Nolte, Ernst. *Der europäische Bürgerkrieg 1917–1945: Nationalsozialismus und Bolschewismus*. Berlin: Propyläen Verlag, 1987.

Nolte, Ernst. "From the Gulag to Auschwitz." In *Fascism and Communism*, edited by François Furet and Ernst Nolte, 23–30. Lincoln and London: University of Nebraska Press, 2001.

Nolte, Ernst. "The Past That Will Not Pass: A Speech That Could Be Written but Not Delivered." In *Forever in the Shadow of Hitler? Original Documents of the Historiker-*

streit, the Controversy Concerning the Singularity of the Holocaust, 18–23. New Jersey: Humanities Press, 1994

Nora, Pierre. "Between Memory and History: Les Lieux de Mémoire." *Representations* 26 (1989): 7–25.

Olusoga, David, and Casper Erichsen. *The Kaiser's Holocaust: Germany's Forgotten Genocide.* London: Faber and Faber, 2010.

Overy, Richard. *The Dictators: Hitler's Germany and Stalin's Russia.* London: Penguin, 2005.

Panteleev, Mikhail. "Repressii v Kominterne (1937–1938)." *Otechestvennaia istoria* 6 (1996).

Paperno, Irina. "Exhuming the Bodies of Soviet Terror." *Representations* 75 (2001): 89–118.

Passerini, Luisa. "Introduction." In *Memory and Totalitarianism*, edited by Luisa Passerini, 1–20. New Brunswick: Transaction Publishers, 2005.

Patryliak, I. K. *Viis'kova diial'nist' OUN (B) u 1940–1942 rokakh.* Kyiv: Kyivs'kyi natsional'nyi universytet imeni Tarasa Shevchenka Instytut istorii Ukrainy NAN Ukrainy, 2004.

Paxton, Robert. *The Anatomy of Fascism.* London: Penguin, 2005.

Pellicano, Luciani. "Modernity and Totalitarianism." *Telos* 112 (1998): 3–21.

Perrault, Gilles. *Le livre noir du capitalisme.* Paris: Le Temps des Cerises, 1998.

Persson, Fredrik. "Den blodiga jorden." *Sydsvenska Dagbladet*, 1 June, 2011.

Peukert, Detlev. *Inside Nazi Germany: Conformity, Opposition, and Racism in Everyday Life.* New Haven and London: Yale University Press, 1987.

Pietsukh, Mariana. "Muzei strakhu v 'nichnomu' formati. Reportazh z Nochi Muzeiv." *Istorychna pravda*, 27 May 2013, http://www.istpravda.com.ua/articles/2013/05/27/124888/. Accessed 23 October 2013.

Pipes, Richard. *Communism: A History.* New York: The Modern Library, 2001.

Platt, Kevin. *Terror & Greatness: Ivan and Peter as Russian Myths.* Ithaca and London: Cornell University Press, 2011.

Pohl, Dieter. "Anti-Jewish Pogroms in Western Ukraine—A Research Agenda." In *Shared History—Divided Memory: Jews and Others in Soviet-Occupied Poland, 1939–1941*, edited by Eleazar Barkan, Elizabeth A. Cole, and Kai Struve, 305–13. Leipzig: Leipziger Universitätsverlag, 2007.

Pohl, Dieter. *Nationalsozialistische Judenverfolgung in Ostgalizien 1941–1944: Organisation und Durchführung eines staatlichen Massenverbrechens.* Munich: R. Oldenbourg Verlag, 1997.

Popiński, Krzysztof, Aleksandr Kokurin, and Aleksandr Gurjanow. *Drogi śmierci. Ewakuacja więzień sowieckich z Kresów Wschodnich II Rzeczypospolitej w czerwcu i lipcu 1941.* Warsaw: Karta, 1995.

Popper, Karl. "Historicism and the Soviet Union (1991)." In *After The Open Society: Selected Social and Political Writings*, by Karl Popper, 378–82. London and New York: Routledge, 2008.

Popper, Karl. *The Open Society and Its Enemies. Volume One: The Spell of Plato.* London and New York: Routledge, 2010.

Priestland, David. *The Red Flag: Communism and the Making of the Modern World.* London: Allen Lane, 2009.

The Progress Report of Latvia's History Commission: Crimes against Humanity Committed in the Territory of Latvia from 1940 to 1956 during the Occupations of the Soviet Union and National Socialist Germany, http://www.mfa.gov.lv/data/file/e/HC-Progress-Report2001.pdf. Accessed 26 January 2015.

Prusin, Alexander. *The Lands Between: Conflict in the East European Borderlands, 1870–1992.* Oxford and New York: Oxford University Press, 2010.

Prusin, Alexander V. "A 'Zone of Violence': The Anti-Jewish Pogroms in Eastern Galicia in 1914–1915 and 1941." In *Shatterzone of Empires: Coexistence and Violence in the German, Habsburg, Russian, and Ottoman Borderlands*, edited by Omer Bartov and Eric D. Weitz, 362–77. Bloomington: Indiana University Press, 2013.

Rachlin, Samuel. "Stalin's Long Shadow." *International Herald Tribune*. 5 March 2013.

Ramlow, Rudolf. *Herbert Norkus?—Hier! Opfer und Sieg der Hitler-Jugend*. Berlin: Union Deutsches Verlagsgesellschaft, 1933.

Randeria, Shalini. "Entangled histories of uneven modernities: Civil society, caste solidarities and legal pluralism in post-colonial India." In *Unraveling Ties: From Social Cohesion to New Practices of Connectedness*, edited by Yehuda Elkana, Ivan Krastev, Elisio Macamo, and Shalini Randeria, 284–311. Frankfurt am Main and New York: Campus Verlag, 2002.

Rentschler, Eric. "Emotional Engineering: Hitler Youth Quex." *Modernism/Modernity* 2 (1995): 23–44.

Rich, David Alan. "Armed Ukrainians in L'viv: Ukrainian Militia, Ukrainian Police, 1941 to 1942." *Canadian-American Slavic Studies* 48 (2014): 271–87.

Roberts, David D. *The Totalitarian Experiment in Twentieth-Century Europe: Understanding the Poverty of Great Politics*. New York and London: Routledge, 2006.

Rodden, John. *Textbook Reds. Schoolbooks, Ideology, and Eastern German Identity*. University Park: Pennsylvania State Press, 2006.

Rohdewald, Stefan. "Post-Soviet Remembrance of the Holocaust and National Memories of the Second World War in Russia, Ukraine and Lithuania." *Forum for Modern Language Studies* 44 (2008): 173–84.

Rolfe, Ella. "Addressing the Baathist Legacy in Iraq." *ICTJ in the News*, 26 February 2010.

Romaniv, Oleh, and Inna Fedushchak, *Zakhidnoukrains'ka trahediia 1941*. Lviv and New York: Naukove tovarystvo im. Shevchenka, 2002.

Rosefielde, Steven. *Red Holocaust*. London and New York: Routledge, 2010.

Rossoliński-Liebe, Grzegorz. "The 'Ukrainian National Revolution' of 1941: Discourse and Practice of a Fascist Movement." *Kritika: Explorations in Russian and Eurasian History* 12 (2011): 83–114.

Rotherhäusler, Paul, and Hans-Ueli Sonderegger. *Erinnerung an den Roten Holocaust*. Roth: Werner, 2000.

Rousso, Henry, ed. *Stalinism and Nazism: History and Memory Compared*. Lincoln: University of Nebraska Press, 2004.

Rudling, Per Anders. "Bogdan Musial and the Question of Jewish Responsibility for the Pogroms in Lviv in the Summer of 1941." *East European Jewish Affairs* 35 (2005): 69–89.

Rudling, Per Anders. "Multiculturalism, Memory, and Ritualization: Ukrainian Nationalist Monuments in Edmonton, Alberta." *Nationalities Papers* 39 (2011): 733–68.

Rudling, Per A(nders). *The OUN, the UPA and the Holocaust: A Study in the Manufacturing of Historical Myths*. Carl Beck Papers in Russian & East European Studies, Pittsburgh: Center for Russian & East European Studies, University Center for International Studies, University of Pittsburgh, 2011.

Rudnyts'ka, Milena, ed. *Zakhidnia Ukraina pid bol'shevykamy, IX.1939—VI.1941*. New York, 1958.

Rummel, Rudolf J. *Lethal Politics: Soviet Genocide and Mass Murder since 1917*. New Brunswick and London: Transaction Publishers, 1996.

Runia, Eelco. "Burying the Dead, Creating the Past. *History and Theory* 46 (2007): 313–25

Rüsen, Jörn, ed. *Approaching Humankind. Towards an Intercultural Humanism*. Göttingen: V & R Unipress, Taipei: National Taiwan University Press, 2013.

Rüsen, Jörn, ed. *Geschichtsbewußtsein. Psychologische Grundlagen, Entwicklungskonzepte, empirische Befunde*. Köln: Böhlau, 2001.

Rüsen, Jörn. *Historik. Theorie der Geschichtswissenschaft*. Köln: Böhlau, 2013.

Rüsen, Jörn. "Holocaust Memory and Identity Building: Metahistorical Considerations in the Case of (West) Germany." In *Disturbing Remains: Memory, History, and Crisis in the Twentieth Century*, edited by Michael S. Roth and Charles G. Salas, 252–70. Los Angeles: The Getty Research Institute, 2001.

Rüsen, Jörn. "Holocaust-Memory and German Identity." In *History: Narration, Interpretation, Orientation*, edited by Jörn Rüsen, 189–204. New York: Berghahn Books, 2005.

Rüsen, Jörn. "Humanism: Anthropology—Axial Ages—Modernities." In *Shaping a Humane World. Civilizations—Axial Times—Modernities—Humanisms*, edited by Oliver Kozlarek, Jörn Rüsen, and Ernst Wolff, 55–79. Bielefeld: Transcript Verlag, 2012.

Rüsen, Jörn. "Verstörungen in der Geschichtskultur. Historikerstreit und Holocaust-Deutung im Wechsel der Generationen." In *Singuläres Auschwitz? Ernst Nolte, Jürgen Habermas und 25 Jahre 'Historikerstreit'*, edited by Mathias Brodkorb, 105–14. Banzkow: Adebor, 2011.

Satzewich, Vic. *The Ukrainian Diaspora*. London and New York: Routledge, 2002.

Schenzinger, Karl Aloys, *Der Hitlerjunge Quex*. Berlin: Zeitgeschichte-Verlag, 1932.

von Schirach, Baldur. *Die Hitler-Jugend. Idee und Gestalt*. Leipzig: Koehler & Umelang, 1934.

Schlögel, Karl, ed. *Russian-German Special Relations in the Twentieth Century: A Closed Chapter?* New York and Oxford: Berg, 2006.

Schreckenberg, Heitz. *Ideologie und Alltag im Dritten Reich*. Frankfurt am Main: Lang, 2003.

Sekules, Edith. *Surviving the Nazis, Exile and Siberia*. London: Vallentine Mitchell, 2000.

Seixas, Peter, ed. *Theorizing Historical Consciousness*. Toronto: University of Toronto Press, 2004.

Service, Robert. *Comrades! A History of World Communism*. Cambridge, MA: Harvard University Press, 2007.

Shafir, Michael. *Between Denial and "Comparative Trivialization": Holocaust Negationism in Post-Communist East Central Europe*. Analysis of Current Trends in Antisemitism 19, Jerusalem: The Hebrew University of Jerusalem, The Vidal Sassoon International Center for the Study of Antisemitism, 2002.

Shearer, David. *Industry, State, and Society in Stalin's Russia, 1926–1934*. Ithaca and London: Cornell University Press, 1996.

Shermer, Michael, and Alex Grobman. *Denying History: Who Says the Holocaust Never Happened and Why Do They Say It?* Berkeley and Los Angeles: University of California Press, 2000.

Shirer, William L. *The Rise and Fall of the Third Reich: A History of Nazi Germany*. New York: Simon & Schuster, 2011.

Shore, Marci. "Conversing with Ghosts: Jedwabne, Żydokomuna, and Totalitarianism." *Kritika: Explorations in Russian and Eurasian* 6 (2005): 345–74.

Slyvka, Iu. et al. *Litopys neskorenoi Ukrainy. Dokumenty, materialy, spohady*, book 1. Lviv: Prosvita, 1993.

Snyder, Timothy. *Bloodlands: Europe between Hitler and Stalin*. London: The Bodley Head, 2010.

Snyder, Timothy. "A Fascist Hero in Democratic Kiev." *The New York Review of Books* Blog, 24 February 2010, http://www.nybooks.com/blogs/nyrblog/2010/feb/24/a-fascist-hero-in-democratic-kiev/ Accessed 30 October 2013.

Solonari, Vladimir. "Patterns of Violence: The Local Population and the Mass Murder of Jews in Bessarabia and Northern Bukovina, July–August 1941." *Kritika: Explorations in Russian and Eurasian History* 8 (2007): 749–87.

Solzhenitsyn, Alexander. *One Day in the Life of Ivan Denisovich*. New York: Bantam Dell, 1963.

Statiev, Alexander. *The Soviet Counterinsurgency in the Western Borderlands*. Cambridge: Cambridge University Press, 2010.

Stenfeldt, Johan. *Dystopiernas seger. Totalitarism som orienteringspunkt i efterkrigstidens svenska idédebatt*. Höör: Agerings Bokförlag, 2013.

Stern, Kenneth. *Holocaust Denial*. New York: The American Jewish Committee, 1993.

Stites, Richard. *Revolutionary Dreams, Utopian Vision and Experimental Life in the Revolution*. New York and Oxford: Oxford University Press, 1989.

The Stockholm International Forum on the Holocaust. A Conference on Education, Remembrance and Research, Stockholm, Sweden, 26–28 January 2000. Proceedings. Stockholm: Regeringskansliet, 2000.

Straub, Jürgen, ed. *Narration, Identity, and Historical Consciousness.* New York: Berghahn Books, 2005.

Struve, Kai. "Komanda osobogo naznacheniia 'L'vov', ukrainskaia militsiia i 'Dni Petliury' 25 i 26 iuliia 1941 g." *Problemy istorii Holokostu* 6 (2013): 102–24.

Struve, Kai. "Rites of Violence? The Pogroms of Summer 1941." *Polin* 24 (2012): 257–74.

Struve, Kai. "Tremors in the Shatterzone of Empires: Eastern Galicia in Summer 1941." In *Shatterzone of Empires: Coexistence and Violence in the German, Habsburg, Russian, and Ottoman Borderlands,* edited by Omer Bartov and Eric D. Weitz, 463–84. Bloomington: Indiana University Press, 2013.

Struve, Kai. "'Vergeltung' und Exzess. Gewalt gegen Juden während des Sommers 1941 in Ostgalizien." Habilitationsschrift, der Martin-Luther-Universität Halle-Wittenberg, 2013.

Suny, Ronald Grigor. "Russian Terror/ism and Revisionist Historiography." *Australian Journal of Politics and History* 53 (2007): 5–19.

Szporluk, Roman. *Communism and Nationalism: Karl Marx versus Friedrich List.* New York: Oxford University Press, 1991.

Tal, Uriel. "Aspects of Consecration of Politics in the Nazi Era." In *Judaism and Christianity under the Impact of National Socialism,* edited by Otto D. Kulka and Paul R. Mendes-Flohr, 49–102. Jerusalem: Historical Society of Israel and Zalman Shazar Center for Jewish History, 1987.

Thurston, Robert W. *Life and Terror in Stalin's Russia, 1934–1941.* New Haven: Yale University Press, 1996.

Tillett, Lowell. *The Great Friendship: Soviet Historians on the Non-Russian Nationalities.* Chapel Hill: University of North Carolina Press, 1969.

Tillmanns, Jenny. *Was heißt historische Verantwortung? Historisches Unrecht und seine Folgen für die Gegenwart.* Bielefeld: Transcript Verlag, 2012.

Tischler, Carola. *Flucht in die Verfolgung: Deutsche Emigranten im sowjetischen Exil 1933 bis 1945.* Münster: LIT, 1996.

Tismaneanu, Vladimir. *The Devil in History: Communism, Fascism, and Some Lessons of the Twentieth Century.* Berkeley, Los Angeles and London: University of California Press, 2012.

Todorov, Tzvetan. *Hope and Memory: Reflections on the Twentieth Century.* London: Atlantic, 2005.

Todorov, Tzvetan. *Mémoire du mal, tentation du bien. Enquête sur le siècle.* Paris: Editions Robert Laffont, 2012.

Todorov, Tzvetan. "Totalitarianism: Between Religion and Science." *Totalitarian Movements and Political Religion* 2 (2001): 28–42.

Tucker, Robert C. *Stalin in Power: The Revolution From Above, 1928–1941.* New York: W. W. Norton & Company, 1992.

Tumarkin, Nina. *Lenin Lives! The Lenin Cult in Soviet Russia.* Cambridge: Cambridge University Press, 1983.

Uhl, Heidemarie. "Of Heroes and Victims: World War II and Austrian Memory." *Austrian History Yearbook* 42 (2011): 185–200.

Ulbrich, Lilli, ed. *Buch der Erinnerung. Juden in Dresden: Deportiert, ermodet, verschollen 1933–1945.* Dresden: Eckhard Richter & Co., 2006.

Vatlin, Alexander. "Kaderpolitik und Säuberungen in der Komintern." In *Terror: Stalinistische Parteisäuberungen 1936–1953,* edited by Hermann Weber and Ulrich Mählert. Padeborn: Ferdinand Schöningh, 1998.

Vatlin, Alexander. *Komintern: Ideii, resheniia, sud'by.* Moscow: Rosspen, 2009.

Viola, Lynne. *Peasant Rebels under Stalin: Collectivization and the Culture of Peasant Resistance.* New York and Oxford: Oxford University Press, 1996.

Völter, Bettina. *Judentum und Kommunismus: Deutsche Familiengeschichte in drei Generationen.* Leverkusen: Leske & Budrich, 2003.

Waddington, Lorna L. "The Anti-Komintern and Nazi Anti-Bolshevik Propaganda in the 1930s." *Journal of Contemporary History* 42 (2007): 573–94.

Vaiskopf, Mikhail. *Pisatel' Stalin*. Moscow: Novoe literaturnoe obozrenie, 2002.

Wehler, Hans-Ulrich. *Das Deutsche Kaiserreich 1871–1918*. Göttingen: Vandenhoeck & Ruprecht, 1973.

Wehner, Herbert. *Zeugnis: Persönliche Notizen 1929–1942*. Halle: Mitteldeutscher Verlag, 1982.

Weiner, Amir. "Nothing but Certainty." *Soviet Studies* 61 (2002): 44–53.

Weiss-Wendt, Anton. *Murder without Hatred: Estonians and the Holocaust*. Syracuse, NY: Syracuse University Press, 2009.

Weiss-Wendt, Anton. *Small-Town Russia: Childhood Memories of the Final Soviet Decade*. Gainesville, FL: Florida Academic Press, 2010.

Weitz, Eric. *A Century of Genocide: Utopias of Race and Nation*. Princeton: Princeton University Press, 2003.

Welch, David. "Education, Film, Propaganda, and the Nazi Youth." In *Nazi Propaganda: The Power and the Limitations*, edited by David Welch, 65–87. London: Croom Helm, 1983.

Werner, Michael, and Bénédicte Zimmermann. "Beyond Comparison: *Histoire Croisée* and the Challenge of Reflexivity." *History & Theory* 45 (2006): 30–50.

Werner, Michael, and Bénédicte Zimmermann, "Penser l'histoire croisée: entre empirie et réflexivité," *Annales HSS* 58 (2003): 7–36.

Werth, Nicolas. "A State against Its People: Violence, Repression, and Terror in the Soviet Union." In *The Black Book of Communism: Crimes. Terror, Repression*, edited by Stéphane Courtois et al. Cambridge, MA: Harvard University Press, 1999.

Wheatcroft, Stephen. "The Scale and Nature of German and Soviet Repression and Mass Killings, 1930s–1945." *Europe-Asia Studies* 48 (1996): 1319–53.

von Wiese, Leopold. "Die gegenwärtige Situation, soziologisch betrachtet." In *Verhandlungen des Achten Deutschen Soziologentages vom 19. bis 21. September 1946 in Frankfurt am Main*. Tübingen: J. C. B. Mohr, 1948.

Wieviorka, Annette. *The Era of the Witness*. Ithaca and London: Cornell University Press, 2006.

Wippermann, Wolfgang. *Fascismustheorien. Die Entwicklung der Diskussion von den Anfängen bis heute*. Darmstadt: Primus Verlag, 1997.

de Zayas, Alfred M., with the collaboration of Walter Rabus. *The Wehrmacht War Crimes Bureau, 1939–1945*. Lincoln and London: University of Nebraska Press, 1980.

Żbikowski, Andrzej. "Local Anti-Jewish Pogroms in the Occupied Territories of Eastern Poland, June-July 1941." In *The Holocaust in the Soviet Union: Studies and Sources on the Destruction of the Jews in the Nazi-Occupied Territories of the USSR, 1941–1945*, edited by Lucjan Dobroszycki and Jeffrey S. Gurock, 173–79. Armonk and London: M. E. Sharpe, 1993.

Żbikowski, Andrzej. "Pogromy i mordy ludności żydowskiej w Łomżyńskiem i na Białjstocczyźnie latem 1941 roku w świetle relacji ocalałych Żydów i dokumentów sądowych." In *Wokół Jedwabnego, Vol. 1: Studia*, edited by Paweł Machcewicz and Krzysztof Persak, 159–271. Warsaw: Instytut Pamięci Narodowej, Komisja Ścigania Zbrodni przeciwko Narodowi Polskiemu, 2002.

Zlochyny komunistychnoi Moskvy v Ukraini v liti 1941 roku. New York: Proloh, 1960.

Index

Adenauer, Konrad, 146
Adorno, Theodor, 39
Ahmadinejad, Mahmoud, 151
Aly, Götz, 33
Anti-capitalism, 62, 64, 68
Anti-comintern, 83, 96
Anti-communism, 5, 21, 61, 62, 63, 64, 68, 72, 73
Anti-Nazism, 61, 62, 63, 64, 65, 68, 69
Anti-semitism, 21, 37, 64, 67, 69, 115, 144, 158
Antonescu, Ion, 153
Applebaum, Anne, 15
Arendt, Hannah, 31, 44, 64, 67, 68, 146
Aryan race, 4, 17
Auschwitz, 3, 14, 17, 21, 23, 41

Babi Yar, 27
Baird, Jay W., 105
Baital'skii, Mikhail, 124
Bakunin, Mikhail, 21
Bandera, Stepan, 143, 144, 147, 152, 154, 156
Baran, Ivanna, 155
Barner-Barry, Carol, 107
Barry, Damon, 115
Bartov, Omer, 16, 155
Bateson, Gregory, 111
Bauman, Zygmunt, 32, 33, 128
Behrenbeck, Sabine, 105
Bemborad, Elisabeth, 115
Beria, Lavrenty, 92, 93, 126, 128
Berk, Leon, 148
Berlin, Isaiah, 67
Bernstein, Eduard, 67
Blacker, Uilleam, 142, 151
Bracher, Karl, 31
Brandt, Erna Asta, 85, 88, 92, 93, 96
Brezhnev, Leonid, 129
Broda, Ihor, 156

Brown, Kate, 37
Browning, Christopher, 146
Brzezinski, Zbigniew, 64, 66, 107
Buber-Neumann, Margarete, 22
Bukharin, Nikolai, 123

Casquete, Jesús, 108
Chase, William, 81
Chornovil, Viacheslav, 138
Chuprun, Gertruda Evgen'evna, 128
Cohen, Stephen, 22, 23
Cold War, 13, 26, 62, 64, 73, 167, 170, 172, 175
Colonialism, 62, 64, 72
Comintern, 64, 67, 78, 79, 81, 82, 85, 86, 87, 88, 90, 91, 95, 96
The Communist Manifesto, 64
Conquest, Robert, 23, 71
Courtois, Stéphane, 21, 24, 26, 27, 28, 62, 64, 70, 71, 72, 82

Dal, Oleg, 80
Denialism, 7, 169, 172, 176
De-Stalinization, 128, 132
Dlugosh, Wolodymyr, 154
Dornberger, Emma, 87
Dostoyevsky, Fyodor, 84
Druzhnikov, Yuri, 105
Duncan, Linda, 156
Dyak, Sofiya, 142

Einarsson, Mats, 43, 44
Eisenstein, Sergei, 112, 113
Ellis, Bill, 115
Engels, Friedrich, 64
Enlightenment, 39
European Union, 15, 41, 42
Ezhov, Nikolai, 77, 79, 123, 128, 173

Fabri, Ernst, 87, 88

About the Authors

Nanci Adler is Division Head of Holocaust and Genocide Studies at the NIOD Institute for War, Holocaust, and Genocide Studies (Royal Netherlands Academy of Arts and Sciences, University of Amsterdam), Senior Researcher, and one of the editors of *Memory and Narrative*. She has worked with oral histories and memoirs of Gulag survivors since the late eighties. She is the author of *Keeping Faith with the Party: Communist Believers Return from the Gulag* (2012), *The Gulag Survivor: Beyond the Soviet System* (2002), *Victims of Soviet Terror: The Story of the Memorial Movement* (1993), and numerous scholarly articles on the Gulag, political rehabilitations, and the consequences of Stalinism. Her current research focuses on transitional justice and the legacy of Communism.

Johan Dietsch, PhD, is post-doc Fellow in East and Central European Studies at Lund University, Sweden. Educated at Umeå and Uppsala Universities, he received a PhD in history from Lund University, where he defended his dissertation *Making Sense of Suffering: Holocaust and Holodomor in Ukrainian Historical Culture* (2006). He has specialized in Soviet and contemporary post-Soviet history, historiography, and uses of history. His articles on history culture, genocide, totalitarianism, and politics have appeared in *Holokost i Suchasnist*, *Krytyka*, and *Ab Imperio* among others. His most recent publication is "Textbooks and the Holocaust in Independent Ukraine," in *European Education*, 3 (2012). At present he is working on a project entitled *Textbook Totalitarianism — Comparing Nazi Germany and Stalinist Soviet Union*.

John-Paul Himka (PhD, Michigan 1977) is a professor in the Department of History and Classics at the University of Alberta (Edmonton, Canada). He is the author of four monographs on Ukrainian history, most recently *Last Judgment Iconography in the Carpathians* (2009). He is currently working on a monograph tentatively entitled *Ukrainian Nationalists and the Holocaust: Pogroms, Police, and National Insurgency*. His 2009 Mohyla lecture has been published as a separate brochure: *Ukrainians, Jews, and the Holocaust: Divergent Memories*. He is also the editor or co-editor of seven other books, including *Bringing the Dark Past to Light: The Reception of the Holocaust in Postcommunist Europe* (co-edited with Joanna Michlic, 2013). His articles on the Holocaust, the Ukrainian famine of 1933, and historical memory have appeared in *Canadian Slavonic Papers*, *Kritika*, and elsewhere.

202 *About the Authors*

Klas-Göran Karlsson (PhD, Lund 1987) is professor of history at Lund University, Sweden. He has published extensively in three fields of contemporary international history: terror and genocide studies, Russian and Soviet studies, and European history culture and uses of history. In the years 2001–2008, he was at the head of the large research project *The Holocaust and European Historical Culture*, which resulted in three anthologies: *Echoes of the Holocaust. Historical Cultures in Contemporary Europe* (2003), *Holocaust Heritage. Inquiries into European Historical Cultures* (2004), and *The Holocaust—Post-War Battlefields. Genocide as Historical Culture* (2006). His latest books, both in Swedish, are *European Encounters with History. Perspectives on the Second World War, the Holocaust, and Communist Terror in Historical Culture* (2010), and *"Those Who Are Innocent Today Can Be Guilty Tomorrow." The Armenian Genocide and Its Aftermath* (2012).

Maria Karlsson holds a PhD in history from Lund University. Her primary areas of interest include the modern history of genocide and mass murder, as well as the subsequent collective and societal processes of remembering, repressing, and forgetting. Her dissertation, *Cultures of Denial: Comparing Holocaust and American Genocide Denial.* (2015), compares and contrasts Western denial and trivialization of the Holocaust and the American genocide of 1915–1917.

Jörn Rüsen, Professor emeritus, historian, and philosopher of history, formerly professor at Bielefeld University and Director at Kulturwissenschaftliches Institut in Essen, Germany. He has for many years been one of the world's most prominent history theorists, and he has published extensively on important theoretical concepts such as history culture, historical consciousness, identity, meaning, and orientation. Among his publications are *History: Narration, Interpretation, Orientation* (2005), *Meaning and Representation in History* (2006), *Shaping a Humane World: Civilisations, Axial Times, Modernities, Humanisms* (ed., 2012), and *Historical Memory in Africa: Dealing with the Past, Reaching for the Future in an Intercultural Context* (ed., 2010).

Johan Stenfeldt holds a PhD in history from Lund University, Sweden. His thesis on totalitarianism as a concept and theme in the public debate of post-war Sweden is titled *Dystopiernas seger. Totalitarism som orienteringspunkt i efterkrigstidens svenska idédebatt* ("The Victory of the Dystopias. Totalitarianism as a Point of Orientation in the Public Debate of Postwar Sweden"). Among his earlier publications on the Communism-Nazism nexus and the role of the Nazi-Communist comparison in different historical cultures can be mentioned "Positioning in the Cold War—Swedish and Danish History Textbooks and the Totalitarianism Doctrine. Historical Cultures in Comparison," in *Scandinavian Journal of History* 4 (2012).

Anton Weiss-Wendt has a PhD in modern Jewish history from Brandeis University, United States. He is currently Head of the Research Department at The Center for the Study of the Holocaust and Religious

Minorities in Oslo, Norway. His research interests include comparative genocide, Soviet and East European history, modern Jewish history, war crimes trials in the Soviet Union and Eastern Europe, and local collaboration in the Holocaust. Among his publications are *Murder without Hatred: Estonians and the Holocaust* (2009), *Eradicating Differences: The Treatment of Minorities in Nazi-Dominated Europe* (ed., 2010), and *Racial Science in Hitler's New Europe, 1938–1945* (ed., 2013).

Ulf Zander (PhD 2001, Lund) is professor of history at Lund University. He is author of three monographs. Among his recent works can be mentioned "Preoccupied by the Past—The Case of Estonia's Museum of Occupations" (with Stuart Burch), *Scandia*, No. 2, 2008, "Oskar Schindler and Raoul Wallenberg—National, European and American Heroes," in Teresa Pinhero et al. (eds.), *Ideas of Europe/Ideas for Europe, An Interdisciplinary Approach to European Identity* (2012), and "Swedish Rescue Operations during the Second World War—Accomplishments and Aftermath," in Irene Levin et al. (eds.), *Holocaust as an Active Memory. The Past in the Present* (2013). He is also co-editor for a number of anthologies, among them *Echoes of the Holocaust, Historical Cultures in Contemporary Europe* (2003), *Holocaust Heritage. Inquiries into European Historical Cultures* (2004), and *The Holocaust—Post-War Battlefields. Genocide as Historical Culture* (2006).

CPSIA information can be obtained at www.ICGtesting.com
Printed in the USA
BVOW03*2209120715

407129BV00010BA/4/P